VIVA LA RAZA!

THE STRUGGLE OF THE
MEXICAN-AMERICAN PEOPLE

VIVA LA RAZA!

THE STRUGGLE OF THE
MEXICAN-AMERICAN PEOPLE

BY Elizabeth Sutherland Martínez AND

Enriqueta Longeaux y Vásquez

Introduction by
Mae Durham Roger

Doubleday & Company, Inc., Garden City, New York

Excerpt from article on Juan Nepocena Cortina, Vol. I, No. 2 issue of *Magazín*. Reprinted by permission of *Magazín*.

"Brown Is Beautiful" by Olivia de San Diego. Reprinted by permission of Olivia Reynolds.

Excerpt from statements by Sevedeo Martínez, March 30, 1971, issue of *El Grito del Norte*, excerpt from *Papel Chicano*, excerpt from "Police Murder Campesino," June 5, 1971, issue of *El Grito del Norte*. Reprinted by permission of *El Grito del Norte*.

Random lines of poetry from "I Am Joaquin" by Rodolfo "Corky" Gonzáles. Reprinted by permission of the author.

"Today, History, and Time" by Guadalupe Saavedra. Reprinted by permission of the author.

Letter by Manuel Gomez to draft board on December 8, 1969. Reprinted by permission of Manuel Gomez.

Excerpt from "Notes on Chicano Theater" by Luis Valdez from the book *Aztlán* by Luis Valdez and Stan Steiner. Published by Vintage Books, 1972.

"Stupid America" by Abelardo Delgado. Reprinted by permission of the author.

Contents

Contents

Introduction

HERE IS THE MANIFESTO of two women who want to tell the factual story of the Chicanos. It is often said that history, as many of us have learned it, is not necessarily what actually took place. This depends, of course, on the interpretation of the historians, their insight and their prejudices.

Elizabeth Sutherland Martínez and Enriqueta Longeaux y Vásquez reconstruct the history of North America from the early days before the coming of the white man to the present time, and its effect on the second largest minority in the United States. With passion and fervor they help the reader understand what lies behind the stabbing efforts to attain a rightful place in history and in society today. Their picture is not a pretty one; they paint it with a sense of pride, determination, and outrage.

In reading their account we are immediately drawn closer to the heart of these people, gaining insight into their proud roots, their traditions, their emergence as a people fighting for equality. This gives the book a vitality. As events are traced and as effects are interpreted, we begin to understand the reasons for what has happened and is happening among Chicanos, between Chicanos and other ethnic groups, between Chicanos and society as a whole.

The authors' examination and re-examination of the orthodox telling of history have catapulted them into writing their version of "the story behind the story." They write vehemently of their Indian ancestors, their "conquerors," their people's treatment and condition since that time. As they present their viewpoint, we become aware that perhaps we haven't been told the whole story. They want us to listen to them.

Viva La Raza is an outcry that echoes the anguish, the anger, the bitterness, and the impatience of a large group of people—a nation within a nation. Their voice must be heard; their story must be told as they know it, not as it has been told for them. Theirs is a strong voice that will not be tempered, and their audience will be vividly aware of this.

The book will be read by La Raza; it should be read by non-Chicanos if there is to be recognition and acceptance of their deep-rooted contributions to the patterned fabric of our past, present, and future, toward a genuine human understanding.

MAE DURHAM ROGER

University of California
Berkeley, California

VIVA LA RAZA!
THE STRUGGLE OF THE
MEXICAN-AMERICAN PEOPLE

1

Viva La Raza, Raza, Raza . . .

PEOPLE ONCE SAID that the Mexican-American was one of the United States' best-kept secrets. We, the second largest minority group in this country, were almost unknown people outside our own communities and we were hardly to be seen in the history books. No one even knew how many of us lived here. But today we are becoming aware as a people, we are finding ourselves as a people, we are uncovering our history. And as we do so, we are arising to be heard. We want to be heard by all but we especially want our own people to hear—and to rise in united pride, united action.

Across the country we see the stirring of our people everywhere. From Denver to Delano, from the fields of

Texas to the big city barrios of Los Angeles, from Oregon to Florida and in the middle states of Wisconsin, Indiana, Kansas, everywhere the Raza lives and works, there is movement. With the rousing Chicano handclap and cheers of "Raza, Raza, Raza, Raza," and the stamping of feet, we can feel that a new era has begun for the Chicano. We feel it in the air, it is written in the wind, it is on people's faces everywhere. Like a volcano we stir, and in the rumble we hear "Chicano Power," "Brown Is Beautiful," "*Somos Hijos del Sol*," (We are Children of the Sun), "*Viva La Raza*," "*Viva Zapata*," and the rumble and the echoes grow louder with more harmony and unison each day.

Our people are on the march in all levels of life, awakening and demanding justice in the schools, in employment, civil rights, housing, the welfare program, the churches, on the land, in the military, and even behind prison walls. After decades of being lynched and displaced; after decades of being herded into migrant camps for mere survival; after decades of being pushed off our land and being forced into the cities where we end up on welfare; after decades of being punished and shamed for speaking our own language and living our own culture; after decades of giving our bodies for dying in wars that are not ours, our people are saying *BASTA YA! ENOUGH!*

We want to determine our own destiny. We do demand justice and equality within this country, but we want to decide that equality on our own terms. In all the stirring and movement that can be seen today, there is something more than a drive for "first-class citizenship." There is a deep probing—a deep search for self. We move to be ourselves, to be brown, to assert our Mexican roots. We say that we have millions of brothers and sisters to the south of us and our strength lies in the fact that we are a *majority* and not a *minority* in America—the continent. We seek to be something other than white, Anglo, gringo, something other than what the majority of this country imposes upon us and would like us to be. To the Chicano of today, equality does not mean becoming a carbon copy of white middle-class America. It means "to be" in the deepest sense.

As archaeologists dig up the cities of old Mexico and of the southwestern United States, we are bringing up our true past from its long burial and listening to old voices. We marvel as the hidden treasures of our farsighted forefathers come to light again. We learn more and more that our cultural roots have long been here, and that the border between Mexico and the United States is but an imaginary line—a line which does not break up culture and kinship ties. We are rediscovering our Indian roots and heritage that date back twenty-five thousand years. We see the common elements that unite us and refuse to be divided any longer as the white man has tried to keep us divided for centuries. With these discoveries, we know that we do not need to try to be something we are not. We do not need to live in conflict with ourselves.

We call ourselves by various names today but most of them suggest the new affirmation of who and what we are. "La Raza" means in Spanish "the race" and stands for the blending of predominantly Indian and Spanish peoples who were our ancestors—the blend that we are today. The essence of La Raza is that we are a mestizo people, a mixed people, a blend of races and culture.

Today among many young men and women, the most popular name is Chicano (or Chicana). We are not sure about the origin of this word. Some say Chicano is derived from a word used by the Aztecs which they pronounced "Meshicano." Since the Spaniards had no "sh" sound in their language, they tended to write the word as Mexicano. However, the last part of the word as pronounced by the Aztecs survived—"shicano" or Chicano.

It isn't clear, in this theory, whether "Meshicano" referred to the Aztecs themselves—our indigenous ancestors—or to the children of mixed Indian and Spanish parentage, which is what we are. But there does seem to be good reason to think the word is old. Then, some thirty years ago, "Chicano" became common again in the slang of the streets—especially in California. Because of that "lower-class" association, many conservative Raza have not liked the term. The young people like it and have adopted it, "because it is something that I choose to be called, not something Mexico chose to call me or, even more important, not something the gringo has named me."

There are Raza who call themselves "Mexican-Americans." This is a term most often used by the white society, along with "Spanish-surnamed" or "Spanish-speaking Americans." The problem with Mexican-American is that it suggests Mexicans are something different from Americans, when in fact we were "Americans" long before the pilgrims or anybody else

from Europe landed. Of course, "America" is a European term itself. But if we use the word, and we
don't have much choice, then we should remember
that America is a continent—not a country. We must
realize that the United States has assumed the name of
the whole continent for itself, much to the disgust of
many Latin Americans. The "America Love It or Leave
It" slogan is laughed at by Chicanos and Indians, who
say: "I buy that. When are they going to leave?"

And there are still more terms used by our people
to describe themselves: Indo-Hispanos, Latinos, Hispanos. It depends on what village, town, city, or state,
what age group, what social class, the person belongs
to. In many mountain villages, where families date
back for several hundred years, some of our people call
themselves "Hispanos" or even "Spanish." The term
Spanish-American is preferred by many middle-class
Raza who have "made it" and wish to relive the gen-
tlemanly *patrón* of the era of Spanish colonization.
Among our people the most widely used word is probably Mexicano—not the English "Mexican" but our
Spanish word, *Mexicano*, which has a brotherly feeling
of warmth and acceptance.

This discussion of names is not just a matter of ar-
guing over words. It reflects our whole struggle for
what some people call "identity"—the affirmation of
who and what we really are; and learning to be proud
of it instead of ashamed. This new pride has come to
us from the feeling we today call Chicanismo. It is often a difficult thing for the Anglo to understand. The
concept and understanding that if you do not know
your roots, your past culture, you are nothing.

White America might understand our demands for civil rights or decent pay, because that is demanding what is ours under *their* rules. But it cannot comprehend the idea that we may not want to be part of the so-called "mainstream of society." It does not occur to them that we may frown upon the non-culture imposed on us. That we may not totally believe that life consists of working for money to buy things. That we may not want to sell ourselves to "get ahead in the world," because in the United States that means forgetting other human beings for the sake of a new color TV. That we have joy in being what we are, in discovering ourselves. That we are a very strong people.

We have found sanity in being Chicano, for it is in our Chicanismo that we have come to see all of the cancer in the dominant white society and we know that we don't want to be that sick. We want a society that will function for human beings, we have solutions and we refuse to become robots that walk in death.

One of the best ways to judge the values of a society is by looking at how it defines *freedom*. The Anglo society, like other Western societies, thinks mostly in terms of freedom *from* something. The heritage of La Raza talks in terms of freedom *to be* something—to be productive, to be loving and participate in care for others, to be alive as a full human being. It is like the difference between being free from responsibilities, and being free to have responsibilities. We thrive on human involvement and devoting time to others, be they our family or close friends. The majority society may think that when they put their old people in "rest homes," they are freed from a burden. For us, caring and learning from our elders is a part of living. After all, if one does not love and care for one's family and others, what else is there worth doing?

These are but a few of the beliefs and reasons for our new pride in being Raza. Our new sense of identity is not just a matter of taking pride in talking our own language or eating our own food and loving our own music. Chicanismo is *carnalismo*—blood brotherhood and sisterhood, a feeling of unity among our people. And this goes beyond, to a feeling for all people. *"Mi casa es tu casa"* or *"Ésta es tu casa"*—my house is your house, this is your house—the phrase expresses a basic openness toward people as fellow creatures on this planet.

Today we often hear the Mexicano or the Indian described as "passive," "humble," or "meek" when in fact the person is simply open and honest and not playing the role game of the Western world. Many times words such as these show us the conflict between cultures. In English, "humble" means low in station, unimportant, like a servant. In Spanish, *humilde* describes a person with a deep feeling for others, a respect and a kind of human concern. It is a good thing to be called. It helps explain the endurance of La Raza and the Indians—an endurance far beyond anything the white society understands or is capable of feeling.

All these values we assert as we cease to be the nation's "best-kept secret." And as we stand up to speak, to be heard, the world has begun to listen. For although we may be looked upon as a minority here, we are a minority with an ancient geography and history on our side. A minority with a history of our own, that was here long before the "majority." A minority that, like the Indians, has specific legal treaties with the United States to protect our rights as a people.

We are, above all, a "minority" with indestructible deep roots in the land. The relationship of Raza to the land is one of the most important facts of history. Raza relates strongly to the land, not only in terms of written treaties and in terms of ownership but also in terms of the land being an ever-existing power; a spiritual link; a source of life and a hope that never ceases.

La Raza has drawn a deep strength from many of these basic feelings and we find them contained in the concept of Aztlán—the name of the Chicano nation, the homeland which many of us are committed to rebuilding. The homeland of Aztlán lies not only in the countryside but also in the cities, everywhere that Raza may be. Rebuilding it means not only claiming our rights but restoring our unity as a people, affirming our historic values, our culture, our spirit—the source of our enduring strength.

As La Raza becomes more alive, more awake, more intense, the dominant society with all its power looks on in puzzlement, wonder and fear. Sometimes it tries to crush us with brute force, and sometimes it tries to buy us off. And all the time, it is making more and more "studies" of us, more evaluations, more investigations. Today we are being studied, surveyed, observed, and studied again. Colleges have made studies, agencies have made studies, everybody is studying us. And what is our answer to all this studying and surveying? All around, La Raza is saying BASTA YA!

We are learning more and more that the ones who

need to be studied are the majority society and its freak mentality that guides this country. We have learned that it is not we who are the problem, but the gringo mind. We have understood his system and his misguided attitudes, we know well how he operates and thinks. We have learned what he stands for. We are tired of listening to him talk about us. We are going to be the ones to talk about us. We are going to make our own studies, tell our own stories, write our own books. We are going to speak for ourselves—and in a language that La Raza understands, with concepts and ideas that existed long before English was used in the Southwest.

As we affirm our worth as a people, as we become more and more conscious that we have a noble past, a rich culture, and beautiful human values, we begin to wonder why they built a bad image of us, why they tried to destroy something that is ours—something that is beautiful. And as we find some answers, we question even more and more and more. WHY? WHY? WHY? The more we look, the more answers we find.

It becomes clear that in the search for the truth about ourselves, we must recognize and throw off the BIG LIES of the Anglo society and its institutions. We must question the actions and teachings of every branch of that society. By institutions we mean the political, educational, spiritual, judicial, all of them, large and small. We must tear away the shroud of distortion, hypocrisy, and just plain falsity that has been wrapped around us—and all other oppressed peoples—for centuries.

The biggest lie, the root of all the other lies, is that

the Anglo belongs here and we are the immigrants—
that this country with all its wealth should be the property of the gringo, and we are foreigners in his land. The
gringo has called Mexicans "wetbacks" because there
is a river that draws a so-called border between Mexico
and the U.S.A., and people have often crossed it by
swimming or just walking. The gringo forgets about his
own great swim across the Atlantic Ocean, when our
ancestors had already been here for centuries. Among
Raza, we know who the real "wetback" is.

From the first lie comes still another: that only the
Anglo society's values—competition, "getting ahead,"
consuming—are good values, and that this is a way of
life that everybody should accept. White makes right,
so get with it, they say. But what about our ancestors
and their way of life? Is it possible that these so-called
savages could teach the white man some basic lessons?
Is it possible that they have much to tell Raza today, as we struggle to create a new society?

A vital part of the present Raza movement is up-
rooting those lies and putting the truth back into history. The real history of our Raza is one of the most
important issues of the day for us. All other issues, all
the oppression we face, arise from the past. We cannot
draw sharp lines between past, present, and future, as
many Western cultures do. We have a different sense
of time. We see that the occurrences of today are the
result of past history, and we need to reveal all that
history in order to build for the future. Because our
roots and part of our ancestry lie in America, we have
a strong base on which to build our own destiny.

To us, history is not just an abstract study of facts,

but a study of human beings—their societies and their ideas. Our history must be treated as a history of peoples, cultures, and a land. This means looking at history without the borderline between the United States and Mexico, it means recognizing that the Southwest was once the northern part of Mexico, it means seeing that there are links between us and Mexico that have not, and cannot, be destroyed. So when we speak of Mexico, we are speaking of a land before there were borders, before there were the concepts of property and land ownership as the Europeans know them. We cannot think of our history merely in terms of the United States. Our history is largely a history of the natives of this continent, a history of the very roots of civilization in America.

This brings us to another of the big lies: that American history began with the arrival of the white man on this continent, and nothing really important or worthwhile existed before that. Columbus "discovered" America, Cortés "discovered" Peru—all the history books talk that way, as if the Indians who lived here never existed or never had any kind of civilization. They were labeled superstitious "savages" by ignorant Europeans, who say that the Indians' life style and values have no use or meaning in today's modern world. This is, of course, the way white society looks at all of us—brown, black, red, yellow. The only history worth talking about began with the white man, according to him.

Let us take a look at life in America before Columbus, for it is through this that we will learn who the "savage" really is, and we will take pride in realizing that we come from a very "civilized" people. Let us not look just at the monuments people built or the wars they fought, but also at the kind of human beings they were—how they related to the universe, the land, and to each other; how they thought of life and death, how the young and old related. Let us begin by learning and writing *our* kind of history.

2

Our Indio Ancestors

THE FIRST HUMAN BEINGS to settle in America are said to have been Asians. These, our ancestors, brought with them ideas from the East that are still found today among the Indians and the Mestizos of Las Americas. Many philosophical ideas of the East are still part of *El Corazón de La Raza*—the heart of La Raza.

Our ancestors lived by hunting or farming, not commerce and manufacture, so they never lost sight of nature and the powerful forces ruling it. Their awareness of nature, with its destructive as well as creative power, made them see human life as a very precious gift. And it was clear from nature that no one could survive alone. People had to live as a group, had to co-operate.

So one of the most important traditions among the Indians was the tribal or communal way of organizing human society. This is a society based on co-operation, not competition. It is the opposite of the modern Western society that makes human beings into isolated individuals fighting separately for survival and growth, whose worth is judged primarily by the possessions they acquire for themselves and their immediate families.

The Indians of what is now Mexico included many different groups in different areas at different periods between 1700 B.C. and A.D. 1521. The kind of society each had depended on how the tribe survived—how the people got their food—and developed. The nomadic hunters in the north had no system of landholding, while the societies in Central Mexico and Yucatán were based on agriculture and had definite ways of distributing the land. There was variation in these systems but usually each tribe was made up of clans, groups united by family ties and by living in the same area. Under the clan system, the whole community lived off the fruits of the land and so it was believed that the community as a whole should own and control the land.

Among the Azteca (or Mexica) and other tribes, a central tribal council divided the land among the clans. The leader of each clan assigned plots to the heads of the different families according to need, size of the family, and so on. The family cultivated the plot, living from its produce. When a tenant died, the plot passed to his sons; if he had no children, the clan assigned it to another family. Divisions of land were marked off by

low stone walls, rows of thorny agave, irrigation ditches
or paths. But these were not like fences; they did not
mean ownership in the modern sense. The family could
not sell its land to anyone, or mortgage it. They just
had the right to its produce, based on the fact that
they worked it. This was called the *calpulli* system,
basically the same as the system of the Pueblo Indians
in what is today the southwestern United States.

The only kinds of private property that existed were
agricultural produce, tools, household and personal
items. Our ancestors had no domestic animals, like cattle or horses. Some of them did have finer clothes or a
bigger variety of food than others, but on the whole
everyone prospered or suffered together—according to
the ups and downs of the entire society.

People helped each other to build homes, to clear
cornfields, to do all kinds of labor that required more
than two hands. People didn't have to sell their labor
to other individuals in order to survive. There were no
beggars in America at a time when Europe had thousands. It was just taken for granted that the community
would meet the basic needs of all its members. The in-
dividualism that we see in capitalist societies would
probably have struck the Indians as very uncivilized.

Everyone saw themselves as part of a much larger
world and subject to its laws. This was the universe,
the world of nature. For our Indian ancestors, the key
to life was living in harmony with the various rhythms
of nature: the cycle of birth to death; of day to night;
of the seasons; of the planets' movements through the
sky. Nature taught that life was not rigid like a straight
line but more like a piece of music, with certain events

repeated from time to time in a certain rhythm. So the Indians saw and thought about things as part of a giant circle—a whole—rather than according to the single-line logic of the European or white man.

The Indians studied the stars and heavens constantly, in order to have a better understanding of these rhythms. They would watch the birds ride the air currents, and study the weather with all its changes. They became master astronomers. The Maya knew planets that we have discovered only in this century. They were particularly aware of the moon's cycles and how they affected human life. To this day, it is considered a fact among many Raza that hair grows with the moon and so an Indian girl who wants healthy, plentiful hair will cut it at the time of the new moon while a boy who wants to keep his hair short will cut it during the old moon.

The Indios saw the forces of nature as acting for good or evil, and they embodied these forces in gods and goddesses. The goal was to understand how the forces acted, and then carry out rituals that would make the divine powers act in the most favorable way for the whole tribe. The gods ruled while the priests interpreted the divine actions and performed rituals on behalf of the community. The priests thus had great power. Sometimes, when they abused that power, the people did away with the priests and moved on to build another city.

Being creative was an essential and natural part of life among los Indios. Neither the craftsman nor the artist was seen as someone essentially different from other members of the community. Their creations were simply another expression of the Indian sense of life's rhythms and the divine powers. And although people traded crafts objects for other things they needed (the Indians had a moneyless society), never did they think of an object as created primarily for buying and selling. There is a "song of the painter" in Náhuatl, the language of the Aztecs and other tribes, which expresses all this:

The good painter, understanding God in his heart,
defines things with his heart, dialogues with his own heart.

Raza today is of a craft culture and our creations often move with the same sense of unity and mystery, the same lack of commercialism.

This heritage can be seen today in Mexico and Latin America as well as the Southwest. In Mexico, we can see the remains of magnificent cities full of huge but well-proportioned stone temples, monuments, market places, game courts, all decorated with dramatically sculptured and brilliantly painted figures, in vibrant settings of lakes and towering, snow-capped mountains. The Maya alone constructed over a hundred cities like that. Many societies built game courts with such excellent acoustics that a normal human voice could be heard two hundred yards away. The game, by the way, was played with a rubber ball—for our ancestors, the Olmecs, had put rubber to use long before Europeans ever came to America.

It is believed that the Olmecs were the first people in America with a developed society and civilization—the Cultura Madre, or Mother Culture. They cut huge stones in the mountains sixty miles from their home on

the Gulf of Mexico, hauled them overland and built
great temples, statues, and monuments—all without the
wheel or any animals to carry them. Our Indian ancestors also built hundreds of pyramids.

Two of the best-known are those at the great city
of Teotihuacán (Place of the Gods)—the Sun pyramid, over two hundred feet high, and the pyramid of
the Moon. The Aztecs, whose culture flourished about
a thousand years after Teotihuacán, thought that giants
must have built these pyramids. It isn't only their size
and looks that are important. The pyramids, which
served strictly religious purposes, were built in certain
relation to the land and mountains around them—and
to the planets in the sky—so that the religion of the
people could be perfectly expressed on this spot.

People have always thought that pyramid-building
came to Mexico from other parts of the world. But
after twenty-five years of study, a Mexican scholar has
said that three thousand years before Christ a group
of strangers arrived in Egypt and showed how to build
pyramids. The group was headed by an architect named
Im Ho Tep, which in Maya means "son of the fifth
sun." It is the theory of this Mexican scholar that the
Maya civilization is the root culture of the world,
whose influence can also be seen in Greek, Japanese,
and other languages.

The ruins of Mexico show us that we had our
geniuses and we are second to none as scientists and
engineers. The Maya did computations of time going
back four hundred million years. They were skilled in
the use of the zero even before the Greeks and the
Hindus, and thousands of years before the computer

experts began building a system based on the zero and the number one, today called binary math.

Mexico City—then and today called Tenochtitlán—was one of the engineering triumphs of human history. According to legend, the migrating Aztec or Mexica people had been instructed to build their capital where they found an eagle perched upon a cactus growing from a rock, with a serpent in its claws. One day, while hunting in a swampland in the Valley of Mexico, a group of braves saw before them the fulfillment of their prophecy: a giant eagle upon a cactus holding a serpent. Draining of the swampland and building of the capital began immediately. The spot, according to the legend, was exactly where the great plaza called the Zócalo stands now in downtown Mexico City and there is a statue showing the braves at the moment of discovery. The eagle, cactus, and serpent live today as the official emblem of Mexico and its flag.

Under Moctezuma I (Anglo historians make the name Montezuma), the city grew tremendously but in a well-planned, orderly way. An elaborate system of causeways, dikes, and aqueducts was built to deal with the problem of living on top of water but without sweet water. The city had four great causeways, wider than modern avenues, raying out from a central plaza with canals serving as streets. And everywhere there was beauty, cleanliness, constant movement, and colorful life. All this moved a soldier in Cortés' army to exclaim about the city: "It is like the enchantments they tell of in the legend of Amadis! Are not the things we see a dream?"

The creativity of the community showed not only

in buildings but also in many kinds of individual production: pottery-making, weaving beautiful clothing and other goods, making stone utensils, featherwork, producing all kinds of useful or decorative objects from shell, mosaic, wood, gold, and jade, making wooden drums. Even an ordinary cooking pot would have its little touch of creativity. There was also the dance and music; this music was memorized, not written down, and its rhythms can still be heard today. Every craft and art showed the same deep sense of rhythm and nature that dominated all the rest of Indian life. Eagles, serpents, jaguars, tigers, coyotes, rabbits, fish, monkeys, and many kinds of plants were often depicted in the arts of the Indios.

Each of the different Indian cultures had certain crafts in which it excelled. The Olmecs are known for their outstanding sculpture in jade and other stones. The Zapoteca created the elaborate wall paintings on the inside of the tombs at the great city of Monte Albán, while in nearby Mitla the Mixtecs built temples decorated with stone mosaic fitted together perfectly, and they were also probably the first to work with metal—mostly gold. The Mayans carved beautiful picture-writing in stone, did wall paintings rich in color and movement, wove fine garments decorated with gold and dyed with plant substances or sometimes animal substances like the much-valued purple dye obtained from a particular kind of snail.

Los Indios used gold to make exquisite jewelry. They also drilled tiny holes in their teeth and filled them with gold (they were and still are great dentists). They saw gold as a thing of beauty, something to enjoy, while the Europeans who came later saw it strictly as a form of material wealth—for which they killed and destroyed.

In Mexico there were many kinds of schools, huge libraries, exciting theater, and a rich literature. Among the Aztec and the Maya, children studied not only elementary subjects but also advanced mathematics, philosophy, medicine, architecture, engineering. For books, the Indians had long manuscripts called codices that were written in complex picture languages (like hieroglyphics). Here they recorded their history, legends, religious teachings, and scientific observations. Thousands of these manuscripts filled libraries in various parts of Mexico and some can still be seen in Mexico City's Museum of Anthropology.

Besides the written literature, the Indios had poetry and prose that was memorized and passed from one generation to the next. Their poetry sang with many beautiful images, sounds, and rich expressions. We can hear much of those ancient sounds and feelings in the Spanish spoken in Las Americas today. Náhuatl, the Aztec language, is related to languages now spoken in the Southwest of the United States.

In the Indian societies, the woman was a far more developed and fulfilled person than the woman of Europe. She was a good craftsman, a strong laborer, a mechanic, a trapper, a doctor, sometimes a spiritual leader and a warrior. Weaving, a traditional occupation of women, was a sacred act to the Maya. The woman was the symbol of fertility and associated with the earth—with the elements of fire, warmth, earth, darkness; with the colors red and yellow. Men were associated with air, water, rain, and the colors of blue and green. These divisions were seen as two parts of a whole and in some of the Indian religions, man and woman were seen as divine twins. By having both gods and goddesses, los Indios created a unity of the species rather than a division of male and female.

The Indians' obedience to nature, their respect for nature, led to a respect for each other. Male and female are equally necessary for survival in the circle of life. The Indios did not think of *rights* in a competitive way.

Children were treated with a profound respect. They were not raised as belonging only to their immediate parents, although final authority rested there. They also received security and care from many elders. Adults treated all the young of a village as their own. A hungry child could run into any home for something to eat. If a child was hurt or needed to be corrected, any person who saw the need could feel free to help or to correct the child. (Today, an adult who spanks a neighbor's child may find himself with a lawsuit on his hands.) With everyone sharing in the raising of the children, the child grew up with a sense of security as well as love and responsibility toward his fellow human beings. It was a good way to achieve wholeness of spirit and real humanity.

Of all the tribes of Mexico, the Aztecs became the most powerful and warlike. They developed a system of vassal states—people they had defeated on the battlefield, who then had to make regular contributions to the Aztec treasury. Unlike Western colonial powers, the Aztecs did not treat the defeated states as their "property," to be occupied by an army and colonized. However, their actions did create resentment among the smaller tribes.

In its late years, the Aztecs also became more of a class society with a pyramid-kind of structure—the priests on top and the ordinary workers on the bottom. Still, it was never accepted that anyone should go without the basic needs of life—no matter how low in rank.

There was never a central government of what is today Mexico before the Spaniards came, and each clan regulated its own local affairs through a group of elected officers. If a decision had to be made that affected the whole tribe, this was done among the Aztecs by a supreme council composed of a member from each clan. From them, a supreme chief was chosen. All these officials were usually the wisest and most outstanding persons in the community as proven by years of service.

In a communal society where everyone shares the same basic beliefs and where everyone's basic needs are cared for, there is little reason for hyprocrisy, deceit, role-playing. There is little reason for crime. Honesty and order come almost naturally. The Indians had few material goods that people could not make for themselves or acquire through barter, so crimes involving property were not a problem. In business dealings, they had no need for written contracts—a person's word was considered binding.

Of the crimes that did exist, the most serious were those that injured the whole community, not just the individual (unless it was murder). Aztecs drew some fine lines that balanced well with their values. For example, petty theft in the market place brought the death penalty because it hurt a social gathering that was to benefit everyone. But theft of individual property was punished only by a fine, or servitude to the person robbed until he had been compensated. In the same way, brawling and fighting in the market place were dealt with severely while in individual cases of assault, the criminal paid for the cure of the injured person and any damage done. To steal corn, the basis of life, while it was still growing, called for the death penalty or slavery. But no one had to worry about helping himself to a few ears that were already ripe.

The Aztecs did not have prisons. Death or exile were the ways of punishing the most serious crimes. Forced servitude or "slavery" was not what we usually think of when we hear that word. Families headed by a slave could not be broken up at the will of the master; slaves could own property (and even have slaves of their own); and the penalty for murdering a slave was the same as for murdering anyone else—death. Nobody could be born into slavery. The main thing that a slave lost was the right to hold public office, a right that depended anyway on past service. Aztec "slavery" never became key to the economy, to the well-being of a ruling class.

What was daily life like among our Indio ancestors? Corn was the basis of the diet for everyone, as among all the Indians of North America. To the Maya, corn was sacred and even today the Maya speak to the corn in rituals, calling it "Your Grace." Maya hunters and others would also beg forgiveness before killing a

deer, explaining that they did so only out of great need
for food.

The Indios ground their corn on a stone metate
with a stone roller, just as you can see it done in
Mexico today, and then baked it into huge tortillas.
In fact the main foods eaten by our ancestors were
tortillas, beans, and chile—the same that many of us
eat today. Some of the ancient tribes had other dishes
as well: beans, squash, green and red peppers, avocados,
tomatoes, fish, turkey, eggs, sometimes meat, all found
locally, together with products like chocolate and pine-
apples from other parts of the country. Most of these
foods, along with *capulín* (choke cherries), the papaya
fruit, peanuts, and tobacco, originated in Mexico and
were among our ancestors' gifts to the world. So were
cotton and hemp, by the way. The maguey plant was
used by the Indians in many ways: as a vegetable, a
fodder, as a fiber for making sacks and rope, to make
the paper on which manuscripts were painted, and to
brew a strong drink called *pulque*—made from fer-
mented maguey juice. Nothing was wasted—even the
thorns were used for writing.

The Aztecs built their houses of sun-baked adobe,
the same material widely used by Raza in many areas
today. Homes were airy and comfortable but simple and
almost without furniture. People slept on straw mats
and kept their houses very clean. Today in Mexico you
still see Indian women sweeping and mopping not once
a week but every day—just as you find the poorest
Raza homes in the Southwest often the cleanest.

Sanitation, both public and in the home, was very
good and the ecology of the Indians could put us to

shame today. People bathed often, using the roots of the Saponaria for soap, at a time when Europeans might be taking two baths a year. The Indians washed their food with Octli, which acted as a disinfectant. Body waste was collected and taken to the fields to be used as fertilizer while urine was preserved in the home and used for the dyeing of cloth. Sunlight, fresh water, and simple ways of getting rid of human waste kept a people healthy—until the Spaniards came and let loose every kind of pestilence.

When people did get sick, the Indians were ready to give treatment. The Aztecs even performed brain surgery, covering the opening in the skull with a sea shell as surgeons today use metal plates. Europeans in those days were still going to the barber to be bled—to get rid of the devil or bad "humor" that they superstitiously believed to be the cause of the illness.

The Indians treated simple illnesses with massage and hot steam baths, for they knew that relaxation and intensive perspiration can often cure or decrease infection. Herbs were widely used; our ancestors knew and utilized about three thousand medicinal plants including quinine and castor oil. The main difference between much of the Aztecs' medicine and modern science is that the Indians used the natural product while today its equivalent is chemically produced. Many such uses can still be found today among Raza. It is no secret in the Southwest that marijuana, for example, can be boiled and then used in a hot bath as an effective remedy for rheumatism or arthritis.

The Indians often used datura, peyote, and other mushroom products to relieve mental stress and disorders. They also used such plants for ceremonial purposes, and much of the deep spiritual development of our ancestors can be credited to that. Our people developed their knowledge of inner space by using drugs in a communal, organized way. They knew what many of today's youth have yet to learn: that these drugs are not to be played with, that you don't pop a mushroom like an aspirin. They did not abuse their drugs or allow drugs to become a crutch. They did use them fully, knowingly, and with respect.

The Indians' awareness of nature's powerful forces also explains the practice of human sacrifice. Many people today condemn this practice. But let us remember that it was in the interest of the Spanish conquerors to make the Indians seem like bloodthirsty savages who needed to be "saved" by Christian Europeans. And let us try to understand the human sacrifices in terms of native American ideas.

The Aztec and Maya believed that for their society to survive, for the heavens not to fall on the earth or the waters engulf it, the gods must be nourished properly. Sacrificing things of little or no value would not be sufficient. The most precious offering was human life, centered in the heart. Therefore some would give up life on earth for the sake of the whole community. For the Indians, the sacrifices were a creative act—the rise of life from death. The victim was not viewed as an inferior; often he was showered with honors and in one ceremony the victim was treated like a prince for a year before being sacrificed.

We can see that this concept is not so different from the Christian sacrifice of Jesus Christ for the good of humanity. It is not considered that his sacrifice showed a barbarous lack of respect for human life. Yet that is what the Western mind often says about the Indian sacrifices. Even the practice of cannibalism, which sometimes occurred in the ancient civilizations, is not so different from eating Jesus Christ as is done today in some Christian religions by the drinking of wine—symbol of his blood—and consuming the host.

The human sacrifices of los Indios were based on an acceptance of death, as opposed to the Westerner's fear of death. If a person died, it could certainly be sad but life continued through the family, clan, and tribe. This is what gave a person immortality. People were not seen as isolated individuals, each trying to achieve personal immortality. The Indians saw death as part of the rhythm of continuing life.

Another important fact is that los Indios had no myth of heaven and hell, no belief that after death you would be rewarded or punished according to how you had acted on earth. They did have different places where you went after death, according to whether you had died on the battlefield, by drowning, in childbirth, or some other way. But the Western concept of human good versus human evil, the concept of personal guilt, all the ideas that have made people feel so divided within themselves, were not part of the indigenous way of life. They did have rituals where people performed acts of penance as well as ordinary fasting. But these were social acts, carried out for the good of the whole community. It was not to save your private soul, just as the long fasts of César Chávez today in the farmworkers' struggle are not for his sake but for the good of humanity.

The religious beliefs of our ancestors, and of the Indians in the United States today, are scorned by the same people who take Adam's rib and the rest of the Old Testament very seriously. People read that Jesus Christ walked on water, that he turned water into wine, and that he rose from the dead—and they do not call that superstition. But when it comes to native American ideas about creation and human life—these are labeled "superstition." It is often suggested that there is something evil about the Indians' basic beliefs—something "dark," as the white society in its racism likes to call everything it cannot understand and fears.

The beliefs and myths of the native Americans were deep, rich, and every bit as full of guidance for living as those of Christianity, Judaism, Buddhism, or Islam. Our ancestors in Mexico created great works comparable to the Christian Bible. One of these, *Los Libros de Chilam Balam*, a giant book of the Maya civilization, is still being translated. *Los Libros*, written in Mayan hieroglyphics, contain many texts, dealing with religion, history, medicine, astrology, astronomy, and other subjects.

This is only one example of the rich literature of native American religion. How much more existed and was destroyed, we will never know. But we do know that Spain had a policy of searching out and destroying every possible record of los Indios. In July 1562, the Spaniards by order of Diego de Landa destroyed twenty-seven codices (manuscripts) together with about five thousand inscribed pillars.

The Aztec calendar or Stone of the Sun, Piedra del Sol, is one record that survived. It was found in 1790 by men working to fix the foundations of the main cathedral in Mexico City. Far more than a calendar, this disc—weighing more than twenty tons and measuring thirteen feet across—not only shows the time elements ranging from years to centuries but also gives a history of creation and prophecies. It is a statement of the entire, infinite universe. The calendar stone itself was carved by the Aztecs but it contains symbols and concepts used in other Indian calendars as much as seven hundred years before Christ. The Maya had a calendar called Tzolkin, or wheel of days.

The Aztec calendar was made in a circle, with no beginning and no end, as the native American to this very day believes life to be. The center of the calendar, called the Eagle Bowl, shows the sun god. According to the calendar, earth and Man have passed through four ages—or suns—and we are now in the fifth, El Quinto Sol (The Fifth Sun). There are different explanations of the four previous suns, which had names like "Four Wind" and "Four Rain," but all of them say that these ages ended in total destruction—by flood, storm, and other disasters.

The calendar served as the key to the whole religion and indicated the days for fasting, feasting, sacrifice, mourning. It was not only a guide for the community but also for individuals in their daily lives—what days were favorable or unfavorable for certain actions. Today in certain parts of Mexico, such as Oaxaca, people still look to the calendar for guidance. The Stone of the Sun reminds us of where we came from and where we may go. It is the symbol of a way of life and a symbol of the spirit of the original American people.

As the calendar shows, the Indians had many gods and goddesses, each associated with a natural force or an animal. A powerful god of great importance was Tlaloc, the Rain God, whose face with its fangs and eye rings shows up in Mexican sculpture everywhere, and who had a companion goddess with a beautiful name—Our Lady of the Turquoise Skirt. The best-known female goddess was the earth or mother goddess, often called Tonantzin. She lived in a palace on Tepeyac Hill—the same hill where, after the Spanish conquest, an Indian had his vision of the Virgin of Guadalupe. This brown-skinned saint became a symbol of Mexico, of Raza, of our endurance as a people.

One of the most ancient, important and mysterious gods among the Indios was Quetzalcoatl. He is found among the different tribes with different names, meanings, and symbols but he seems to have been seen most often as a prophet and bringer of civilization—a teacher and spiritual leader. He is pictured as the Feathered Serpent—a serpent with the plumes of the quetzal bird (we should remember that the Indians did not associate snakes with evil but with mystery and power). According to some legends, Quetzalcoatl was born of a virgin who became pregnant after his father's death when she swallowed a piece of jade. He is said to have civilized and then ruled the Toltecs for twenty years, living in Tula, close to Mexico City. When Tula became involved in a civil war, Quetzalcoatl escaped and sailed away with the prophecy that he would return on a certain day.

Quetzalcoatl is often shown as having a black or red beard and a white face. The whiteness was nothing unusual, since the faces of gods were often shown as painted and white symbolized the color of corn (black or red could have symbolized the corn tassel). But after the Spanish conquest, the Catholic priests tried to use the legend of Quetzalcoatl to justify Cortés and his savagery. So the story has come down to us that Quetzalcoatl was blond and blue-eyed and that when Hernán Cortés appeared in Mexico with his strange horses and guns the people thought it was their wise and powerful god returning at last. This story aimed to make the people willing to accept the great white father—Spain.

What does seem true is that a series of frightening omens occurred at the time of Cortés' arrival in 1519, which led the Aztecs to expect some great disaster. A column of fire at midnight all year long, the destruction of one temple by fire and another by lightning, the daytime appearance of a comet, waves appearing suddenly on the Lake of Texcoco, and then the war chief's vision in a mirror of a host of armed men—these and other reported events unnerved the people and their leaders.

Meanwhile, the Indians heard rumors from the southeast of strange four-legged creatures with human bodies rising from their backs. These were, of course, Cortés and his four hundred men with their horses, an animal never seen before by the Aztecs. The Spaniards moved slowly but surely toward Mexico City, with the help of an Indian woman named Malinche and her followers. Finally Moctezuma II received Cortés in a cautious but hospitable way. Cortés immediately seized Moctezuma as a hostage.

The full story of the conquest is a long tragedy, in which the Indians defeated the Europeans at one point and had them on the run—but then lost. Moctezuma was killed—some say by his own people, supposedly angry at his weakness, but others say by the Spaniards. He was succeeded by his brother, who died, and then by their nephew Cuauhtémoc. This strong leader fought with great courage until the Spaniards captured him and his family. They imprisoned and tortured him, but Cuauhtémoc never lost his dignity. He died years later, murdered on Cortés' march to Honduras.

Despite the courage of Indians like Cuauhtémoc, and some Spanish defeats, the story almost had to end as it did. People were demoralized by the omens of disasters. The conquistadores had cannon and muskets, weapons totally unknown to the Indians as well as terribly noisy and hard to understand—how could something kill you without touching you? They also had crossbows, steel swords, armor, savage dogs, and the horses—all equally unknown to the Aztecs. And the conquistadores had entirely different ideas about war from the Indians.

Aztec war always had a strong spirit of ceremony and its main purpose was not to kill but to take live prisoners for the sacrifices. The Spaniards fought a dead-serious war of total conquest and annihilation if necessary. On the battlefield, the Indians' basic tactic was simply one of mass, frontal attack for a single, decisive battle. The Europeans had various military techniques that included the splitting of the enemy's

forces and then destroying each part separately, pro-
longed campaigns, mobile maneuvering. The Indians
would never have thought of war as justifying the
destruction of all the houses in an area so as to fill the
canals with debris—an action taken by Cortés to give
the troops ground for maneuvering.

The Spaniards also had a secret weapon—smallpox.
The Aztecs had no previous experience with it and
therefore no immunity to it. When an epidemic of
smallpox swept through Tenochtitlán not long after
the arrival of Cortés, the people died by the thousands.

In all these ways, the war of conquest represented a
confrontation between two cultures. It was symbolized
by the fact that when the Spanish demanded precious
objects, the Indians offered jade and turquoise, their
most precious substances. Cortés and his men wanted
gold, which the Aztecs valued only in a minor way, and
the Spaniards became very irritated. They would kill
for gold.

The Indians fighting Cortés also had a serious internal problem. This was the neighboring tribes from
whom the Aztecs had long taken tribute, including
people to sacrifice. Many of them joined with the
Spaniards as a chance to revolt against the Aztecs and
share in the expected Spanish victory. No one, not
even Cuauhtémoc, managed to unite the Indians in
the Valley of Mexico against their common enemy.

In 1521, the Aztecs made a last stand against Cortés
in the northern part of Mexico City. So many of their
people died that the canals turned red with blood. This
final defeat left the people dazed and overwhelmed
by destruction and sickness. Not only hunger, thirst,

and wounds plagued them but all the diseases just
imported from Europe. Smallpox and a type of in-
fluenza turned Mexico into a ghost of its former self. As
an unknown Aztec poet said in 1528:

> Broken spears lie in the roads;
> we have torn our hair in our grief.
> The houses are roofless now, and their walls
> are red with blood. . . .
>
> We have pounded our hands in despair
> against the adobe walls
> for our inheritance, our city, is lost and dead.
> The shields of our warriors were its defense,
> but they could not save it.
>
> We have chewed dry twigs and salt grasses;
> we have filled our mouths with dust and bits of adobe;
> we have eaten lizards, rats, and worms. . . .

Two worlds had met, the East and the West, and
the "Christian" West massacred thousands upon thousands to quench its thirst for gold. Swarming through
the sea of Aztec blood, Europe would brand with a
hot iron those who survived but refused the new religion. All this it did in the name of Jesus Christ. And
all this we, the mestizo, feel in our blood today, all
this makes us cry out from the heart with a *grito* of
sorrow and rage.

> Before the coming of the mighty men and Span-
> iards there was no robbery by violence, there was no
> greed and striking down one's fellow man in his
> blood, at the cost of the poor man, at the expense of
> the food of each and everyone . . . It was the be-
> ginning of tribute, the beginning of church dues, the
> beginning of strife with purse snatching, the begin-
> ning of strife with guns, the beginning of robbery

with violence, the beginning of debts enforced by
false testimony, the beginning of individual strife, a
beginning of vexation.

From a Maya commentary

Gun in one hand and cross in the other, the Spaniards began their self-appointed task of raping a land
and a people—and a whole philosophy of life. Cortés
expressed their attitude: "I came to get gold, not to
till the soil like a peasant." The Spaniards let the
highly developed agriculture of Mexico die out while
they went racing after minerals.

To get the minerals, the Spaniards needed workers.
But the Indians did not want to work for the Spaniards, to sell their labor. The *encomienda* system was
then applied. It provided for a Spaniard to be granted
one or more entire villages and the right to exploit
everything in them—including the Indians. High-ranking Spaniards received huge grants of land—as much as
two and a half million acres—and perhaps also an
encomienda of Indians from other places.

The Spaniard would then build his big hacienda
home and control everything in the area from food
distribution to fiestas. In return, he supposedly provided the natives with food, housing, and religious
instruction. This *patrón* has been pictured by many
as a guardian, benefactor, a colorful figure. In Mexico,
we can remember that he came, he conquered, and he
was the man with the whip.

Spain passed many laws, known as the Laws of the
Indies, which were supposed to protect the natives from
abuse. These laws said that the persons and property
of the natives must be respected and that no transfer
of land from the natives to the Spaniards could be

made without approval of the viceroy (the Spanish ruler of Mexico). Many times a strong effort was made to carry out these laws and pass still stronger ones. But the greed and racism of the Spaniards in Mexico proved too strong over the years.

They grabbed up the land. They destroyed the old communal economy and replaced it with feudal exploitation, making the Indians into serfs. Slowly but surely the natives lost their traditional, individual plots and were left with nothing but the common lands or *ejidos*, which could not provide enough food. The Indians ended up working in the mines, on the big estates, or building churches. They ceased to be a free people.

A society with concern for everyone in the community was destroyed and replaced by a society ruled for the benefit of the rich. Upper-class Western ideas of privacy and ownership were forced on the Indios. To the European, privacy meant shutting out everybody except one's immediate family. The Spanish hacienda was the home of a single family unit, the nuclear family, with the father as dictator. The Europeans did not understand the humanitarian, tribal ideas of the Indios.

No one suffered more from this breakdown of communal life than the Indian woman. She had been a vital and respected pillar of the whole Indian social structure. In order to destroy that structure and establish their own, the Spaniards had to dominate the women completely. This process began when Cortés took as mistress an Indian woman named Malinche, who had organized some of those tribes we mentioned before which were opposed to the Aztec imperial rule. It continued with the rape of Indian women. The Spaniards set about building up a strong male figure, the *macho,* whose masculinity was based on how superior and dominating he acted. This concept of machismo was wrapped up and forced on the Indians as a "tradition." The new religion brought by the Spaniards—including the story that woman was responsible for "original sin"—also was used to justify oppressing the Indian women.

The Spanish declared women to be inferior and said that their first commandment was to build up the male ego. Spanish machismo went hand in hand with this thing called "ego," the habit of regarding one's self as the center of everything. Egoism makes the "I" opposed to "we," and alienates people from their fellow human beings. It encourages greed, envy, jealousy, dishonesty, hypocrisy. It is the product of every competitive society, for it tells people to think that being alive means acquiring possessions, and to think only of self. Of all the new illnesses that the Europeans introduced in the Americas, none was worse than the disease of egoism.

Yet the egoism and materialism brought to Mexico by Spain were a mild form of the disease, compared to what we see today as a total life concept. Spain was still a feudal country without big business, and it was not so European a country as other nations which became the world's major colonial powers. The Spanish people and culture were strongly influenced by the Moors, who had occupied Spain for five hundred years. They were an African people, a non-"Christian" people, far more advanced than the Europeans of those times. It was the Moors who had introduced rice, sugar, and cotton to Spain; beautiful styles of architecture, music, poetry; advanced irrigation methods; a breed of horses that enabled Spain to develop the world's finest horses. Four thousand words in the Spanish language are of Moorish origin. The Moorish influence helped to make Spain more human in some of its attitudes and practices than the other colonial powers in the Americas.

Still, most of the Spaniards who came to Mexico saw the native peoples as "dark savages," more animal than human, fit to be branded with hot irons or slaughtered at will. The priests thought the same way—but said the Indios could be saved by becoming Christians. For the Indians, Christian baptism meant another kind of oppression.

When an Indian was baptized, he was given a new name—a Spanish name—which made him two people. He was also told of a soul, separate from his mind and body, and this divided him further within himself. He was threatened with a fate after death, which sounded horrible. He was filled with feelings of guilt for supposed sins. Up to the conquest, the Indian had been a whole person. Now all the separations and divisions of the Western mind were set to work on him. Spain's military conquest was followed by psychological warfare on the Indio.

It can never be said that the Indian of Mexico gave up without a struggle, or that the Indian spirit was totally broken. There were many rebellions by the native peoples such as the one led by Jacinto Canek in Yucatán in 1761. Canek was finally captured by the

Spanish, tortured, killed, his body burned and the ashes scattered in the air. But no wind was strong enough to blow away the spirit of revolt in Yucatán, home of the Maya, who refused to learn Spanish and who assert their independence even today. The Yaqui Indians in northern Mexico have been no less defiant. Even after Mexico became independent from Spain, thousands of Yaqui joined a revolt led by Juan Banderas and Dolores Gutiérrez to win a separate, independent Indian state in northern Mexico. They fought with bows and arrows until both Juan and Dolores were captured and executed in 1833.

The Indians were often joined in revolt by the black slaves, whom the Spaniards had brought to Mexico. There were great numbers of these Africans. Records show that up to 1575, the Blacks—not counting mulattoes—outnumbered Spaniards throughout North America. Eric Wolf tells us in *Sons of the Shaking Earth* that during the rule of Spain over Mexico, 300,000 Spaniards came—and 250,000 African slaves. It was a slave of Cortés named Juan Gattido who found three grains of wheat in a sack of rice and planted them—thus becoming the first person to plant wheat in the Americas. The slaves not only joined in the Indian rebellions but also had revolts of their own—like the one led by Yanga in Veracruz, or the revolt near Córdoba in 1735, which took 500 Spaniards to put down.

The Spanish conquistador—unlike other European colonizers—brought almost no women to the Americas. When Cortés took Malinche as his mistress, there began an intensive mixing of Indian and Spanish that produced a new people—the mestizo. Malinche can be called the mother of the mestizo, of our Raza. This mixing of racial groups, and the creation of the mestizo, was officially recognized by Spain in its Laws of the Indies of 1680. Over the centuries, the Indian prevailed.

Two thirds of the native Indians died between the Spanish invasion and 1650, but they built back their population and today only 5 per cent of Mexico's people can be called "pure" Spanish. The backbone of Mexico is Indio and mestizo, not Spanish. The *huaraches* that the *campesino* wears today are the same that the Toltecs put on their feet centuries ago. The subways of Mexico City today follow the same routes as the canals of the Aztecs. Cloth is still made from the maguey plant, and so is the liquor called *pulque*. Today in Mexico we see the use of urine for curing hides, much as the Aztecs used the same human waste to dye cloth. Everywhere we can see traces of the old native ways of living, feeling, thinking.

And los Indios themselves are still there. Today one can visit the state of Chiapas, Mexico, and view the very much alive, very pure-bred Maya peoples. San Cristóbal de Las Casas in Chiapas is a market center where indigenous tribes gather to sell their goods. There live the Chamula, the Sinacantan, the Oschux (made up of the Tzeltal Tzotzil tribes) and others. They are very much the majority of the population; the Tzeltal tribe alone numbers one hundred thousand. They are living day to day with their philosophies and old ways of life, even though they are being pushed into the jungle by a system and mentality alien to them.

In San Cristóbal de Las Casas we find the international center for anthropologists known as Na-Bolom Centro de Estudios Científicos, established by Frans Blom and Gertrude Duby Blom (known as Trudi Blom). Frans Blom was an archaeologist who brought much attention to the ruins in Campeche and the ancient Maya city of Palenque. Trudi now devotes her life to exposing the poverty and oppression of the Indians; the burning and clearing of the forest, erosion of land and the looting of Maya monuments. She helps develop programs for the conservation of nature and of humanity—the native tribes of Mexico.

The tribes continue to speak their own native tongues. There are many of these: 260 between the northern border of Mexico and the southern border of Guatemala. People often speak another language as well, which is a common tongue between tribes. So in Chiapas we hear Spanish, a tribal tongue, and a third tongue which is a common language between tribes of certain areas.

The Church is still hard at work to clamp the guilt chains on the Indios of Chiapas. Since they are very poor, they often have only one or two tunics—and sleep naked at night, using their tunics as blankets. The Church tells them that they should wear clothes to sleep, because "God comes at night and he doesn't want to see you without clothes." We doubt that the Indios believe this. Although 90 per cent of Mexico's people are Catholic today, the native belief in living in harmony with nature is far from dead.

There is a saying that "a man who obeys nature cannot tolerate the idea of obeying man." This spirit explains much of the native American survival. And so "the conquest" is a term that may apply to the Indian lands and governments, but the Indian spirit and values have never been wholly conquered for they have a basic concept of total freedom. Like the two volcanoes that tower near Mexico City—each over seventeen thousand feet high—they were just too large, too close to the grand forces of nature, too enduring, for any complete or final submission.

In those thousands of years stretching between the first civilizations of our Indian ancestors and full establishment of the European in America—from about 1700 B.C. to A.D. 1700—we of La Raza can see that our past is rich in beauty and wisdom. Our ancestors were not "savage" or "primitive" at all—neither in technology and the arts nor in human values and life style. The myth of the savage Indian is just that, a myth.

This holds true for all native Americans. In this chapter, we have talked mostly about the Indios of central and southern Mexico, but of course our Indian ancestors also included people from the many tribes and pueblos of what is now the United States. They were here thousands of years before the Spanish. The Chicano or mestizo of today is not just a mixture of Spanish and Mexican Indian, but also North American Indian. When we study their cultures, we find that they, too, should hardly be written off as "savages."

Near Pecos, New Mexico, about A.D. 1100, Pueblo Indians were well settled in villages along the streams. By A.D. 1450, the Indians there had multistoried buildings built around a central plaza, with some 660 rooms for living quarters and storage together with at least 22 kives (ceremonial chambers). And even earlier, in about A.D. 900, Pueblo Indians at Chaco Canon, New Mexico, had built many large pueblos including one of the biggest "apartment houses" in the history of the world. Five stories high, Pueblo Bonito housed more than 1,200 people around a large outdoor plaza that was the center of a busy social life.

These people ate corn ground on the metate, lived in the tribal way, and also had a rich craft culture. They made tools from obsidian, beautiful pottery, fine ornaments and jewelry of turquoise, and majestic robes from the bright feathers of birds that they got from the Indians of Mexico in exchange for Chacoan pottery. And they had the same basic philosophy in their arts and crafts as the Indians of Mexico: a communal and spiritual philosophy.

In our present search for self, we are finding many answers in our own history, life values, and styles. We can see why we have, to this day, such a conflict with the Westerner's thinking and society. We find much strength in the values of the Indios. This does not mean that we see no value in modern technology but that we recognize the value of our roots, of our native knowledge. The two need not conflict; they can strengthen each other.

The society of our Indian ancestors was a society geared to PEOPLE-living and PEOPLE-development and PEOPLE-relations. Technology and machines are valuable when they serve people, not when people serve them. Perhaps that is why the white mind and system seem so sick and shattered today. The gringo does not view nature with respect, he only seeks ways to conquer it. He does not ally himself with nature, toward the goal of world-wide human growth. Instead he destroys it, in a rush to make more money that benefits only the super-rich. He has separated people from nature, he has separated them from one another, and he has divided them inside as well.

Many people in the United States today—including Anglos—sense that something important is missing from life. They thirst for something spiritual and are told to compete—which only creates more thirst. Raza today feel we have answers to many gringo problems, and that is why we aim to develop as a people within our own cultural knowledge.

The real, *original* American way of life existed for thousands of years among the native peoples on this continent, from Alaska to Tierra del Fuego. Cooperation and communalism are as native to this continent as corn itself, and still live today in many places. We still have a strong sense of family ties and we call our extended family "La Familia de La Raza." We can all learn much from the non-competitive life of the native Americans. We can draw deep inspiration from our ancestors, the first Americans.

3

Why Remember the Alamo?

WHEN WE LEARN in school about the history of the United States, we are always told how it began with the Pilgrims, Plymouth Rock, and Thanksgiving. Yet many years before the *Mayflower* landed, men had already come from Mexico to explore and colonize a large part of this country. Years before the first English settlement, Spaniards already had a capital city in what is now the United States. And of course long before the Spaniards, there were the natives who lived here—the original Americans called Indians.

It was in 1539—almost seventy years before the first English colony—that Spain began spreading its empire from Mexico to the north. Spanish explorers traveled as far north as Canada. On their maps, they drew a line between what is now the United States and Canada, and wrote above it "Acá nada"—meaning "here, nothing." The words combined to made the name "Canada."

Spain's first expedition to what is now the Southwest consisted of one Spaniard and a Christianized Moor from Africa named Estevanico or Estebán—sometimes called "the Black Mexican"—together with a small number of Mexican Indian servants. Estebán is one of the most dramatic figures in the history of what is now the United States. Born in Africa, he had traveled in North America with another Spanish explorer and learned six Indian dialects as well as the arts of the medicine man. He explored more of the Southwest and probably learned more about its history than any other man of his day. Estebán became a legend to the Indians, who had never before seen anyone like this tall African, and among certain tribes he was treated like a god.

Leaving from Mexico City in 1539, on foot and without maps or arms, Estebán would march several days ahead of his group—leaving markers on the way. The group reached Arizona, then made their way to the Zuñi settlements in western New Mexico. They were looking for "the seven cities of gold" that the Spaniards had heard about as places of fabulous wealth. They found one of them—but it turned out to be an ordinary little village built mostly of mud. As for Estebán, he met a sad end. Apparently his popularity with the Indian women became too much for some of the native men, who banded together against Esteban and killed him.

The other six "cities of gold" turned out no better than the first. Francisco Coronado was the next major explorer to go looking for them. When he arrived at a village called Tiguex, near what is today Albuquerque, he was so angry about the lack of gold that he burned two hundred Indians at the stake. Coronado went on across Texas and into Kansas, looking for still another golden town. When this one turned out to be a myth too, Coronado had his Indian guide killed and then headed back to Mexico. These actions by Coronado were not forgotten by the Indians, who later killed one of Coronado's men when he went back into their lands. This man is now called "the first Christian martyr on American soil" by people who have forgotten why he was killed.

When the Spaniards didn't find those "cities of gold," they slowed down their exploration. They concentrated on a few areas of what is today the Southwest. These were declared part of "La Nueva España"—New Spain—the name for the entire Spanish empire in America. New Spain was a colony, with Spain as the so-called "mother country." Spain considered it a possession; the native peoples and their natural resources were also considered possessions. As in all colonies, Spain's goal was to take out those resources with the cheap labor of the native peoples and then process those resources to sell them in Spain or to other countries. The "mother country" also sold finished products to the natives of the colony. The people in the colony stayed poor while the "mother country" got rich. This is how our people, the mestizos of "La Nueva España," first became colonized in our own land.

The main base of Spanish power in the Southwest was the Provincia de Nuevo México de Santa Fe—an area that today would include New Mexico and Colorado together with parts of Texas and Utah. The colonization of Nuevo México began when a man named Juan de Oñate set out from Mexico toward what is now El Paso. He had made a huge fortune from Mexican silver, and took with him four hundred soldiers, seven thousand head of livestock, and eighty-three carriages of goods—including velvet and satin suits, linen shirts, feathered hats, and many servants. His group moved north from El Paso and in 1598 they established the first capital city of what is now the United States at the village of San Juan Pueblo, New Mexico. This capital was later moved to Santa Fe in 1609.

Within twenty more years, Spain had set up a chain of settlements in the area. But the Indians revolted in 1680 and drove out the colonizers within three short days. Later Diego de Vargas restored Spanish rule, treating the Indians in a more civilized way than Oñate had done. Vargas made treaties with them, promising respect for their customs and culture in return for the use of their lands. The Spaniards also drew up documents recognizing Indian land ownership.

The Spanish settlements would not have survived without the help given to them by the Pueblo Indians— the Indians who lived in settled villages called pueblos. Until the summer of 1608, the Spaniards failed to produce a single crop on their own. They had to live off the Pueblo Indians, who had carried on irrigated farming for centuries. The Indians taught the Europeans how to stay alive. They provided not only food and shelter, but served as guides and did household work for the Spaniards.

Perhaps the most important asset that the Spaniards took from the Indians was: women. Unlike the English colonizers, the Spanish did not bring women to this country. Instead they took the native women as wives, as they had done in Mexico. They had many children and these children were mestizo—of mixed races. The new mestizo generation soon outnumbered the so-called "pure male Spaniards." One historian says that in 1846 there were a thousand Spaniards in Nuevo México and sixty thousand mestizos.

What was life like in those early Spanish settlements? In the capital city of Santa Fe, there were big hacienda-like palaces and a handful of rich people lived a comfortable life provided for them by thousands of Indians and mestizos, who were all housed in the poor man's section of town, a barrio. But outside the capital of Nuevo México, we find a very unusual kind of society. You could call it communalism, *comunidad*.

Spain settled Nuevo México by giving grants of land—called *mercedes*—to different kinds of people. In some cases, the king of Spain would grant a large private estate to one of his favorites. This man would then build a big house, a hacienda, and have the land worked by the Indians and mestizos. But there was another, more common type of land grant. The king would make a grant of land to a family or a group of families, who would then build a whole village. Each family would get its own small plot of land to cultivate. But most of the grant would be for the use of the entire village. This would be the grazing lands, the forests, and certain other areas. All of that land was owned in common by the whole village community. The individual plots could be passed on to heirs, divided up among heirs, or sold. The common land, called the *ejido*, could never be sold and had to remain the property of the whole community. Sometimes as much as 95 per cent of the land in a grant would be *ejido*.

This second kind of grant was made mostly for security reasons—to create settlements that would serve as outposts against the Indians. Not only was the land held in common, but work was done communally. Planting and caring for the crops, building homes, slaughtering animals for food, tanning hides, canning and drying food, making and washing mattresses—all these tasks were shared. Life, with all its joys and sorrows, was shared. If one family was short of food, another would help out. If one man had a successful hunt, the meat was shared with the whole community. People worked together, not for money but because they knew it was the best way for all of them to survive.

Theirs was not a money economy. They lived off of what they could grow, the crops and the livestock. If they needed something else, they got it by making it themselves—handicrafts—and by barter. There was little to buy and, since most people shared, they did not feel their poverty in a lonely, bitter way.

The mestizo people of those villages had very few material comforts or conveniences. But they created many things of beauty by themselves: fine silverwork, tinwork, weaving, and wood carving. One of the high points in their culture was the art of making *santos*— images of saints, carved from wood or painted on wood in strong simple lines and with great feeling. These can be seen in the museums of Santa Fe, New Mexico, and other places today. The village people also created a strong literature and a people's theater, of which we know very little because it was either printed in Mexico or not written down at all. But we can find enough of it to know that it combined the Spanish and Indian languages, ideas, feelings. A poet who came to Nuevo México with Juan de Oñate in the year 1610 wrote the first epic poem in what is now the United States. This poet was Don Cristóbal Becerra y Moctezuma, grandnephew of Moctezuma.

Life in the Spanish province of California was very different from Nuevo México. In California, Spanish colonization did not begin until 1769. Spain used the mission system—large estates of land that were given to the Catholic Church and worked for the benefit of the Church. The missions were strung out along the California coast from San Diego to San Francisco. The priests ran them and the local Indians did all the work. It was semislavery for the Indians, who died by the dozens while the Church's profits boomed. In 1834, the property of the missions had a total value of seventy-eight million dollars. That year the mission propperties were taken away from the Church and put into the hands of fewer than eight hundred families. These few rich families stood at the top of the social ladder with the Indians and poor mestizos at the bottom. It was like feudalism.

In other parts of the Southwest, like Arizona and Texas, Spain did not succeed in setting up any permanent colonies. Every time a mission, village, or a big hacienda was established, it would be wiped out by Apache, Comanche, and other nomadic Indian tribes. They did not help the Spaniards as the settled Pueblo Indians had done but instead put up a constant, fierce resistance to the invaders. The Apache and Comanche soon learned how to ride horses even better than the Spanish—and did not need saddles or stirrups. With no settlements to worry about defending, the nomadic Indians could carry out lightning raids on a mission or village and then disappear again.

The whole Spanish empire in the Southwest had only a few thousand soldiers, officials, and priests to hold it under control. All through the 1700s and into the 1800s, the colonies did not grow very much. They were isolated from each other and they were isolated from Mexico. They were also isolated from the United States. The mestizos and Spaniards living in Nuevo México or California knew very little about what was going on in the rest of North America. They could not suspect in the early 1800s that their lives were about to change very suddenly—and for the worse.

In the United States, to the east, lived some men who had greedy eyes on the Spanish colonies of Mexico,

Nuevo México, and California. These men controlled the industries of New England and the big cotton plantations of the South. The industrialists were reaching the point where they needed new markets, new places to sell their products. The southern plantation owners also needed to expand, to get more land for planting cotton and more labor. Both groups were interested in the Spanish colonies.

The United States drove Spain out of Florida in the early 1800s by a series of military operations and wars that were conducted without the approval of Congress. The United States also acquired from France the huge Louisiana Territory, which ran from the Mississippi River to the Rocky Mountains and from Canada to the Gulf of Mexico. By 1820, the United States had control over all the eastern area and it was right at the backdoor of the Spanish colonies in the Southwest.

In those same years, the Spanish empire was falling apart in Europe. Spain was losing its grip on its colonies in America. The businessmen in the eastern United States were happy about this. They could see the possibility of moving into a big area of the West, once Spain lost control. So they watched, and they waited. When Mexico won its independence from Spain, it was like a green light for the Anglo businessmen of the East.

Our struggle for independence from Spain officially began on September 16, 1810. On that day, a parish priest named Miguel Hidalgo went into his small church early in the morning and rang the church bell. The people of the parish, which was named Dolores and located about two hundred miles north of Mexico City, were mostly Indians. They liked Father Hidalgo, who was different from most priests and who had taught them carpentry, textile-making, and other skills. They hated the Spaniards. So when they heard the bell, they went to the church where Father Hidalgo raised his voice to cry out the famous words: *"Viva Nuestra Señora de Guadalupe, viva la independencia!"*—Long live our Lady of Guadalupe (the Brown Virgin), long live independence! These words, known as the Grito de Dolores—the Cry of Dolores, were taken up by the Indians. September 16 would later become Mexico's official Independence Day.

It was a long and bloody struggle against Spain. Father Hidalgo was defeated and shot the next year, 1811. Then another revolutionary priest, José María Morelos, arose to carry on the struggle. He stood barely five feet tall, with broad shoulders and burning eyes, and he dreamed of an independent Mexico in which the big estates would be broken up. The wealth of the rich would be divided among the poor and the government. Morelos inspired many people to join the struggle for independence.

Hidalgo and Morelos are the two great names of Mexican independence, but there were many other heroes and heroines. One of these was Gertrudis Bocanegra, sometimes called Mexico's Joan of Arc. She worked in the underground, transporting clothing, food, and weapons to the soldiers. When both her husband and son died in the fight, she still continued her work under Morelos. After seven years, Gertrudis was captured and tortured by the Spanish forces. But she never gave them the names of her fellow workers, she never betrayed anyone. The Spaniards finally executed her.

Morelos himself was captured and tortured in 1815. The Church did nothing to save his life, just as it had done nothing save Hidalgo—it was on the side of the Spaniards and interested only in protecting its own wealth. But new guerrilla leaders like Guadalupe Victoria (his real name was Felix Fernandez) and Vicente Guerrero carried on the fight.

Finally, in 1821, the Spanish surrendered. With independence, the government of Mexico took over the Spanish colonies to the north. Nuevo México, California, and the other areas now became *departamentos* (departments) of Mexico.

The U. S. Government helped Mexico win its independence—but why? They knew that Mexico, free of Spain, would be a weak new nation. It could not defend itself—or its northern territories. The door would be wide open for the businessmen and plantation owners of the East to step in.

Their first stepping stone would be Mexico's Departamento de Téjas.

> The occupation, separation and annexation (of Texas) were, from the inception of the movement to its final consummation, a conspiracy to acquire territory out of which slave states might be formed for the American union.
>
> President Ulysses S. Grant

The whole process of taking over Texas was planned from the beginning by President Andrew Jackson and

his friends, most of them Southerners. By 1830, the
northern industrialists and the southern plantation owners had become real economic rivals. Southern agriculture was fighting against northern industry for national power. The southern interests knew that if they
didn't expand, they would be defeated by the economic
power of the North. So the South had special reasons
for wanting to take over Téjas. Both North and South
wanted that territory for new markets and resources,
as we mentioned before.

Men from the East had already begun to arrive in
Téjas—part of Mexico—in the 1700s. There were no
great mountain ranges to separate Téjas from Anglo-
America, and there were rivers as well as coast line to
encourage travel. These first men, called filibusterers,
fought their way in—killing and laying waste in the area
around San Antonio. Most of them came from the
slave states and they brought with them a racist superiority attitude. They treated the Mexicans living in
Téjas the same way they treated Black people, and
they showed no respect for the laws of Mexico. When
Mexico abolished slavery in 1826, the filibusterers just
ignored the new law and kept on bringing in slaves.

President Jackson and his friends wanted to do more
than filibuster their way into Téjas, especially since the
law against slavery did make it a little hard to establish big plantations. So they drew up a plan. The
United States would try to buy Téjas from Mexico.
But in case that didn't work, Anglo settlers would be
brought into Téjas until there were enough of them
there to declare a "revolution" against Mexico. The

Mexicans would be kicked out, and then the United States would annex Téjas.

The conspiracy was in full operation by 1829. Jackson's good friend Sam Houston went to New York and Washington looking for people to invest in the conquest of Téjas. Houston sent agents all over the country to recruit "settlers" for Téjas. These agents used a secret code to report back; Jackson and Houston also communicated secretly. Another person who played an important part in the whole plan was Moses Austin and later his son, Stephen.

Moses Austin asked the Mexican Government for a large grant of land in Téjas, where he would establish a settlement of three hundred Anglo-American families. All the families would be Roman Catholics and of good character, he said, and they would swear allegiance to the Mexican Government. Mexico in good faith agreed to grant this land to Moses Austin. Later his son, Stephen, got more contracts to settle Téjas. By 1833, he had issued land titles to two thousand Anglo families. Austin and also Sam Houston even became Mexican citizens to convince Mexico of their honorable intentions.

In 1836, it was clear that Mexico would not sell Téjas. But there were enough Anglos there for the other plan to be put into effect. So the Anglos decided that they would declare their "independence" from Mexico. Having received the land from Mexico on certain conditions, they simply broke the agreement and called it a "revolution." Sam Houston himself recognized that they were nothing more than thieves when he said: "So long as we don't choose a government and declare war and proclaim independence, we are just pirates." To make the so-called revolution look more legal, Houston and his friends set up a so-called government. They wrote a Constitution. Everybody knew it was just a trick; as Houston later told a friend, "We signed the constitution on my birthday and then went on a two-day drunk."

The United States whipped up a tremendous national enthusiasm for helping "Texas" win its "independence." In New York, Boston, Philadelphia, and many other cities, rallies and benefits were held to raise funds for the "Texans" against what was called "the Mexican tyrants." Money poured in. Sam Houston was named commander of the army and Téjas was named Texas.

The President of Mexico quickly sent in troops to put down the phony revolution, and they won several victories in a row. The most famous of these was retaking the Alamo fort in San Antonio. "Remember the Alamo" is the famous cry that has come down to us from that battle. We are told that the Mexicans massacred hundreds of helpless Anglos who had taken refuge in the Alamo. "Remember the Alamo" has always meant: remember the massacre and get revenge on Mexico. But what really happened at the Alamo?

When Mexico's troops began winning in Texas, many Anglos panicked and took refuge in the Alamo fort. A small number of Mexicano women and children also went there. Houston ordered that the fort be abandoned, because it couldn't be defended and he couldn't promise any help. But Jim Bowie, the man in command at the fort, didn't want to give up. Bowie, a supposed hero of "the Wild West" who was actually a businessman and politician, had acquired millions of acres of land in Texas. So he stubbornly insisted on staying in the Alamo.

With Bowie were William Travis and Davy Crockett. Travis was a well-to-do Southerner who had come to Texas after letting a slave be sentenced to death for a crime that he, Travis, had committed. Crockett was a businessman from Tennessee who dreamed of making a fortune in Texas. He had volunteered for the gringo army with the idea of getting in on the fight at an early stage, to pave the way for making that fortune. Bowie and Travis both owned slaves and each had a slave with him inside the Alamo.

The Mexican attack on the Alamo began on February 23, 1836. Soon after, General Santa Anna sent word to the people inside that if they would just put down their arms and swear never to take them up again to fight Mexico, their lives and property would be respected. This offer was answered with a volley of cannon fire. The Mexican troops continued to shell the fort and then stormed it on March 6.

They took the fort, but paid dearly for the victory. Mexico lost many more men at the Alamo than the Anglos. Bowie, Travis, and Crockett all died fighting as did the other men. It was not a massacre, it was a battle. The women and children were all removed safely from the Alamo and given money and quilts. The two slaves who had been inside were freed by the Mexicanos.

That is the true story of the Alamo. Yet "Remember the Alamo" has come down to us as a cry of anger and bitterness from the Anglo. It is we Chicanos who can really feel bitter, because we see the hypocrisy and deception of "Remember the Alamo." That cry is taught to promote hate toward Mexico, Mexicans, and ourselves. For us, the Alamo was a victory in the struggle by Mexico to defend itself against invasion and aggression. For us, the Alamo was the birth of the gringo—when the gringo first showed us his true colors.

The Alamo was the last of Mexico's victories. Soon after, General Santa Anna was defeated and captured in a surprise attack and he signed a treaty recognizing the "independence" of Texas in exchange for his freedom. The Mexican Government did not confirm that treaty so the war went on. The gringos in Texas even sent a band of 270 men to invade Nuevo México. They were defeated, but that was the beginning of a new move—to take over still more of Mexico's territory.

This move began with Anglo trappers and traders—just plain businessmen, who are called "frontiersmen" and "pioneers" by most history books. They started going into Nuevo México to make money, without buying permits and without paying for what they took as Mexican law required. Their headquarters was a so-called trading post, actually a fort, which protected and helped these businessmen. The fort was run by Charles Bent and his friends. Later men like Bent also began to buy up land, secretly.

Then came another move. The gringos in Texas claimed that part of Nuevo México belonged to them, and they sent soldiers there in 1841 to claim it. But these men were captured and jailed. Still, that didn't stop the greedy Anglos.

The President of the United States in 1845 was James Polk, and he badly wanted an excuse to attack Mexico so that his country could grab Nuevo México and other Mexican territory. The United States couldn't just invade, they needed some excuse. Ulysses Grant would later write in his memoirs, "We were sent to provoke a fight, but it was essential that Mexico should commence it."

The next year, 4,000 U.S. troops invaded Mexican territory and Mexico fought back. That became President Polk's eagerly awaited excuse for a formal declaration of war. "Mexico has invaded our territory," Polk said in his war message, turning the facts completely around. In his diary, he said something more like the truth: "I declared my purpose (in a private meeting of the Cabinet) to be *to acquire for the United States California, New Mexico and perhaps some other of the northern provinces of Mexico*."

The truth was that the United States had decided it would drive all the way to the West Coast, so as to acquire ports on the Pacific Ocean and build up its commerce. A name was invented for this plan: "Manifest Destiny." The war on Mexico was just a matter of "destiny," of "God's will," the U. S. Government officials said. It was the God-given destiny of the United States to expand all the way to the Pacific. The magic words "Manifest Destiny" were played over and over again, like a song, in official speeches and in the press. They were used to justify the takeover of anything and everything.

And so the United States invaded Mexico. One army came down from the north, overland, and later another was landed at the port of Veracruz. Both headed toward Mexico City. General Winfield Scott, who headed the second invasion force, himself admitted the horrors of the war. He said that the invaders had "committed atrocities to make Heaven weep and every American of Christian morals blush for his country. Murder, robbery and rape of mothers and daughters have been common." Mexicans charged that the Anglos also desecrated the Catholic Churches, "sleeping in the niches devoted to the sacred dead . . . drinking out of holy vessels."

U.S. forces shelled the civilian section of Veracruz, destroying hospitals, churches, and homes. They burned down whole villages. And they even *scalped* many Mexicanos. A seventeen-year-old Yankee soldier later wrote a book in which he described the horrors he had seen with his own eyes. He tells of coming to a cave where some Mexicanos had been caught. "The cave was full of our volunteers," said the soldier, "yelling like fiends, while on the rocky floor lay over twenty Mexicans, dead and dying in pools of blood. Women and children were clinging to the knees of the murderers shrieking for mercy . . . Most of the butchered Mexicans had been scalped."

Two hundred and fifty U.S. troops, mostly Irish immigrants and Catholics, couldn't take it and they deserted. They joined the Mexican Army as the San Patricio Battalion. In the United States, there was a rise of protest against the war and its brutality—much as we have seen in recent years against the war in Vietnam. Abraham Lincoln lost a congressional election because of his opposition to the war. Henry David Thoreau went to jail briefly when he refused to pay taxes because of the war. But the war and atrocities went on anyway.

While the U.S. troops continued marching toward Mexico City, another attack was launched in Mexico's lands to the north. Colonel Stephen Kearny began marching from Fort Leavenworth, Kansas, to Santa Fe in Nuevo México. He was then supposed to march on to southern California, where his forces would join another, sea-borne force to conquer that province.

Our people in Nuevo México prepared to make a stand against the invaders east of Santa Fe. But their governor, Manuel Armijo, surrendered without having a single shot fired. It is said that he received about forty thousand dollars from a U.S. agent for his co-operation. Chicanos today know the name of Armijo as the first big sellout—*vendido*—in our history. The United States appointed as governor of Nuevo México the man named Charles Bent who had helped the trappers and traders to sneak into the territory.

Armijo's betrayal angered the Mexicanos and Indios in Nuevo México. They began planning to rise up against the invaders. The leaders of this revolt came from Taos, about ninety miles north of Santa Fe. They included Taos Pueblo Indians and Mexicanos. One of the original leaders was Father Antonio José Martínez, a priest.

Padre Martínez had always been worried about the Anglos moving into New Mexico. He tried to stop the trappers, traders, and land grabbers. He had worked hard to help the poor mestizos and Indians in other ways, too. For example, he refused to collect from them a sort of forced tax that the Church demanded; he wouldn't exploit the people like other priests did. Born in Abiquiu, Nuevo México, on January 7, 1793, he opened a public elementary school in the early 1800s, a time when only the rich and the powerful learned to read and write. He also began publishing a newspaper called *El Crepúsculo de la Libertad* (The Dawn of Freedom), which was not only the first paper published west of the Missouri River but also a paper that spoke out against injustice. Because of his activities, Padre Martínez found himself in a constant fight against the officials of his own church, a white hierarchy, and he was excommunicated. But the poor people ignored this decree, and Padre Martínez went on working with them.

On January 19, 1847, the people rose up against the United States. They killed Charles Bent, the invader who had been named their governor, and other officials. A revolutionary government was set up and rebellion spread all over the region. Soon about two thousand mestizos and Indians were marching on Santa Fe from the north.

But the Anglos had the big guns. Armed with twelve-pound howitzers, they forced the rebels back to Taos. The people barricaded themselves in the church at Taos Pueblo. At dawn on January 30, those big guns began pounding on the church until finally the roof caught fire and collapsed, and the walls broke down. About 150 mestizos and Indios were killed in this attack while some 30 prisoners were immediately executed by firing squads. The Anglo troops are said to have been so drunk that it was more of a massacre than a battle.

Six leaders of the rebellion were put on trial before an Anglo judge. Naturally they were all found guilty and condemned to be hanged for "treason." After the hanging, the Anglos went back to the tavern to drink straight brandy and a batch of eggnog which they had ordered in advance. One of the more sober observers of that day's events later wrote: "It certainly did appear to be a great assumption on the part of the Americans to conquer a country and then arraign the revolting inhabitants for treason."

In California, also, our people fought bravely against the invaders. Led by Captain José María Flores, they rose up in September 1846 against a U.S. occupational force stationed at Los Angeles. Another leader in the Los Angeles revolt was Serbulos Varela, who issued a proclamation that year saying: "Shall we wait to see our wives violated, our innocent children beaten by the American whip, our property sacked, our temples profaned, to drag out a life full of shame and disgrace? No! A thousand times no, compatriots! Death rather than that!" In this spirit, our people fought off the United States for four months.

But in Mexico the war against the invaders was going badly. On September 12–13, 1847, a proud last stand was made on the outskirts of Mexico City. The battle took place on Chapultepec Hill, where a military academy was located in a castle. For fourteen hours, the gringos pounded away with their big guns while fewer than a thousand poorly armed soldiers and cadets tried to defend the hill. The United States began a final assault on the hill and it was obvious that the Mexicanos would have to surrender. To prevent the flag of Mexico from falling into enemy hands, two of the young cadets from the academy wrapped themselves in the flag and jumped from the heights to their death. Four others followed rather than surrender. They were all teen-agers, just young boys, and today we Chicanos honor them as "Los Niños Héroes de Chapultepec"—The Heroic Children of Chapultepec. Their names were: Juan de la Barrera, Juan Escutía, Fernando Montes de Oca, Vicente Suárez, Francisco Marques, and Agustín Melgar.

Among the people watching that last battle were thirty Anglos—with nooses around their necks. They were members of the San Patricio Battalion, the men who could not stand U.S. barbarity any longer and had gone to fight on Mexico's side. The battalion had been captured shortly before the battle of Chapultepec, and fifty of its members sentenced to be hanged. Twenty were already dead. Now, on the day of the Chapultepec battle, the thirty men left were seated with nooses around their necks on boards placed across wagons. "You will be hanged when the U.S. flag rises above Chapultepec Castle," they were told. And when the flag was seen on the highest tower of the castle, the wagons were driven off and the thirty bodies were left dancing in the air before they became still. Today the U.S. victory at Chapultepec is commemorated by the red stripe that the U. S. Marine Corps wears on the trousers of its dress uniform. A disgrace is thus honored.

The North American Invasion of Mexico—which

U.S. history books call the Mexican-American War—officially ended on February 2, 1848, when the Treaty of Guadalupe Hidalgo was signed. With that treaty, our life as victims of gringo exploitation, racism, and oppression began. With that treaty, our long struggle as Chicanos began.

According to the treaty, the United States took over an area that included what is today Texas, California, New Mexico, large parts of Nevada, Utah and Colorado, most of Arizona and a piece of Wyoming. This added up to half of all Mexico (many gringos wanted ALL of Mexico). The United States paid Mexico fifteen million dollars for this area, which was as large as all of England, Ireland, France, Germany, Italy, and Poland together. Almost a third of the United States is land taken from Mexico.

Yet the Mexicans who negotiated the treaty were less worried about that loss of land than they were about protecting the rights of the people living in the area. Mexico was even ready to give up more territory to win more protection. Long discussions took place. As the treaty finally came out, Article VIII said that in the new U.S. territories, "property of every kind . . . *shall be inviolably respected.* The present owners, the heirs of these, and all Mexicans who may hereafter acquire said property by contract, shall enjoy with respect to it guarantees equally ample as if the same belonged to citizens of the United States." The treaty also said that the people living in those areas would, unless they chose to keep Mexican citizenship, have "the enjoyment of all the rights of citizens of the United States, according the the principles of the Constitution, and . . . *shall be maintained and protected in the free enjoyment of their liberty and property,* and secured in the free exercise of their religion without restriction."

In the original treaty, there was still another promise of protection—Article X—which said: "All the land grants made by the Mexican government . . . will be respected as valid, with the same force as if those territories still remained within the limits of Mexico." But this article did not get into the final treaty. The big businessmen who ran the United States knew that they could not expand and develop their economic power if they couldn't grab up the land. So the government refused to approve the treaty unless this article was taken out. President Polk even threatened to start the war again if this article wasn't removed.

Mexico had to agree. But to sugar-coat this pill, a U.S. representative signed a special document called a protocol. The protocol said: "The American government, by suppressing the Xth article of the treaty of Guadalupe Hidalgo, *did not in any way intend to annul the grants of lands made by Mexico in the ceded territories.* These grants . . . preserve the legal value which they may possess, and the grantees may cause their legitimate (titles) to be acknowledged before the American tribunals."

The Treaty of Guadalupe Hidalgo also created a two-thousand-mile-long border between the United States and Mexico—the basis of today's border. This border cut in half a country united by geography, people, and culture. It runs mostly through empty desert and has little connection with any kind of natural frontier. The border wasn't even patrolled by the U. S. Government until 1924; until then, people just walked from one country to the other. And sometimes they still do.

The lands that fell on the U.S. side of that border were a huge gain for the Anglo government. But it wasn't enough to satisfy the gigantic appetite of "Manifest Destiny." The ink had hardly dried on the treaty before the Anglos were violating it. Groups of filibusterers burst into Mexican territory below Arizona, California, and elsewhere along the border. In 1850 two of the biggest cattle barons in Texas, Richard King and Mifflin Kennedy, sponsored another "revolution" to steal more land for the United States. They wanted to grab one of Mexico's northern states, and hundreds of armed gringos rushed across the border to help that so-called "revolution." This new grab did not succeed. But today the King Ranch in Texas is still the biggest in the nation, and the family owns many lands in Mexico as well.

In 1853, "Manifest Destiny" took another big chunk of Mexico. James Gadsden was sent there to buy a large area of northern Mexico—what is today southern Arizona and part of New Mexico. This area was very rich in minerals. The history books tell us that the U.S. paid ten million dollars for this area but they don't often tell us that Mexico agreed to sell because Gadsden said that if she didn't, "we shall take it."

We might wonder why Mexico agreed to the Gadsden Purchase, and to the treaty before it. First of all, Mexico knew it could not win on the battlefield and the U.S. invasion had cost many Mexican lives. If

Mexico did not agree to what the United States wanted, it could expect more war and more hardship for its people. It is also important to know that Mexico had many internal problems at that time. Independence from Spain had not rid the country of big landowners and other rich men. Some members of this class thought they could benefit personally by wheeling and dealing with Uncle Sam. Santa Anna became such a man, and today he is regarded as a traitor in Mexico—a man who sold out his people.

When we talk about all this history, and how the United States took the Southwest by force, there are always people who will say, "Well, the United States paid for it, didn't they?" It is useful to remember the wealth that these lands later produced. The mines of Arizona alone, in an eighty-year period, produced three billion dollars' worth of metal for the benefit of U.S. companies. Compared to money like that, ten or fifteen million dollars is nothing but pennies—what we call a *hueso*, a bone left over from the big feast.

Today our people see those years of "Manifest Destiny" as something that gringos should be ashamed of. As we see it, the gringo gobbled up more than half of Mexico, leaving a trail of blood and a bone at the wayside. But there was worse to come. The Treaty of Guadalupe Hidalgo and the protocol would soon be violated a thousand times over, and all their promises of protection broken (perhaps this is why it is difficult even to find a copy of the treaty or the protocol in U.S. libraries today). The rights of our people in the Southwest would be violated in every possible way. The gringo would also destroy the communal ways of living that existed in the Southwest and replace them with his individualistic laws of "private property." He would replace tradition and trust with fences. He would make his own greed the law of the land.

That is the story that comes next—the story of how the West was *really* won.

4

How the West Was Really Won

SO OFTEN we see the tough, romantic cowboy with his guitar, singing "Git along, little dogie," "Home on the Range," or "Yoddily yoddily yooo." And the TV series like "Gunsmoke," "Bonanza," "Alias Smith and Jones," "Big Valley"—exciting stories that supposedly show how the West was won and settled. In books and movies, too, we see the portrayal of the kind, hard-working pioneers as they bravely struggled to survive in the "Wild West," the "virgin land," "the savage country."

But where are the real builders of the West? Where are the Indians, who worked the first fields and mines, dying by the thousands from illness and exhaustion?

Where are the Mexicanos, who taught the Anglo how to mine, who built and tended the railroads, who made possible the huge cattle industry? Somehow the true builders of the West are left out of history. Yet as we look at life in the West after the United States took over, we realize that they were the Anglo's teachers. They taught him how to survive and get rich.

Let's begin with that cowboy. Everything about the cowboy came from the Spaniards or the Mexicanos, beginning with the cow itself. It was Coronado who first drove a Spanish type of cattle into the Southwest, the original breed from which the range cattle of the United States were later developed. By 1846, when the war began, there were three million cattle on Mexicano ranches in Texas. The huge cattle industry of Texas began with the stealing of those herds by Anglos.

The word cowboy itself is a literal translation of the Spanish word *vaquero*—meaning cow man. The cowboy took all his equipment from Spanish-speaking people. His saddle was an adaptation of the horned saddle used by the Spaniards. The bridle, bit, spur, lasso or lariat, cinch, halters, chaps, stirrup tips, chin strap for the hat, feed bag for the horse, and the ten-gallon hat all came from the original vaquero.

The Anglo cowboy also took over or adapted dozens of Spanish words such as lasso, rodeo, corral, hondo, mesa, vamoose, canyon, barranca. All kinds of techniques or procedures were also taken over: horse-breaking, branding and the registration of brands, the round-up, the laws of the range. The dried meat called jerky that sustained many cattlemen was the Mexican charqui. Our people have a long tradition of expert horsemanship, artful use of the rope and other skills of cattle raising. But in the mythology of the cowboy, credit is never given to this world of Spanish and mestizo know-how. The Lone Ranger calls his buddy "Tonto"—which in Spanish means stupid or dumb. Yet there definitely would have been no Lone Ranger without "Stupid" and his fellow Americans.

Like the cattle industry, sheep raising was also a well-developed art long before the coming of the Anglo. Juan de Oñate brought to New Mexico the herds of sheep that later formed the basis of that area's economy—and with them came a sheep culture based on six hundred years of Spanish experience. It included techniques for pasturing sheep and establishing trails to march them over. The Spanish system of having sheep raised and handled by men who did nothing else, with each step of the work handled by a different group of experts, produced fine animals.

The pastor or shepherd was, by long tradition, a man who knew how to handle sheep in the right way, how to train sheep dogs, how to read the weather, how to defend his flock against wolves and other animals. The Mexican sheep shearers were also specialists, who had high status and dressed beautifully. They would migrate across the Southwest, doing their job in one place and then moving on to another. Thanks to the skill of Mexicanos like these, gringo businessmen in the East got rich with their textile factories.

When the Anglo came West, he knew little about cattle or sheep—and still less about irrigated farming. Again, it was the Indian and the Mexicano who taught him how to do it. The Pueblo Indians had been irrigating for almost a thousand years before the *Mayflower* docked and they taught what they knew to the mestizo. Since irrigation systems take many years to develop and perfect, the Anglo who came along in the late 1800s was able to put a huge amount of experience to work for him. An interesting part of this story is that when the Anglo first began irrigating, he didn't understand that it is a job which should be done communally. In dry areas, people must share water, and the ways of sharing must be decided by the whole community. So at first the Anglo tried to impose his ideas of private property on irrigation. But soon he realized this just wouldn't work and he finally had to adopt some of the Mexicano procedures.

With irrigation under control, Anglos began building the big ranches of fruits and vegetables that would bring them millions of dollars in the twentieth century. On the California mission farms, mestizo and Indian workers had proved how well one could grow oranges, lemons, limes, grapes, olives, peaches, pears, figs, apricots, strawberries, raspberries, plums, dates, cherries, walnuts, tomatoes, lettuce, and other plants. Wine making and raisin culture were also developed by our peoples, and so was the type of cotton that became a major source of Anglo wealth in Texas.

Another big source of new wealth for the Anglos was mining, and here again they learned everything from the people whose lands they had invaded. The ancient mining culture of Spain had been combined with Aztec methods to make a very advanced mining technology. Mexico had a "silver rush" in 1548, three hundred years before the Anglo discovery of gold in

California, and our people had learned a great deal about mining techniques. In fact, gold itself was discovered in California six years before the big rush—by a Mexican herdsman named Francisco Lopez. When James Marshall did find gold in 1848, he is supposed to have rushed into town shouting "Gold! Gold!" But what he really said was that he had found a *chispa*, a Spanish term for bright speck.

The gringos who came West for gold took over not only the mining language but also basic tools and techniques. We could not list all of these here, but they include basic tools like the batea, a kind of flat pan widely used in the early days of creek-bed mining, and the first successful technique for dry diggings. Mexicanos were the first quartz miners of gold, and they not only put to use techniques developed in Mexico but they also invented new equipment that could be built on the spot and was easy to operate. Thanks to Mexican technology and Mexican labor, two million dollars in gold was taken in just one year (1850) from just one quartz mine—now owned by Anglos.

As far back as 1557, Mexicans had developed a process for separating precious metals from ore by using quicksilver. It was also a Mexicano who discovered quicksilver near San Jose, California, in 1845. His discovery made it possible to exploit the gold and silver of the entire West. In the mining of silver itself, we find the same story. Comstock, who made a fortune in Nevada from the famous Comstock Lode, had to be told by a Mexican miner that he had discovered silver. Comstock himself didn't know what "that blue stuff" really was. And it was equipment invented by Mexicans that made possible the early development of the incredibly rich Comstock Lode.

With copper mining, we learn that it was a Spaniard who discovered the big copper and silver mines of western New Mexico. Here, Mexican workers developed the techniques that would later be used at the famous Bisbee mines of Arizona and across the Southwest. They also built the first furnaces to smelt copper ores in Arizona. Anglos who wanted to develop those mines went to Mexico to get the men with the know-how.

Even in the laws that governed mining, the Anglos took from our people. There was no U.S. mining law in 1848, but the Mexicanos had long had a complete set of rules and codes that were well tested by experience. They became the basis for the Anglo's mining law. Yet many California historians still try to tell us that this law shows "the great natural, Anglo capacity for self-government."

With mining, agriculture, and raising animals, the Anglos found a ready-made economic base in the Southwest. This was partly because of the Indians who had been living there for centuries and partly because of development through Spanish colonization. The Anglos even found a ready-made transportation system and trade routes. These, too, the Anglos took over—and without them, the other industries would not have developed.

As far back as 1486, the Spaniards were using pack trains in Europe. These trains had as many as fourteen thousand mules and burros, and could travel great distances. Spain brought not only the mule and burro to this continent but also the ox and, of course, the horse.

Like sheep herding, the pack train depended on several kinds of specialized workers with traditional knowledge and traditional dress. Their skills went into very fine detail—the loading process by itself included complicated techniques of roping, with all sorts of different knots and splices. Even the Anglos agreed that nobody could handle burros and mules as well as the Mexicans. In the 1880s, the pack trains were replaced by the railroads as the main type of transport—and there were our people again, as laborers. From 1880 until recent years, they made up 70 per cent of the section crews and 90 per cent of the extra gangs on the main western lines.

There is one other kind of know-how that we should mention, housing. The Anglo of the East had no idea of how to live in the semidesert and rugged mountains of the Southwest. He was lucky to learn from the mestizo how to build homes from adobe—an architecture developed by the Indians and later the mestizos. Adobe houses can be kept warm in winter, cool in summer, and they are fireproof.

When we look at all the technology that the Anglo got from the non-white people of the Southwest, we wonder why he is called a "pioneer." He seems more like a Johnny-come-lately. We also wonder why the Anglo is so often described as the "practical" person, the master of technology, while our people were actually his teachers. The Anglo made his life and fortune in the West thanks to technology developed by Indians, Spaniards, and Mexicans. But why do most history books teach us a different story? Why don't we learn the truth?

The answer to that question can be found in the story of what the Anglo did to our people after he took over the Southwest from Mexico. It is another story that we don't often hear.

At the time of the U.S. takeover, there were about sixty thousand of our people living in Nuevo México, seventy-five hundred in California, five thousand in Texas, and a thousand in Arizona. For Raza, as for the Indian peoples, the years after 1848 were one long struggle against genocide—against being simply wiped out as a group. The treaty had promised our people all their rights, but often they didn't even have the right to live. To the Anglos who poured into the Southwest, we were a conquered people—and that meant they could do anything they wanted to us.

There were lynchings in every part of the Southwest. Nobody has ever been able to count the total number of Mexicanos lynched or murdered in cold blood, but it must have been in the thousands. In one part of Texas, the total was the same or even higher than the number of Blacks known to have been lynched in the South during the same period. California, where crimes of violence were very rare before the Anglo came, had more murders in the year 1853 than all the rest of the United States. Most of the victims were Mexicans and Indians. In 1854, a killing a day was reported in Los Angeles alone. The reports of all this bloodshed came from the Anglos themselves—who saw nothing wrong with what they did. (The lynchings did not stop in modern times. As late as the 1930s, there were lynchings of Chicanos reported in California.)

In Texas, gringos used the fact that Mexicanos often helped Black slaves to escape as one excuse for attack. In 1856, they claimed to have discovered a plot in which Black slaves were going to rise up against their masters and fight their way across the border with the help of local Mexicans. All the Mexicanos in two counties were then ordered to leave immediately, and in a third county they were forbidden to travel without passes. The following year, the gringos started the "Cart War"—to prevent Mexican oxcart trains from doing a valuable business of hauling goods between San Antonio and other points. In organized bands, the Anglos attacked these trains and killed the drivers, then stole the goods.

Then there was the "Salt War" of 1877 in El Paso. At that time, only about eighty of the twelve thousand people living in El Paso were not Mexicans—but those eighty had already moved to take over. One of them, by a series of tricks, got control of a salt mine which had traditionally been used by the Mexican community. This man announced that from then on, the mine would be a private monopoly. The people of El Paso, for whom salt was, of course, an important item in the daily diet, were outraged. They "rioted," killing three Anglos and destroying Anglo property. The Anglos then killed or lynched dozens of Mexicans.

Sometimes lynching was just a sport to the gringo. In Bee County, Texas, it was reported that several gringos killed a Mexican simply because he would not play the fiddle for them. Their attitude is shown in the famous words of gunman King Fisher. Asked how many notches he had on his gun, he said: "Thirty-seven—not counting Mexicans."

The three main reasons for all the bloodshed were: *gold*, *cattle*, and *land*. Those were the three big attractions for the Anglos who came west, hoping to get rich quick.

Gold

Beginning in 1848, thousands of Anglos raced to California from across the country, shouting "gold, gold, gold!" When they arrived, they found that miners from Mexico and other Latin American countries were already there, working mines in the southern part of California. So the Anglos at first stuck to gold fields in other areas. But they could not resist for long the temptation to take over the efficient camps of the south.

In 1850, California passed the Foreign Miners Tax Law, aimed at cutting out competition from non-Anglo miners. By calling the Mexicanos "foreigners," the law denied them and their property any kind of legal protection. This clearly violated the Treaty of Guadalupe Hidalgo, but it didn't matter to the miners. They saw the law as a big, green light. That same year, California passed another law that was actually called the "Greaser Act," and it said that any Mexican could be arrested on sight if he couldn't prove that he had a job and home. This, too, was like declaring open season on our people.

Two thousand Anglo miners swept down on the southern camps that year. They burned them to the ground and shot every Mexican they saw. In the course of one week, they lynched and murdered dozens of our people. That became the pattern for the whole area. Within twenty years, the Anglos had driven out all but a few of the Raza miners.

The Anglos always blamed any petty theft in the mining camps on some Mexican and then carried out the accepted penalty—hanging him on the spot, without the pretense of a trial. Women, too, fell victim to the gringo brutality.

In the small mining town of Downieville, northeast of Sacramento, there lived a young Chicana whom we know only as Josefa. She was married to a man named José, who worked in town as a card dealer because Mexicanos were almost never allowed to stake claims in the local gold mines. On July 4, 1851, the gringo miners were all busy getting drunk and late that night one of them—a man named Fred Cannon—broke into the cabin of José and Josefa. She was alone because José had not yet come home from work. Another miner persuaded Cannon not to bother her, and the two men finally left.

The next morning, José demanded that Cannon pay for the broken door but he refused. He began to insult Josefa, calling her immoral and many bad names. As he went on with his insults, Josefa finally grabbed a knife and killed Cannon. By nine o'clock that same morning, a so-called trial had been arranged—with the verdict already decided against Josefa. A lawyer who protested was attacked and beaten by the drunken, bloodthirsty mob. Josefa was sentenced to be hanged in two hours, and José was ordered to leave town within twenty-four hours. At four o'clock on that afternoon of July 5, she was hanged from the bridge—our first Chicana martyr —and then the gringos went back for more drinks.

This kind of behavior by the Anglo miners made some of our people into revolutionaries. Joaquín Murrieta is one of the most famous, and he is as important in our history as George Washington has been made in Anglo history.

Joaquín was born of a respected family in a little mining and ranching town of northern Mexico. His father may have been a Maya Indian, while his mother's family came from Spain. Joaquín's family lived near Varoyeca, a center of revolt by the Indians who were worked like slaves in the local mines. Joaquín probably learned guerrilla warfare tactics through the Indian struggle.

He was well educated and later went to California as a miner. Gringos came to his mining claim and told him to abandon it, as they had forced so many other Mexicanos to do. Joaquín refused. Then a band of gringos came and raped his beautiful sixteen-year-old wife, Rosita Felix. It is said that thirteen of them did this, one by one, and she died. They also beat Joaquín almost to death.

According to some historians, Joaquín then left the area and went to make a claim in a new place, near the town of Murphys, California. They lynched his brother before his eyes and whipped Joaquín.

These horrors drove Joaquín to action. He organized a small army of Mexicanos, including the famous

three-fingered Jack García. Operating from a base in
the hills, they carried out a campaign of guerrilla warfare against the gold-crazy gringos for two years. To
most Anglos, the name of Joaquín Murrieta became
something to make the biggest bully shake in his boots
with fear. Among our people, he was known for his
generosity and decency to the poor. He had supporters
all across California, including some Anglos, so that
he always had a place to hide if needed. Our people
saw him not as a fearsome "bandit" but as El Patrio—
the native. They knew that he was not just a man looking for personal revenge, but the leader of a revolt
against invaders.

The Anglo government also realized that his revolt
could become a revolution. So the California legisla-
ture named a former Texas Ranger named Harry Love
to find and kill Murrieta. Love, who had fought in the
war on Mexico, was such a vicious adventurer that he
was later shot while mistreating his wife. His troops, a
company of U. S. Cavalry and Rangers, have been described by one Anglo historian as "a disreputable group
of thugs."

On July 5, 1853, Love and his men came upon a
small group of Mexicanos. One of the Anglos said he
recognized Joaquín, so they riddled the whole group
with bullets. The head of this Joaquín was cut off,
preserved in alcohol, and presented to the governor.
Later it was put on public display and sent around the
state. In San Francisco, people paid a dollar each for
the privilege of looking at it.

But they were looking at a gringo lie. It wasn't
Joaquín Murrieta's head, and the Anglos themselves al-

most admitted this. The Ranger who had claimed to recognize Joaquín was in a bar drinking and told a friend that "one pickled head is as good as another if there is a scar on the face and no one knows the difference." The real Murrieta returned to his homeland in Mexico and people there reported having seen him in the 1870s. He died and is buried in the desert mountains, above the village of Magdalena. Today the Indians there call it the grave of El Pistolero.

Another hero in the resistance struggle against the gold-crazy gringo was Tiburcio Vásquez. He was born in Monterey, California, on August 11, 1835, of a large respected family. As a student, he wrote well in Spanish and learned English after the U.S. takeover. Only thirteen years old when the war on Mexico ended, he soon came to hate the gringos. It is said that both his mother and sister were raped by them. Tiburcio dreamed of an uprising against the Yankee invaders.

One night, when Tiburcio was seventeen, he and two friends attended a dance in Monterey. During the event, a fist fight began and an Anglo constable came to the dance. Just what happened is not clear, but the constable was killed. Tiburcio was never officially accused of the killing, but the Anglos said they wanted him for "questioning." Tiburcio and one of his two friends knew that the "questioning" could easily turn into a lynching, so they fled into the hills. The other friend was caught and hanged without a trial—which proved how right Tiburcio had been.

Vásquez became a fierce fighter against the gringo colonizer, and a hero to his people. It is said that he never killed or stole from a fellow Mexicano. The people hid and sheltered him whenever necessary. But in

1874, with the help of a traitor, the Anglos captured Tiburcio. He was tried and hanged in San José on March 19 of that year. A reporter who saw the hanging wrote that he died with beautiful dignity and courage. Thirty-nine years old, well-dressed, with a neatly trimmed beard and mustache, he went to his death in the quiet, brave way of a noble warrior. The grave of Vásquez can be seen in Santa Clara today, a small monument to a great fighter.

Tiburcio Vásquez and Joaquín Murrieta are only two of the better-known resistance fighters in California. There were many, many more. The gringos labeled them all "bandits," ordinary criminals. But they were really leaders of a people's struggle for independence, not just bloodthirsty individuals out for their own gain.

To our people at that time, it was the Anglos who brought the terror. Our people knew who the real bandits and killers were: the gringos, a name that represents all the murder and theft experienced by our people. The word gringo may come from *griego*, a Spanish term for foreigner. In any case, the word came to represent a racist mentality, a way of life that oppresses and exploits others. We might mention here that while all gringos are Anglo, not all Anglos are gringos. Also, Chicanos have other names for the white man—such as *gavacho* or *gabacho*, which means a nicer kind of gringo. But in this book we use only Anglo and gringo.

Cattle

It was gold and silver that brought the Anglos to California, while others went West looking for a different kind of wealth: cattle. The grazing lands of Texas, New Mexico, and Arizona soon became a battleground just as bloody as the mine fields.

The gringo cattlemen stole millions of cattle from Mexicanos and killed the owners. They drove their cattle across the unfenced ranges of Raza farmers, killing all who resisted and their families. They carried out a full-scale war against our sheepmen to take over their grazing lands. The Lincoln County War of New Mexico is one example of this, and movies have been made about it. But the movies don't always make it clear that the sheepmen were defending lands where they had lived for centuries—and the cattlemen were invaders.

Everywhere, the law enforcement officials supported the gringo cattlemen against the Mexicanos. They were gringos themselves, and they believed that killing a Mexican was no crime. They had a double standard of justice, and would pull out their guns when a white person was bothered in any way by a Mexicano—but they showed no interest when one of our people was viciously murdered by a white. Historians say there are no examples from the 1800s of a white man being punished for a crime against a Mexicano.

Sometimes the authorities played a direct role in the theft and murder by the cattlemen. The most famous example of this is the Texas Rangers. Their history begins with the Ranger bands formed by Stephen Austin in the 1820s, to protect his "settlers" in the big conspiracy to take Texas from Mexico. When Texas declared its "independence," the Rangers were formally organized as a band of mounted riflemen. They became famous during the war on Mexico, when there were about fifteen hundred Rangers in action together with the U.S. troops.

About thirty years later, in 1874, the Rangers were reorganized and called "peace officers." They also dropped in numbers. But their reputation for racism and brutality against our people did not disappear. The story is still told in Texas of how a group of gringos went one night to a village where there was some land that they wanted to take over. During the night, they fenced in the land. Then some Texas Rangers set fire to the village. When the people began jumping over the fence to escape the fire, the Rangers shot them down as "trespassers." Today our people continue to feel hatred toward the Rangers for their violent attacks on striking farmworkers organized by César Chávez's union.

In Phoenix, Arizona, tension between Mexicanos and gringos grew as more and more cattlemen came in. One day in 1879, a thousand Mexicanos who had been working on the Southern Pacific railroad were suddenly dumped off in Phoenix without jobs. The workers gathered in a park and were talking angrily against the railroad, against the gringo. With such a large crowd, the local Anglos didn't dare to make a direct attack. Instead, they went to the jail and took out two Anglo prisoners—then lynched them in the park. They told the Mexicanos that the same thing would happen to them if the meeting didn't break up at once. It did —but what we can remember is that the gringos would even murder their own in order to terrorize our people.

Mexicanos fought back against the brutal invasion of

the cattlemen in many ways. Some Raza sheepmen adopted the old tactics of the Indians, and called themselves Los Comancheros. They would carry out raids or other actions to defend their people against the gringo cattlemen. A well-known fighter in this resistance war was Elfego Baca of New Mexico, who held out alone against eighty Anglo cowboys in a famous gunfight that lasted a day and a half.

Elfego was born February 27, 1865. When he was nineteen years old and working in the town of Socorro, in the southern part of New Mexico, a deputy came to see him. The deputy said that he just couldn't deal with all the shooting that was going on between the cattle and the sheepmen. Elfego told him that he would take over the deputy's job if the man would go with him to the place where the fighting was most severe—San Francisco Plaza, today Reserve, New Mexico. The deputy agreed and the two men left.

On October 29, 1884, cowboys came into the town, shooting up the place, and then went to have some drinks. Baca saw one cowboy hitting another over the head with his pistol, and went to stop the beating. The cowboy shot his hat off, and ran. Baca then chased the man, caught him, and arrested him.

That night, twelve cowboys armed to the teeth came to Baca's house where he was holding the prisoner for safekeeping. They demanded that the cowboy be released at once. Baca told them that he would count to three and then start shooting. He did, and killed one of them. The next day, a trap was set for him. Elfego suspected this and rounded up all the people in the settlement and put them into a church so they wouldn't get hurt. Then he went out to deliver his prisoner to the Justice of the Peace.

Eighty cowboys appeared on the scene. Baca walked up to two of them and threw their guns on the ground. Someone behind him fired a shot. Elfego drew his guns and backed up into a small frame hut, a jacal. He put the women and children out of the house, and the famous gunfight started.

During the next thirty-six hours, an estimated four thousand shots were fired at Baca in the hut. He killed four and wounded eight of the Texas cowboys. When he got hungry, he made some beef stew, tortillas, and coffee while he kept on shooting. Inside the hut there stood a large statue of a saint that was supposedly six hundred years old. It was never hit by the bullets, and neither was Baca.

After a day and a half, Elfego finally surrendered to a deputy sheriff, whom he knew, but not until he had set certain conditions. First, that he would not give up his gun and second, that when the deputy sheriff took him to the town of Socorro, there would be six cowboy guards riding a good thirty paces in front of Baca. Elfego himself would ride next to the deputy sheriff. He had his life insurance.

They made the trip to Socorro and Elfego was later taken to Albuquerque, where he was tried for murder—and found innocent. Some years later, he became a criminal lawyer and went into politics. He died not many years ago—in 1945—at the ripe old age of eighty. During all that time, the spirit of resistance stayed alive in New Mexico. Underground organizations like Las Gorras Blancas (White Caps) and La Mano Negra

(Black Hand) fought the gringo invaders with such
tactics as cutting Anglo fences, destroying railroad
tracks, and freeing our people when they were imprisoned.

Land

When the Treaty of Guadalupe Hidalgo was signed
in 1848, our people held an estimated thirty-five million acres of land in the Southwest. By the early 1900s,
they had lost 70 per cent of this. The worst losses
were the *ejido*, the common lands, because they were
used by all the people. The U. S. Congress simply
said it would not recognize them; U.S. law didn't allow
for anything except private, individual property. Much
of this land was therefore taken over by the U. S. Government while other parts were grabbed up by Anglo
businessmen. As for the lands held by individuals, these
were lost to the Anglos also—through violence, trickery,
cheating, and U.S. "laws."

The treaty had promised "inviolable respect" for the
property of Mexicans. But three years after the treaty
was signed, the U. S. Congress passed new laws saying
that anyone claiming land had to prove that they had
what the Anglos called *title* to it—in other words, a
piece of paper proving that the person really owned the
land. For our people, this was next to impossible.
First of all, the land grants dated back as far as the
1500s. Among Raza, land ownership was usually recognized by tradition and most people did not need pieces
of paper or fences or other boundary lines to know
what belonged to whom. But even if people did have
the right piece of paper, they had to go through the

courts of the Anglo to win their case against an Anglo.

The judges were all Anglos and almost always on the side of the gringo who wanted the land. The courts were conducted in English and few of our people knew much English. The judges talked in a mumbo jumbo of technical legal terms that our people didn't know, terms that represented an entirely different culture and law. To make matters still worse, our people were required to hire Anglo lawyers. They, too, were usually on the side of the gringo.

The Mexicano had to pay the lawyer a big fee, so most people could not even take their cases to court. But even if they could afford it, the case would take so long to go through all the courts that the people would end up broke. Many, many families ended up paying their lawyers with land itself. A whole new class of rich gringos developed: the lawyers. Today, some of the biggest landholdings in the Southwest are the result of lawyers building up their personal kingdoms through such fees. In California, 40 per cent of the land once held in Spanish or Mexican land grants was sold to meet the expenses of lawsuits—and it was sold dirt cheap. The Anglos controlled the banking system too and, unlike Raza, they could get loans to make quick and easy money.

Another way that people lost their land was through the new system of land taxes. Under Spain and then Mexico, the land itself was never taxed—only the produce of the land. But the Anglo came along with a new system that our people did not understand. He sent out surveyors who decided on the value of a particular property, and then taxes had to be paid on it. Needless to say, the surveyors were all Anglos who often worked hand in hand with land-hungry friends. The surveyor would declare a property to be worth some huge sum of money, which meant that high taxes had to be paid on it. Our people could not afford to pay the taxes, or did not understand the system. So by the 1860s, five-sixths of the land in southern California, for example, was officially "tax delinquent." The owners would have to sell their land to pay the taxes. One ranch covering 265,000 acres was bought for $152 in this way.

There were many other ways in which the Anglo took advantage of our people. For example, the law said that land claims, new tax laws, or other important land matters had to be announced in the newspaper. The authorities would then publish this information— but in a newspaper located far from the homes of the people affected, and in English only. As a result, many people lost their land without even knowing it—until they were evicted.

Another favorite trick was to tell some Mexicano landowner that he should sign a certain paper—just a routine document. After the owner signed the paper, which was written in English only, he would find out that he had in fact signed away his land. (This still goes on today; it happened to a seventy-year-old woman in New Mexico as recently as 1969.) A variation on that trick was described by a Catholic nun who lived in New Mexico in the late 1800s and who wrote: "When the men from the states came out west to dispossess the poor natives from their lands, they used many sub-terfuges. One was to offer the owner of the land a handful of silver coins for the small service of making a mark on a paper. The mark was a cross which was acceptable as a signature, by which the unsuspecting natives deeded away their lands. By this means, many a poor family was robbed of all their possessions."

It was in New Mexico that "legal" trickery and cheating reached an all-time high. Because of its isolation, few Anglos moved there after 1848 and the population remained 90 per cent Raza until 1870. As a result, less violence and more trickery had to be used—especially in the northern part of the state. The land-grabbers moved slowly at first, but then the railroads opened up New Mexico and they descended like vultures.

The famous Santa Fe Ring developed: a small, tight group of bankers, merchants, politicians—and especially lawyers. In the 1880s, it is said, one out of every ten Anglos in the state was a lawyer. Almost all of them were there for the same purpose—to grab up land. The Sante Fe Ring invented a whole new bag of tricks. So-called "mysterious" fires broke out in government offices and old land grant documents were conveniently destroyed. Such documents also disappeared "mysteriously" into sewers, cesspools, and trash barrels, or were "unfortunately" stolen from stagecoaches. Even records kept in Guadalajara, Mexico, were burned up in an "accidental" fire—so that there were no copies left anywhere.

A top figure in the Santa Fe Ring was Thomas B. Catron, the biggest lawyer and land-grabber of them all. Catron was a slaveowner in Missouri who was disbarred as a lawyer in his home state after the American Civil War. He went West, became head of the Santa

Fe Ring, and soon he personally owned more land than anyone else in the United States at that time. Only one man ever made a serious challenge to his power, and that man was "mysteriously" murdered. History, and the trials of that time, show that this man was probably killed by Catron's order. But neither this nor his disreputable slave-owning past prevented Catron from being made attorney general of the Territory of New Mexico, and later becoming New Mexico's first U.S. senator when that territory was made a state in 1912. Today, there are many reminders of Catron in New Mexico—Catron County, Catron Street, and the Catron Building on the main plaza of Santa Fe. The Catron family is still powerful; Catron's sons and grandsons became lawyers.

There were a few Mexicano families in the Southwest that held out against land-grabbers like Catron, and kept their land despite all the pressure. Among these was the Cortina family of Texas. One of the Cortina sons, Juan Nepomuceno, led one of our most famous resistance struggles.

The Cortina family had land on both sides of the Rio Bravo—which became the border between Mexico and the United States after the war. They were living on the Mexican side when Juan was born, May 16, 1824. He grew up to be a slight, red-haired youth with passionate eyes and the nickname "Cheno." Although his family was wealthy and influential, he soon showed that he had a strong sense of justice. When Cheno was only seven years old, he noticed a foreman on his family's ranch beating a worker. Cheno rushed toward the man and began pummeling him with his little fists. The foreman laughed, but Cheno took it very seriously.

During the war, Cheno served in the Mexican Army against the U.S. forces. After it was over, his family moved to their lands on the U.S. side of the Rio Bravo. They settled near what is today the city of Brownsville, as U.S. citizens. Cheno was there, too, leading the life of a well-to-do young Mexican gentleman. But on the morning of July 13, 1859, his whole life took a different turn.

He had been sitting in the Brownsville market place having a cup of coffee, and when he had finished, he got on his beautiful horse to leave. Cheno was a splendid horseman, and he rode along the street with pleasure, bowing now and then to people he knew. Suddenly he noticed the local marshal brutally beating a Mexican, whom Cheno recognized as a former servant on the Cortina ranch. He reined in his horse and asked the marshal what he was doing. "Keep out of this, Mexican!" yelled the marshal.

In Spanish, Cortina then questioned the former servant, who said the marshal had accused him of stealing some chickens—but that he was innocent. Cortina then told the marshal in English to let the man go. But the marshal insulted Cheno, and began beating the servant again. Cortina drew his pistol and shot the marshal, wounding him in the shoulder. Then he picked up the beaten man and galloped out of town on his horse.

Cheno knew he had done something that was never allowed, even by a man of his social position. He had shot a representative of U.S. law and rescued a humble Mexican. So he decided to stay on the family's ranch as long as possible. But after a few days, a posse was sent out to the ranch to get him. What happened next has been vividly described by historian Max Martínez in the Chicano publication *Magazín*:

The five men in the posse rode onto the Cortina land and two of them dismounted outside the main house. Cheno's brother stepped out on the porch. "Jes' stop right there, meskin," said one of the men on foot, pointing his gun at the brother.

"What do you want?" asked the brother, whose name was José.

"We want that murderin' brother of yours, that's what we want, meskin." The man spat on the ground, never taking his eyes off José, waiting for an excuse to shoot.

"He didn't kill anyone. And he's not here."

One of the men laughed. "Ain't that jes' like a meskin? Stand there in broad daylight and lie. Standin' there lyin' through his teeth." The man's face hardened, then he said: "Now, where's that brother of yore's?"

"I don't know."

"Then we'll have to search the house, that's all."

"No . . . you can't. There are women in there."

The man who had spat on the ground giggled nervously and said, "Jes' meskin women. Les' burn the place down."

At that moment, Cheno stepped out from the side of the house and yelled, "Hey!" As the man who had spat on the ground turned, a bullet tore into his cheek. He fell to the ground on his back, dead within seconds. Cheno then motioned to the other man on foot to drop his gun. The three men on horseback dropped their guns before being ordered to. Cheno told the posse to pick up the dead man. He promised to return all the guns if the men would

be "more careful" in the future. The posse left, and
the next morning the guns were found in a sack outside the marshal's office—just as Cortina had promised.

Cheno knew that he had to move quickly now, if
he was not to be lynched. He went at once to the
neighboring ranches, to recruit supporters. The
workers there were glad to join him; they had had
enough of their gringo bosses, who worked them
long hours for a few pounds of flour and rancid
meat—and who often beat them.

Meanwhile, the "law-abiding" citizens of Brownsville had asked for the Texas Rangers to come in and
help. After a big welcome, the Rangers went out
looking for Cheno. The marshal, who had recovered from his wound, went with them. But instead
of catching Cheno, they fell into a trap that he and
his men had set.

As the Rangers were riding along, relaxed and
singing "The Eyes of Texas Are Upon You," they
suddenly saw 50 of Cortina's men standing before
them with Cheno himself in the lead. The marshal
spotted his bushy red beard and yelled, "It's Cortina!
It's Cortina!" The Rangers ran as fast as they could.
But they galloped right into another 150 of Cortina's
men, who were lying in wait. The Rangers broke
into several directions, and it was nightfall before the
Ranger captain could find all of them again.

The word went out that Juan Cortina had control
of all of south Texas. His army grew in numbers,
and he decided that it was time to teach the gringo
a clear lesson. He began making plans for the Brownsville Raid of September 28–29, 1859.

Cheno sent word to Brownsville that he was coming and that he intended to bring to justice a small
number of men known to be the cause of misery for
many Mexicanos. As Cortina rode into town with

five hundred men, the town panicked. Cortina's
army killed five men, including a bystander. Several
of the guilty persons that he wanted to find ran and
hid in the homes of other people. Cortina was upset
about the death of the innocent man and afraid of
more deaths like that. So he stopped the raid and
left town after buying supplies and arms, for which
he paid in gold. He never carried out the robbery,
pillage, and rape that some gringos claim.

Cheno then issued a proclamation in which he explained the purpose of the raid and his sorrow about
the innocent victim. He named the criminals that he
had wanted to punish and declared: "All truce between them and us is at end." In this and later proc-
lamations, Cheno said he would not injure the innocent but would strike for justice. He spoke of how
the Mexicanos had hoped for a good life under the
United States but that these hopes had been
smashed. The gringos had tried "to depreciate and
load with insults" the Mexicanos of Texas. He also
talked about how the Anglo lawyers in Texas were
working to steal the lands with the help of certain "law
enforcement" officers. But the gringos, Cheno said,
"shall not possess our lands until they have fattened
it with their gore."

Stirred by Cortina's actions and words, hundreds
more Mexicanos joined his forces and named their
leader "Cheno El Justiciero"—Cheno, the Man of
Justice. The gringos gave him another name, "Red
Robber of the Rio Grande," in honor of his red
beard.

The Cortina forces liberated an area that extended
150 miles, and Cheno became a master of guerrilla
warfare. When the Rangers captured and lynched
one of his close friends without any kind of trial,
Cheno was enraged. He announced that he would
drive the gringo out of south Texas. In December

1859, U.S. federal troops finally defeated Cheno at
Rio Grande City. But they failed to capture him.
With his red beard gleaming in the sun, he flew
south on his famous black stallion—across the border
to Mexico.

Cheno later came back. The American Civil War
was going on then, and he became an officer in the
Union Army. (Perhaps Cheno had the same attitude as
some of our other brothers who fought in the Union
Army: "A dead gringo from the South is one less
gringo.") After the Civil War ended, Cheno continued
his own guerrilla war against the Texas gringos until
1876. In that year, a man became President of Mexico
who was very friendly to the United States. When Cortina came into Mexico, the President had him arrested
at the request of the United States—and he could never
return to Texas.

But Raza resistance in Texas didn't die. Until 1875,
Cheno's men continued making raids fighting to try
and get back the land and cattle stolen by Anglos. In
1915, Mexicanos drew up the Plan de San Diego
(Texas) —a plan for armed revolt and "independence
of Yankee tyranny." That plan, by the way, also called
for the liberation of Blacks and co-operation with the
Indians.

Despite the courage of men like Joaquín Murrieta,
Tiburcio Vásquez, Elfego Baca, and Juan Cortina, the
rule of the Anglo prevailed in the Southwest. By the
early 1900s, gringos had established control over their
new colony. Somehow our people survived that period

—but at a terrible price. They had lost 70 per cent of their land, they had been driven from their homes and their ways of making a living. They had been subjected to a campaign of terror that was aimed at breaking their spirit once and for all. Their language had been outlawed, in one place after another (in California, for example, all government documents had to be published in both Spanish and English at first—but that was stopped in 1879). Except for a tiny group of *ricos*, rich Mexicanos who managed to hang on to some wealth and influence, our people found themselves herded onto the wrong side of the tracks. There they faced a constant struggle to feed themselves, to stay alive.

What happened to the Indian in the Southwest was even worse, of course. Those who had not already died under the Spanish were wiped out by disease, overwork, or just plain murder. In California, for example, the Digger Indians dropped from a hundred and fifty thousand to thirty thousand during a ten-year period of Anglo rule. Any Indian arrested could be sold to the highest bidder as his slave for four months. No Indian could testify in the trial of a white—which created a permanent open season on Indians. So-called "heroes of the Wild West," like Kit Carson, were in fact professional executioners of Indians. U. S. Army generals carried out massive search-and-destroy missions that wiped out thousands of women and children as well as men.

To justify these actions, U.S. history books tell us that the Indians were "savages." The Anglo also put a label on the Mexicano to justify all the theft and the lynchings. A certain image was created of the Mexican: dirty, spendthrift, thieving, immoral, cowardly, and bandit. Instead of getting credit for teaching the gringo how to mine, how to raise cattle, how to irrigate, and so forth, our people were labeled lazy and stupid. It seems clear that the reason why we are not taught about our skills and technology is that the gringo colonizer had to change the truth so as to make his actions seem right. He had to make us believe we were worthless so that we could be controlled. We will say more about this brainwashing process in another chapter.

The gringo took over our land, our technology, and our natural resources. It is these losses that made the mestizo and the Indian into colonized people, people who became not only strangers in their own land but voiceless shadows of the West.

5

"Bandits"— or Heroes?

The enemies of the country and of freedom of the
people have always denounced as bandits those who
sacrifice themselves for the noble causes of the people.

Emiliano Zapata

IN 1910 AN EVENT took place in Mexico City that
would have tremendous effects on the lives of our people. It was in that year that the Mexican Revolution
began—the first real social revolution in American history. A million people would die during that revolution, and millions more would come to the United
States as a result of it. The Revolution also gave us two

heroes of today's Chicano movement: Emiliano Zapata and Pancho Villa.

The causes of the Mexican Revolution go back many years. Mexico won its independence from Spain in 1821, after the long struggle we described in Chapter 3. But that did not change the life of the masses of people, who were mostly Indios. They continued to be poor and at the mercy of the big landlords. Many political struggles took place between leaders but they had little effect on the lives of most Mexicans.

There was one leader who was a man of the people: Benito Juárez, a Zapotec Indio from a poor family of southern Mexico, who came to be known as "The Father of the Constitution." He led a struggle against the conservative Catholic Church and the military, the two forces that controlled Mexico. Juárez was a liberal and wanted to make many reforms. The aristocrats of the Church and the military wanted to keep things the way they were. Some of them decided that the best way to do that was by bringing over a nice, old-fashioned monarchy from Europe.

Napoleon III of France liked this idea. He agreed to send troops who would help the conservatives set up Mexico as an empire. The rulers would be an aristocrat from Austria named Maximilian and his wife, Carlota. Plans were made, and the French troops landed expecting an easy victory. Mexico would be their kingdom.

Instead, they got a big surprise. The troops under Juárez defeated them at the town of Puebla on May 5, 1862. This is a date that Mexicans celebrate as the Cinco de Mayo, a great victory against imperialism. Today, Chicanos in many parts of the United States also celebrate Cinco de Mayo with fiestas, dances, and cultural programs.

Unfortunately the French brought in more troops and soon had the rulers Maximilian and Carlota on their thrones in the Castle of Chapultepec. But Juárez and his people continued to fight. Juárez was determined to bring reforms to Mexico, and he hoped that this could be done through a new Constitution. For five long years, he led the struggle against the French, traveling around Mexico in a cart and carrying the precious Constitution with him in an old black box. Finally his forces were victorious.

But Juárez died a few years later. A new man came into power: President Porfirio Díaz, who ruled Mexico with an iron hand for over thirty years, starting in 1876. Díaz is said to have brought "stability" to Mexico. What he really brought was U.S. influence and exploitation. By 1910, U.S. interests (called investments) in Mexican oil, railroads, mines, and agriculture were worth *billions* of dollars.

Under Díaz, the rich got richer while the poor became poorer. The Church regained the power and wealth it had lost under Juárez. Díaz was the friend of the rich, and he gave huge amounts of land to his favorites. By 1910, a thousand people owned 90 per cent of all Mexico. Those people were not interested in growing the basic foods that fed the people. They were only interested in products that could be exported, and make them rich. The ordinary Mexicano found himself forced to work on huge haciendas that were run like company towns—with their own stores, churches, jails. The owners kept the poor Indio and mestizo in permanent debt, and the debts were passed from fathers to sons.

A revolution *had* to happen. Too many people were hungry and angry.

You could hear the rumblings of revolution not only on the land but also in the mines and factories. One day in 1906, some workers at a big U.S.-owned copper mine just across the border from Arizona decided they would not take it any longer. Two thousand of them went on strike. U.S. troops came in to help Díaz's troops break the strike, and at least thirty miners were killed.

That same year, a strike of textile workers broke out near the city of Veracruz. It was led by Lucretia Toriz, one of many women workers prominent in this and other strikes. The women formed leagues, issued manifestos, and suffered vicious attacks by government troops sent to stop the strikes. On January 8, 1907, dozens of them—men and women—were killed or wounded when troops broke the textile workers' strike.

By this time, more and more brave Mexicans were raising their voices against all the oppression. A number of underground newspapers attacking the regime were started, three of them by women. Juana Belen Gutiérrez de Mendoza published a paper called *Vesper* in the town of Guanajuato, where miners suffered some of the worst exploitation. She was jailed and her paper was suppressed many times, but she carried on the struggle for years.

There were other people who had already begun to organize revolutionary forces. One of them was Emiliano Zapata, from the cotton-growing state of Morelos just south of Mexico City. Only thirty families owned almost all the cultivated land in Morelos. One of them was famous for its hacienda with ten acres of land-scaped gardens, fountains, bowling lawn—and a tomb for the owners' dead dog. The Indios of Morelos knew that that dog had lived better than they did—and they began to rebel. They took down the hacienda fences and reclaimed their land. Emiliano Zapata was their leader and *"Tierra o Muerte!"*—Land or Death—became their cry.

A thousand miles to the north, another man named Francisco (Pancho) Villa had for some time been taking land, cattle, and grain from the rich—and giving it to the poor.

Zapata and Villa did not know each other in 1910. Each man was fighting injustice in his own way in two separate parts of the country. But the whole country was ready to explode. The fuse was finally lit by the Serdan family in Puebla. On November 8, 1910, they fired the first shots against the government from their own house. For many hours, the men and women of this family fought the Díaz police and troops. They were defeated at last, but two days later the Revolution broke out all over the country.

The national leader at this stage was Francisco Madero, a rich young liberal who called for a revolution to overthrow Díaz. Villa and Zapata supported him, as did other forces. Madero won a quick victory, and became the new President of Mexico in June of 1911. When he marched into Mexico City, the people went wild with joy. They saw Madero as their savior. For once, poor people had a reason to care about politics in Mexico. For once, they believed that a political leader would change their daily lives.

Unfortunately Madero could not lead the full-scale social revolution that Mexico needed. He was an idealistic, well-meaning young man, who thought that you could win justice and democracy simply by having elections (and not letting anybody get himself re-elected many times as Díaz had done). Zapata saw the problem right away. He met with Madero and told the President that it was necessary to take away the huge estates of the rich and return the land to the people. But Madero could not see that political reform was useless unless you changed the whole economic structure. Without realizing it, Madero played into the hands of the old order.

Zapata kept on trying to change Madero's mind. On November 28, 1911, he issued the Plan de Ayala (the name of his hometown area) which supported Madero's program for election reforms but said that wasn't enough. People needed LAND, a way to make a living and eat. The Plan de Ayala provided for this kind of land reform in much detail. One of its provisions said that the *ejidos*, the lands once held communally by the people, would be returned. The plan said the present owners of that land would be compensated for their loss, unless they simply refused to agree to the new arrangement. "Tierra, Pan y Justicia" —Land, Bread, and Justice—were the goals of the plan.

Madero refused to accept the Plan de Ayala. He could not see that Zapata and those who supported the plan were his true friends. Instead, he let some of the old Díaz people stay in power. And soon the enemies of Madero moved to destroy him.

A general named Victoriano Huerta, who had important friends at the U.S. embassy, organized his forces against Madero. Zapata saw the danger and offered Madero a thousand troops as help—but the President foolishly refused. Within a short time, General Huerta imprisoned Madero. One day in 1913, Huerta told Madero that he was going to be transferred to "a safer place." Instead, Madero was murdered in cold blood.

Even Anglo historians in this country agree that the U.S. ambassador secretly supported the murder of Madero. General Huerta had convinced the ambassador that only he, Huerta, could keep control over Mexico and protect U.S. investments. That was what the United States cared about. The President of the United States had already ordered twenty thousand troops—*one quarter of the entire U. S. Army*—to the border between the United States and Mexico. They were on stand-by duty, in case they had to invade Mexico again for the benefit of U.S. businessmen.

The murder of Madero enraged many Mexicans. In the North, Pancho Villa swore to defeat General Huerta. In the South, Zapata also organized for the fight against Huerta. Other leaders were on the scene too. The hardest years of the Mexican Revolution now began, yet they were also productive and inspiring years.

Zapata and Villa were very different as human beings, although they both fought for the poor against the rich. They were almost the same age, Zapata born on August 8, 1879, and Villa on June 5, 1877 (or 1878). A quiet, reserved man who often shielded his eyes and his thoughts under his big sombrero, Emiliano Zapata stood small and dark. He was a mestizo from a family that had fought against both Spain and the French—a family well respected in Morelos. When Emiliano was about nine years old, he once saw his father break down and cry after a big landowner took over an orchard belonging to the village where they lived. He promised his father to get the land back and he never forgot that promise.

Emiliano's family had a little property. On holidays he would dress up in the fine outfit of a *charro* and go riding on a silver-saddled horse. But he never had a taste for social-climbing or making deals to get ahead. He hated the city, with all its smooth-talking hypocrites, and he especially hated politicians. One of the few revolutionary generals who didn't want to be President, Emiliano never had personal ambition.

Zapata became one of the leaders of Mexico not because he wanted it but because he had the qualities of a born leader. He was appointed by the elders of his own village and other villages as a leader. So he accepted, because he thought he should serve his people. He never acted as though he was more important than the people. This used to confuse many visitors. They complained that they could not tell Zapata from his followers, because everybody dressed alike and talked alike.

Zapata had very clear political ideas, as the Plan de Ayala shows. He expressed his basic philosophy in these beautiful words: "The land belongs to everyone like the air, the water, the light and the heat of the sun, and those who work the land with their own hands have a right to it."

The plan was actually put into effect for a while, in Zapata's home state of Morelos. The land was redistributed to the *campesinos* (small farmers) as planned. The revolutionaries knew that it is no use owning land if you don't have the means to cultivate it, so they set up an agricultural credit bank where campesinos could get loans to buy tools, seed, work animals. Within a few years, many campesinos had won back their economic independence. They were again growing the crops that people needed to live—beans, corn, chile, tomatoes, onions, and so forth. As a result, less food had to be imported and prices stayed down.

The people governed themselves in a humanistic way. In the areas under Zapatista control, local councils appointed the leaders. Through the councils, the people themselves solved their problems—they ruled themselves. Zapata never set up a state police force; the councils enforced the law. Military chiefs were forbidden to interfere in village affairs. For the first time in modern Mexican history, power flowed from the bottom up—not from the top down. Poor people themselves made the decisions about their lives, instead of some military strong men or some bureaucrats in a faraway city.

All these ways of living and organizing a society had deep roots in old Indian tradition—the traditions of the clan and tribal councils that we described in Chapter 2.

Zapata took the best of those old ideas and put them to modern, revolutionary use.

The army of the Zapatistas was a *people's army*. The soldiers were not professionals but campesinos who would work part time as soldiers and part time as farmers. They knew many guerrilla secrets of survival: how to hide in holes made by animals in the cornfields, how to hide under water for long periods of time, how to survive in the mountains. Their strength lay in the fact that they came from the villages, and the villages were like big families. The community surrounded the fighters like a warm, protective cloak.

Zapata's ideas were not limited to rural areas or to Mexico. He understood the needs of industrial and city workers too, and he called for many labor reforms. He also said that foreign ownership of Mexico's natural resources must end. Zapata sent representatives to the United States, England, Cuba, and other countries to explain the Zapatista movement. He saw that the time had come all over the world when, as he said, "the enslaved men, the men with sleeping consciousness, begin to awake . . ."

Pancho Villa did not put his feelings into long-range programs as Zapata did, but he also had a clear sense of why he was fighting. Pancho was born Doroteo Arango of a family that lived by share-cropping in the state of Durango. His father died young but the family managed to scrape by, with all the sons and daughters working and helping. One day in September 1894, Doroteo came home from the fields and learned that his twelve-year-old-sister had been raped by a rich landowner. The boy, then sixteen, got a pistol and shot the man dead.

That was the beginning of his long flight from the police and certain death. Doroteo became Pancho Villa and hid in the mountains. Up to 1910, he was just a fugitive with a price on his head who managed to collect some friends and supporters. But in that year, when the Revolution began, he suddenly had more to fight for. He never had big political ambitions for himself; as he once told a reporter, "My ambition is to live my life . . . among my *compañeros* whom I love, who have suffered so long and so deeply with me. I think I would like the government to establish a leather factory where we could make good saddles and bridles, because I know how to do that. . . ."

Villa has been called a "bandit" by most Anglo historians, who often said the same thing about Zapata. But to our Raza, he is more like a hero. To us, he is the man who not only fought long years in the Mexican Revolution but also defied the powerful U. S. Government. Today, many *viejitos*—our old people—still remember Villa from personal experience. They tell many stories of his exploits and his humanity.

A big bear of a man with a tremendous laugh, Pancho did not learn to read and write until he was imprisoned in 1911. There, behind bars, a Zapatista taught him how to read. He had been sentenced to death but President Madero—who was in power then—pardoned him at the last minute. The pardon arrived while Pancho was up against the wall, facing the firing squad. He lived to become an outstanding military leader in the Revolution, with the entire North under his control at certain times.

The secret of Villa's success was that he was so much at home with the land and the people. When his fighters were wounded, he had a *curandero* bring them back to health. This man (or woman) used strong herb teas and other remedies of the people called folk medicine. Our *viejitos* also tell of Villa's love for children and how he would feed every child he met. He wanted very much to have them educated in the United States—to learn the skills, industries, and habits of the Anglo. "And then I will laugh at the gringos," Pancho said, "or if I am not still alive, then my little ones will laugh."

Villa traveled through much of the Southwest, as far north as San Luis, Colorado. The border was wide open in those days. He would often trade with Anglo merchants, exchanging cattle for arms and ammunition. Sometimes he would have to make special trips to collect what he was owed.

The most famous of these visits took place at Columbus, New Mexico, in March of 1916. Villa went there to settle accounts with a man who had taken a large number of Villa's cattle but did not send the guns and ammunition that were part of the deal. Arriving in Columbus, Pancho found the man's brother at a hotel he owned. Instead of trying to make amends, the brother became very nasty. Villa and his men were so furious that they tore the hotel apart and shot the brother. The gringos called this a "raid," but Villa was just angry because he had been cheated in business.

General John Pershing volunteered to go into Mexico

with U.S. troops and get Villa. The famous Pershing expedition became a Kill Mexicans expedition. The troops marched into Mexico, killing over four hundred innocent people and singing this song:

> "It's a long, long way to capture Villa
> It's a long way to go;
> It's a long way across the border
> Where the dirty greasers grow."

Even with that song to inspire them, the U.S. troops failed to capture Villa. At one point, there were thirty thousand men assigned to catch Pancho, and the United States spent over $130,000,000 on the Pershing expedition. Still they failed. Villa had too many friends, and Pershing only made him more of a hero to Raza. Villa was once asked in a newspaper interview, "How did it happen that Pershing never caught up with you?" Pancho answered: "Very simple. How could Pershing catch up with me when I was traveling behind him?" It was one of Villa's favorite tricks to send out men who would offer themselves as guides for Pershing. The men would, of course, send Pershing in the wrong direction all the time—so that the gringo general would not be tracking down Villa but wandering off ahead of him.

Zapata and Villa are two of the best-known leaders of the Mexican Revolution but many other people fought bravely for land and justice. Among them were the brothers Ricardo and Enrique Flores Magón, two revolutionary journalists. Born on September 16, 1873, Ricardo began a newspaper called *Regeneración* calling for an end to the Díaz regime and social change. Díaz imprisoned him and his brother, and suppressed the paper; they started another paper and were again jailed. Finally they decided it was impossible to continue working in Mexico so they moved to the United States in 1904 with the idea of publishing a paper there, then smuggling it into Mexico.

The Magón brothers in exile became leaders of Mexico's Liberal Party, which called for land reform, guaranteed minimum wages, breaking the power of the Catholic Church, an end to foreign exploitation, and equal rights for women. Ricardo Flores Magón understood the basic truth seen by Zapata. "When you are in possession of the land and the machinery of production," Ricardo said, "then you will have justice." On another occasion he wrote: "Political freedom doesn't feed the people; it is necessary to win economic freedom, the basis of all other freedoms."

Like Zapata, he finally had to oppose Madero and even fought against Madero's troops in Lower California. The Mágon brothers also became very active in labor struggles and strikes by Mexicano workers both in the United States and Mexico. They saw the importance of organizing Raza on both sides of the so-called border. The United States soon stepped in and imprisoned the Magón brothers with two other men for "violating neutrality laws." The men began serving two years of forced labor at McNeil Island Penitentiary in Washington state. They had many trials and a long legal struggle, but the U. S. Government refused to free them.

Both brothers ended up in Leavenworth, Kansas, federal prison in 1918. Thanks to strong public protest, Enrique was freed and Ricardo was scheduled to be freed at last on November 22, 1918. The day before, at midnight, a guard known as "The Bull" came and strangled Ricardo to death in his cell. It seems clear to us that he did this under the orders from a government that never wanted Ricardo freed. In an interview with a U.S. senator, who was among those protesting the imprisonment of the Magóns, President Woodrow Wilson said: "For heaven's sake, Senator, I am absolutely convinced that the Magóns are innocent. But I don't think it would be convenient, politically speaking, to free them."

This story is not well-known in the United States, but it shows how involved the United States was in the Mexican Revolution. It is also the story of a brave man whose ideas still live today. We can never forget the words of Ricardo Flores Magón: "I have in short lost everything, except my honor as a fighter."

Not only men but also many women played a vital role in the Mexican Revolution. They are remembered today in two popular songs of the Revolution: "Adelita" and "Valentina." Women joined the Revolution in all kinds of ways: as fighters, secret messengers, nurses, suppliers of food, journalists. Thousands were soldaderas—soldier women who followed their men from one camp to another, one battleground to another, moving munitions and setting up camps. In the famous paintings of the Revolution by such artists as Diego Rivera and Orozco, we often see the soldaderas trudging along with the columns of troops, their heads covered by shawls and their feet in sandals, their strong Indian faces sad but uncomplaining.

Many Mexican women got into actual battle by

disguising themselves as men. One of these was
Encarnación "Chenita" Cárdenas. A poor girl married
to a young miner, Chenita decided to go to war when
Huerta killed Madero. She cut off her hair, put on
men's clothing, practiced using a deeper voice, and enlisted in a cavalry regiment. Her husband enlisted too.
In her first battle, Chenita's coolness and courage
under a rain of bullets won the respect of all the
soldiers including her own, surprised husband. As a
reward, she was named standard-bearer—the person
who carries the flag. In a later battle, Chenita's horse
was shot but she grabbed the flag and rolled it around
herself, then put one foot in the stirrup of another
soldier's horse. He pulled her up by the hand, and they
galloped away—with the flag still flying high. Chenita
lived through many more battles and narrow escapes,
was promoted to second lieutenant, and served for
three years.

With Zapata, Villa, and so many other courageous
Mexicans fighting him, General Huerta did not last
long after killing Madero. In 1914, he was forced to
flee. The next year, the government ordered that millions of acres of ejido land, with water and forest rights,
be taken away from the big haciendas and returned to
the villages. It seemed as though the dream of Zapata
and many others would finally come true. But there
were too many rich, greedy people still holding power.

During the next five years, power shifted back and
forth between different leaders. At one point, Zapata
and Villa controlled Mexico City—where the two men

met for the first time. They thought they would soon mop up the opposition. But they failed.

The United States had been watching developments month by month in Mexico. First they would throw support to one side, then to another, wheeling and dealing. They decided that the best man for U.S. interests was a landowner and former supporter of Díaz named Venustiano Carranza. He had jumped on the revolutionary bandwagon and built up an army of his own. The United States officially recognized Carranza as ruler of Mexico and helped him.

By now, Villa was losing strength in the North. One big problem still stood in Carranza's way: the strength of the Zapatistas. So Carranza set a trap for Emiliano. One of his officers pretended that he wanted to leave Carranza and join Zapata. When the officer invited Zapata to a meeting to discuss this, Emiliano was suspicious. But he needed help so badly that he went—on April 10, 1919. When he arrived at the meeting place on his famous white horse, there were troops drawn up in formation—apparently to honor him. A salute was blown and then, as the last note faded away, the troops opened fire and filled Zapata's body with bullets.

After the cold-blooded assassination of Zapata, the Revolution came to a grinding end. Carranza soon gave way to another general. Pancho Villa and the remaining Zapatistas made peace with this new government. Then, in 1923, Villa was also shot down by hired assassins.

The ideas and spirit of both Zapata and Villa lasted long after the two men died. Days after the murder of

Zapata, people said they had seen his white horse galloping through the mountains—without a rider. Zapata was still alive, the people said, and he would return. In Morelos, somebody carved on a post: "Rebels of the south, it is better to die on your feet than to live on your knees." Zapata is, to us, the man of the land. His ideals live because they have roots in the land, in the people. We remember his ideals in today's Chicano movement, as we remember the defiance of Pancho Villa. In the words of a Mexican revolutionary, *"Ya murió el Jefe Zapata y ahora somos todos Zapatistas"*—Zapata has died, and now we are all Zapatistas.

6

Strangers in Our Own Land

THE LONG, bloody years of the Mexican Revolution brought hard times all over the country. Driven by fear, poverty, and the hope of a better life, campesinos and workers left their villages to move north— into the United States. No one knows exactly how many came, but we do know it was millions.

The Mexican heading north did not think of himself as an alien entering a foreign nation. In the early 1900s, a person just walked north. If you traveled across the bridge over the Rio Grande, you paid three cents—but there was no registration, no papers needed. To our people, it was all one country. Many had family or friends already here, people who had come to work in the cotton fields or on the railroads (in 1906 alone, sixteen thousand Mexican railroad workers were recruited at El Paso).

The Anglo businessmen in the United States looked at the situation with enthusiasm. They saw the Mexicanos as a source of cheap labor, as workers who were so desperate for jobs that they would accept the worst kind of wages and living conditions. It was like owning a slave.

It happened that during the same years as the Mexican Revolution, a giant agricultural boom had taken place in the southwest United States. Truck farming (fruits and vegetables) began to grow at a tremendous speed in the early 1900s, in California and other areas. In those days, it took five hundred hours of work to grow and harvest one acre of strawberries. So a huge supply of labor was necessary for such crops. There was another new agricultural industry: sugar beets (for the production of sugar), which began in Colorado and then spread.

To meet the need for workers in all these new industries, U.S. agri-businessmen sent out a call: Bring cheap labor! They brought the Japanese, Chinese, and others. Then the call went out: Bring the Mexicans! And the Mexicanos were ready to come—they had no other choice at that time.

The movement of our people to the north took a giant leap. Between 1900 and 1930, the number of Mexicanos in California alone jumped from about 8,000 to over 368,000. It was mostly Mexican hands that cleared thousands of acres of brush to create the "winter gardens" of the Southwest, as the fruit and vegetable centers were called. It was usually Mexican bodies that stood out in the fields at temperatures up to 115 degrees, doing all the tiring stoplabor and hand labor that few Anglos of the Southwest would tolerate. But of course it was not Mexican pockets that were filled by the huge profits from the new crops. In the 1920s, a number of big Anglo employers told a congressional committee that Mexican labor had been a vital factor in developing five billion dollars' worth of agriculture and industry.

The big Anglo growers were a lot like southern plantation owners. They looked at our people as work animals, and treated them that way. The Mexicano was always willing and ready, yet he did not impose problems. Once the planting was done, or the harvest was finished, the Mexicano could be sent away just like that. Although the grower had recruited the worker, he had no responsibility for the man and his family. The fact that the Mexicano didn't speak English made it even easier to exploit him.

For some years, there were laws that made it illegal to import Mexican labor—laws made to protect U.S. workers. The Anglo growers got around these laws by having Mexicanos smuggled into the country. This added to the suffering of our people.

For example, a worker in Mexico would be picked up by the labor smuggler—called a coyote. This man would fill up cars, carts, old trucks, or whatever with Mexican workers and hide them under some large covering like a tarpaulin. Then he would head for the United States, while the people had to stay hidden and could not come out to eat or go to the bathroom.

Sometimes they had to stand all the way. The coyote would turn the workers over to a labor contractor, who would then sell them to the employer for fifty cents or a dollar a head. The workers themselves had to pay for their own transportation.

Sometimes "man-snatchers" would steal a whole crew of Mexicanos and sell them. The man-snatchers would even sell the crew to one employer, then steal the crew back at night and sell it to another—often several times in a row. To prevent this, crews of workers would often be locked up at night in barns or corrals under armed guard. In all these different situations, the Mexicano was not treated as a human being. He never knew where he was going, he had to stay hidden in silence, he was just a piece of property.

Once the Mexicanos arrived at their place of work, they would be crowded into labor camps made up of broken-down shacks with no sanitation or plumbing. These camps were very isolated, and the workers had to buy their food in company stores where the prices ran sky-high. Often the workers brought their families along, and everyone worked. The children almost never went to school; they would be out in the fields too, helping to boost the family's earnings.

At the end of the season, after paying all expenses, a family of seven—with everyone working—would be lucky to clear two hundred dollars. In the sugar-beet industry, where Mexicanos had the unusual chance of working all year long, the average annual income for a whole family was about five or six hundred dollars.

On top of all this, the Mexicano suffered from racism. On the job, he was never paid the same as an

Anglo for the same kind of work. Whenever he left the labor camp, he ran into hatred for his brown skin. Anglos ignored the fact that the Mexicans had been *recruited* to come to the United States, and they treated our people like unwanted dogs.

The terrible living conditions, the racism, all the oppression, had to produce some kind of protest. And they did. A wave of big strikes began—strikes that were really a kind of rebellion. This story is usually forgotten when people talk about the American labor movement. But it is one of the most important chapters in our history of resistance.

Our people had a tradition of labor protest that went back as far as 1883, when several hundred Texas cowboys answered a call to strike that was signed by a man named Juan Gomez. Twenty years later, over a thousand Mexican and Japanese sugar-beet workers went on strike in California. A wave of strikes started by Mexicano railway workers followed. Then, as more and more Raza workers came to the United States, the protests quickly spread.

In the 1920s, the cry of *"Huelga!"*—Strike!—could be heard from many agricultural workers. A big union called La Confederación de Uniones Obreras, the Confederation of Workers' Unions, was born in southern California and soon had twenty local chapters. In 1928, the Confederación called its first big strike in the Imperial Valley. This area, known for its searing hot temperatures during the daytime, became even hotter as the angry workers and gringo growers clashed.

The response of the growers to that first strike was to arrest large numbers of workers and deport them to

Mexico. But two years later, about five thousand Mexicanos again struck in the Imperial Valley. This time they won their demands. The growers decided they would have to take stronger action. A few months later, when the cantaloupe harvest began, the union was attacked before it could call a strike. Over one hundred Mexicanos were arrested, many were tear-gassed and beaten.

Then came 1933, a highpoint in the strikes. Seven thousand of our people walked out of the onion, celery, and berry fields of Los Angeles County in the biggest strike of farmworkers ever seen. The Cannery and Agricultural Workers' Industrial Union called twenty-five strikes in California that year. The growers were really worried now.

When Mexicanos struck for the third time in the Imperial Valley, the gringos broke up union meetings with tear gas and clubs. They kidnaped labor lawyers and took them outside the county. They arrested almost a hundred people. That fall, one of the bloodiest strikes in U.S. agricultural history took place at Pixley, California. Five thousand cotton pickers walked out. Growers went to the union hall with shotguns and three workers were killed.

For several years, it was like wartime in California. When two thousand workers struck in the celery fields, tear-gas bombs were thrown into shacks where the workers' children were playing. One striker was seriously wounded by a tear-gas bomb fired at close range. Many of the people hurt weren't even on strike. The injured couldn't get medical treatment at the county hospital. During a strike of citrus workers in Orange

County, guards with submachine guns patrolled the area. The sheriff issued his orders: "Shoot to kill." Hundreds of Mexicanos were arrested and put on trial in a bull pen.

Farmworkers struck in seven other states, including Washington and Idaho. In Texas, the sheep shearers cried *"Huelga!"* and more than six thousand pecan-shellers did the same in 1934. Sugar-beet workers had a major strike in Colorado; many of them joined in forming La Liga Obrera (The Workers' League).

Some of the strongest protest—and most violent gringo repression—took place in the mine fields. From 1900 to 1940, Mexicanos made up 60 per cent of the common labor force in the mines of the Southwest. They began striking in 1915, with a total of five thousand men walking out of three copper mines in Arizona. Hundreds were arrested and the National Guard was finally sent to break the nineteen-week strike. Two years later, all Arizona copper miners—Mexicanos and others—walked out. Over a thousand of them were rounded up by a mob of vigilantes and shipped out of town in boxcars, then dumped in the desert.

During the 1930s, several thousand Mexicano coal miners went on strike against the Gallup-American Company in New Mexico (then a subsidiary of Kennecott Copper, one of the world's biggest mining companies). The whole area around Gallup was placed under martial law for six months. Although the workers won some relief, the miners of New Mexico continued to suffer from bad working conditions and racism.

All over the Southwest, the strikes failed to bring any lasting improvements in the workers' lives. The

Anglo bosses had two ways of dealing with them: violent repression and deportation, the gun and "the law." Whenever a leader of the workers would grow strong—like Jesús Pallares in New Mexico and Humberto Silex in El Paso—the owners would get their friends in the U. S. Government to deport him. Since the Mexicanos were often not official citizens of the United States, this could be done easily. Jesús Pallares, a brave man who fought in the Mexican Revolution and later helped to organize the Liga Obrera, was labeled a "Communist"—one of the favorite tactics. He was then deported at the request of New Mexico's Governor Clyde Ringley (for whom a park in Albuquerque is named today).

It wasn't only labor leaders who suffered the hardship and humiliation of being deported. The 1930s were the years of the Depression, and the United States sent about half a million ordinary Mexicanos out of this country. The polite word for this was "repatriation," which means sending people back to their native country. What happened, however, was that many Mexicanos who had been born in the United States— or who had lived here for many years—found themselves sent to Mexico. Some did go voluntarily, but most were forced to leave. Since no records had been kept at the border until 1924, many of us had no proof of "legal" entry—and this was often used as an excuse to kick us out.

The Anglo said that the reason for "repatriation" was to get Mexicans off relief—to save money being spent on poor people during the Depression. But the real reason was to get rid of potential strikers and "troublemakers" and to stop the growth of unions. Many of our people were too proud to accept relief, anyway.

This was a very bitter time for our Raza. We had lost our land, become workers on the land for someone else, and then lost our fight for more rights as workers. We had been brought here to work for the Anglo, treated like animals, and then kicked out. This was also a time when the economic struggle made us become divided among ourselves. The Chicano who had been born in the United States looked down on the Mexicano who had arrived recently. The terrible competition for survival often set us against each other instead of fighting our common enemy.

Then, in 1941 the United States entered World War II. The Japanese, who had provided much cheap labor in the fields, were put in concentration camps. U.S. industry boomed. And the old cry was heard again: Bring the Mexicans!

This time, a special international agreement was worked out for importing Mexican labor for the fields. It became known as "the *bracero* program"—*braceros* means arms, or workers. Under the original agreement, workers were supposed to receive free transportation both ways, and they would have certain guarantees of wages and decent work conditions. Mexican officials could inspect the labor camps and make complaints if the workers were mistreated. The U. S. Government would pay to recruit the workers. This was the program which went into operation in 1942.

But after a few months, the growers found ways to get around the promises of protection for the workers.

They paid rock-bottom wages. They put Mexicanos in the same old broken-down labor camps and made them shop at the same old high-priced company stores. The bracero program became a type of legalized semi-slavery, and the growers made fantastic profits. Since the U. S. Government paid most of the cost of recruitment, the growers didn't even have that expense. The taxpayers were picking up the bill.

Over a hundred thousand braceros came to the United States in 1942–47 and helped to produce almost every major crop. Another eighty thousand were recruited to work on the railroads—at $.57 an hour. Like the Mexican workers before World War II, these families got very little money to take home after the bosses had made all their deductions. In one case, a bracero was supposed to get $19.15 for a week's work, but ended up with only $4.56 after all the deductions were made for food and other items. In another case, the man worked twenty-four hours in three days and got $.14 in actual pay.

While thousands of our people were working to feed the United States during the war, thousands more were fighting and dying as soldiers for the United States. Chicanos had served in all the wars beginning with the Civil War, but in World War II they were outstanding. About half a million went into the Armed Forces and an estimated one third of them were wounded or killed. They won a giant heap of medals for bravery on overseas duty.

But back home in the United States, we were still "dirty Mexicans." The truth about Anglo attitudes toward Raza was shoved in our faces with brutal force in many wartime incidents. The worst of them took place in Los Angeles. It was called the "Zoot-Suit Riots."

At that time jitterbug dancing was very popular. In East Los Angeles, where thousands of Mexicanos lived, the young men liked to wear "drapes"—often called a zoot suit—because the style was suitable for jitterbugging. The zoot suit became a symbol of the young Chicano, called *pachuco*.

On June 3, 1943, a group of sailors on leave were walking down the street, so they said, in a Los Angeles neighborhood where servicemen rarely went. They were attacked by a "gang" of Mexicans, they said, although we believe they probably went into the neighborhood to make trouble and then found themselves outnumbered. The next day, two hundred sailors came into town "to clean up the zoot-suit gangsters." They hired twenty taxicabs and began cruising the streets of East Los Angeles. Whenever they saw a zoot suit, they stopped and beat up the person wearing it— then drove on to the next, and did the same. Soon there were four young Chicanos lying in their own blood on the pavement. The police saw what was happening, but they just looked the other way.

The next night, the sailors were joined by soldiers and Marines. They all walked together through downtown Los Angeles with their arms linked, stopping everyone who wore a zoot suit and warning them to put on different clothes by the following night or else . . . Neither the police nor the Shore Patrol nor the Military Police made any move to stop them. But the police did arrest twenty-seven Mexicanos "on suspicion" of various crimes. And the next day, the police followed the sailors around, letting them do whatever they wanted. They arrested over forty Mexicanos who had been beaten up.

The press reported these events with enthusiastic approval for the sailors, which encouraged more violence. During the next two days, June 7 and 8, thousands of gringos—including civilians now—formed a giant lynch mob. They stormed into movie theaters and bars and stopped streetcars, grabbing the victims out of their seats. Many if not most of the victims weren't even wearing zoot suits, and quite a few were Filipinos and Blacks. Boys of twelve were beaten and a mother who tried to protect her young son was hit by police.

Finally the military authorities declared downtown Los Angeles out of bounds to servicemen. The rioting quieted, but then it spread to the suburbs for two more days of brutality. Again, the police did nothing to stop the vicious attacks.

Why did the police let the brutality go on for such a long time? Shortly after the riot, a police captain revealed that the police had encouraged the violence by the sailors. At that time, an officer was accused of kicking a man to death in the Los Angeles jail. By having a riot, the public would be convinced that harsh police methods were necessary and the accused officer would be more likely to go free. This tactic worked: the cop was cleared while the bodies of our people lay broken and bloody.

As Raza servicemen came home from the war, they became more and more angry. They had just risked their lives for the United States and often been injured, only to come home and face signs on restaurants that said "No Dogs or Mexicans Allowed" and "For Whites—Mexicans Keep Out." Chicanos who had been awarded the Congressional Medal of Honor, the nation's highest decoration, were refused service in cafes. In Three Rivers, Texas, in 1947, city officials refused to allow the burial of a Chicano soldier named Felix Longoria who had been killed overseas (he was finally buried in Arlington National Cemetery).

This kind of incident happened again and again. Chicano veterans began to form protest organizations all over the country. These included the Community Service Organization and the G-I Forum, which are still in existence today. When they began to organize, there was no other large Raza Chicano organization except LULAC (League of United Latin American Citizens), which had been formed in Texas in the 1920s when our people were under attack by the Ku Klux Klan.

The new organizations were not radical or very militant; they simply asked that Chicanos be treated like first-class citizens. But they were a breakthrough. After the unions had been crushed, there had been no organized, public way for our people to protest against racism. The new groups showed that the spirit of resistance had not died.

The life of our people changed in other ways as a result of World War II. Many Chicanos left the rural areas to go to work in the cities, and today there are many more Chicanos living in the city than in the countryside. This broke up the old neighborhoods, the barrios and *colonias*, which had long been places where our traditions and culture could survive. Of course the old neighborhood or barrio also meant segregation, like the ghetto. But it was a source of unity and protection too.

More and more of our people moved outside the Southwest. Although most Chicanos do still live in the Southwest, millions of our people can now be found in industrial areas like Chicago (250,000), Detroit (40,000), Gary, Indiana (25,000), Kansas City (20,-000), and Milwaukee (18,000). We even have people in Alaska—a whole trainload of Raza workers was once shipped there to work in the canneries.

The situation of Chicanos in such areas is a little different from in the Southwest. They cannot see the land and Raza faces all around them, as in much of the Southwest. They do not have the feeling that where they live was once their own country, a non-Anglo country. Yet in the end, they suffer from most of the same problems as our people in the Southwest: no jobs or poor jobs, the welfare system, poor education, housing, health, and so forth. As for racist attitudes toward them, it was not a Texas gringo but a justice of the Supreme Court of New York who said some years ago:

"Diseased, ignorant and belonging to a greatly lower class, the Mexican element are lowering the standard of our population as far north as Wyoming. They are," said the judge, "the most undesirable of all peoples."

7

The Big Brainwash

A HIGH SCHOOL STUDENT sat writing a paper for his civics class. He began it: "When our forefathers landed at Plymouth Rock . . ." The name of the student was Juan Montoya, but he saw nothing strange about writing those words.

A group of Chicano children stood in the plaza of the pretty tourist town in the Southwest. They were staring at a statue of a white man wearing buckskins and holding a rifle—a real frontier fellow. Under the statue, some words were engraved: "To the heroes who have fallen in the various battles with savage Indians."

The TV was on, in the home of the Rodriguez family. A commercial for an underarm deodorant began flashing on the screen. It showed a man with a big sombrero on his head, dressed like a typical Mexican bandit. The man was using the deodorant and the TV voice said: "If it works for *him*, you know it will work for you."

Those are just three examples of what we call the big brainwash. If we think about them carefully, we see that they teach three lessons. The first is that our people have no history of our own, that the history of the United States began with a group of Englishmen. The second is that Indians are savages, so we don't want to say that we are part Indian. And the third is that Mexicans are *really* smelly and dirty.

Why would the schools and TV and other people teach us these things? Why would they want us to believe these lies?

If we look at world history, we can see that every nation or group of people that has conquered another group uses certain methods to stay in power. Guns are one method, but guns are not enough. It's too expensive to keep a big, permanent army on top of the conquered people. You must do something else: you must control the minds of the people in the colony.

This means that you must destroy whatever it is that makes them strong as a people—their spirit and culture. You must make them hate their true selves. You must make them identify with you and your system. You must make them want to be like you, the conqueror. You must make them agree to their own oppression.

All this is very hard to do, and the colonial power must hammer away at it day after day. He must create a certain image of the colonized people. We have seen this done with Indians, Blacks, Asians, and Puerto Ricans. In the same way, the Anglo books, movies, television, advertising, and the press all work to reduce the Mexicano to a certain stereotype image: stupid, lazy, dirty, ignorant, sneaky, violent, unreliable, sinister.

The only good qualities we have been assigned are singing, dancing, grinning, cooking Mexican food, and sometimes having beautiful women. Most of the time, the Mexicano is asleep under a big sombrero. He wakes up just long enough to say a few words in broken *Engleesh* before going back to his endless siesta. So much for the children of Cuauhtemoc, Hidalgo, Morelos, Juárez, and Zapata. They have been washed away.

The whole point of the big brainwash is to make us think that our poverty and oppression are *our own fault*. It is supposed to be our fault that 41 per cent of the Raza families in New Mexico and over 50 per cent in Texas have incomes below the official poverty level, while about one third of the Chicanos across the nation are classified as poor. It is supposed to be our fault that only 17.5 per cent of the nation's Chicanos have white-collar (higher-paying) jobs. It is supposed to be our fault that Chicanos in the Southwest finish three to seven years of school *less than* Anglos.

The big brainwash starts on the first day of school for many of our people. Up to that time, the Chicano child has usually lived in a home where Spanish is spoken and certain foods are eaten and the family is united. Now he goes into the classroom where a different language is suddenly the only one he is allowed to use. The first blow often comes with the child's name. Juan, José, Roberto, Tobias, or Carlos become Johnny, Joe, Bobby, Toby, and Charley. Juana, Gertrudis, María, and Rosa become Jane, Gertrude, Mary, and Rose. When you lose your name, you lose an important piece of your identity.

But it isn't just a problem of your personal identity. The language of a people expresses the soul of that people, their whole culture. Imposing the Anglo's language—English—is a way of destroying our soul. This is what we call cultural genocide.

The language problem gets worse as time goes by in school. When the Anglo children are beginning to learn facts and figures, the Chicano child is still trying to learn the language in which that information is taught. By the fifth grade, according to various studies, the Chicano child is considered two years behind the Anglos. The odds keep on rising and it's a tough kid who is not convinced by junior high school that Mexicans really are stupid—including himself. When the Chicano finally quits school, he is labeled a dropout—as if he ever had a real chance to drop *in*.

Let the Anglo who doesn't understand all this just think of going into a schoolroom where only Spanish is spoken. He is not given permission to go to the bathroom unless he asks for it in Spanish. The rest of the class listens and laughs as he struggles to produce the right words. He falls behind, doesn't get promoted, and soon finds himself in a class where he is older and bigger than the Anglos which causes him to feel stupid.

When he is given one of those official intelligence tests, he does badly on it. The test is in English, and full of ideas that he doesn't understand. He may end up in a class for retarded children. This is no exaggeration. In 1969, it was discovered that forty-seven Chicano children in Los Angeles, who had all been classified as retarded, were really normal or very intelligent when they were tested in Spanish instead of English.

The pressures on the young Chicano to forget his own language and culture are not just social. In most of Texas, it is illegal for teachers to use any language but English. In parts of Colorado, it was illegal for teachers to speak Spanish in the classroom until 1969. The same ban applies to students in many areas. The punishment for speaking Spanish ranges from being made to stand in the corner, to being kept after school, to being beaten—which is still an approved penalty in some of the largest school systems. Whatever happened to the Treaty of Guadalupe Hidalgo with its promise of respect for the rights of La Raza?

But language is only part of cultural genocide. Everything in the classroom works to make the Chicano child feel out of place, lost, like a zero. The reading books that show blond Dick and Jane playing in their middle-class home are just one example. By high school, the Chicano is writing "When our forefathers landed at Plymouth Rock" because he never learned about his real forefathers. The Raza girl is bleaching her hair and trying to powder her face white. Both are being taught to compete, to become "a good American," to make money. They are never taught that their own people have beauty and that their own traditions are co-operative—not competitive.

All this not only drains the young Chicano of his true being. It also tries to fill him with the desire to be somebody else—a stranger, a white person. Soon he is caught in a trap: rejecting his real self, he wants to be like the Anglo, but at the same time he knows this is impossible. Spiritually he has been made an alien in his own land.

The young Chicano becomes a divided person inside. He or she also becomes divided from parents and grandparents. They often speak only Spanish—but it is shameful, the child has been taught, to speak Spanish. His mother packs him a lunch with tortillas and chile in a paper bag—but he is ashamed to eat it among all those ham sandwiches and rosy apples packed into shiny new lunch boxes. For the elders, the process can be heartbreaking. Their child goes from home to school and comes back almost a stranger. The family loses its unity, although never as much as Anglo families.

The big brainwash goes on long after school. On the job, our people are often told by the Anglo boss not to speak Spanish even when the entire work crew is Chicano. In 1969, for example, the janitors at a university in New Mexico were given a written order to speak only English when discussing their work or in the Buildings office. At stores, in government offices, at the post office, our last names are often Anglo-cized. The social worker complains about not being able to pronounce Spanish names like Gallegos or Jimenez, and hints that we should change them.

Some of us even begin to believe that we really are "culturally deprived," as Anglo professors like to say. We forget to ask: how can we be culturally deprived when we speak two languages and have a culture with roots that are thousands of years old? We forget all this, and go on trying to be like the Anglo.

Again and again, we are told that we lack "incentive" and "motivation" and "ambition." The social scientists are worried about this, they say. They want to give us "goals." We forget that in this society "incentive" and money usually mean the same thing. Our best achievements come out of a different kind of incentive, but they are not appreciated. So our people begin thinking they really are lazy. Some of them buy Arrow shirts and ties and alarm clocks and *Time* magazine and start trying to "get ahead." They learn the gringo's lingo about business and success. Then they tell their Chicano brothers who don't succeed: you just didn't try hard enough. Anybody can make it if he works hard and has "incentive." The big question has been forgotten by now: incentive for what? For money? For things? For happiness? What is happiness?

The pressure to act white and think white continues all through life. We are taught that the Spanish heritage in the United States is something to celebrate, but not the Mexican heritage. The Spanish label is all right because it means non-Indian, white—not "savage." So we are told about the Spaniards who founded the city of Los Angeles, for example. But when we check the historical records carefully, we find that out of the twenty-three men and women who founded Los Angeles, only two were really Spaniards. The rest were Indios from Mexico (nine), mulattoes (eight), Blacks, mestizos—and one Chinese.

In the Southwest every year, there are often big fiestas to celebrate the arrival of Juan de Oñate—the millionaire from Mexico who came to Nuevo México. This is supposed to be a fiesta for the Spanish tradition. But Oñate's own wife was a mestiza, the great-great-granddaughter of Moctezuma and great granddaughter of Cortés. Most of the men who came with Oñate were mestizo.

It is very important for the Anglo to make Chicanos *not* want to identify with their Mexican history and culture. As we said before, the colonizer must make the conquered people identify with him and his system. The Anglo had a special problem with La Raza that he didn't have with Black people. No ocean separated us from our original homeland. It was right here in the Southwest, or right next door. Mexico is so close; it can always remind us of who we were and what we had been. The Anglo colonizer had to break this down. He had to prevent unity between the two branches of the same family—the one living in the United States and the one living in Las Americas.

This has been done in many ways, but one of the most important has been by making our people feel like enemies on the job. In other words, make the Chicano and the Mexican compete for work—for economic survival. This tactic is called "divide and conquer."

The big Anglo growers have done this with agricultural workers again and again. When Chicano workers go on strike in the United States, the boss brings in Raza from Mexico to break the strike—as scabs. It is hard to blame the Mexicanos who become scabs because we know they are desperate for work. It is also hard to blame the Raza who become angry at them, because the strikes represent their struggle for a better life. The result is a tragic situation of brother pitted against brother, sister against sister.

Many of us remember how our people were divided during the Depression years. The divisions showed in the names we called each other. Those who had U.S. citizenship called the man from Mexico such names as *cholo*, *suramato*, and *mateo*, while the people from old Mexico called those who were already here *pocho* and *manito*. We yelled the word "outsider" at our brother from Mexico because we were hungry, because we were suffering, and because that was what the Anglo wanted us to do. The Chicano from the United States began calling himself a "Spanish-American" to show that he was different from those "dirty" Mexicans.

We fought against each other, never realizing that we were both being taken. Never realizing that we were all in the same mess and being used against each other. Never realizing that our fight was just what the gringo wanted. Never realizing that the Anglo himself saw us all as the same, basically—a bunch of foreigners, "wetbacks." The joke was on us.

The Anglo has divided us not only from the Raza of Mexico but from all our other mestizo brothers and sisters on this continent. We learn a lot in school about ancient Greece and Europe, but how much are we taught about Latin America? The Anglo image of Latin Americans is not very different from his image of the Chicano. Both are seen as foreign and inferior. So we learn to look at our brothers and sisters that way.

Another way that we have been brainwashed is by Red-baiting—having the label of "Communist" put on people or groups that are trying to work for real social progress. This weapon was used a lot during the 1950s, when Senator McCarthy and men like him were active. It hurt many Chicano organizing efforts then, and even today we can see Chicanos who are scared off by that label.

How else are we brainwashed? There are many more ways. All through life, we are divided inside ourselves personally and among ourselves as a people. This is why, in the last few years, our people have been talking about an "identity problem." This is why many Chicanos are now asking: Who am I? Who are we? What shall I call myself?

Today many of our people are confused. There are those who call themselves Hispanos or Spanish. No matter how Indian they may look, they still insist that they are Spanish. Of course we are all Hispanic in a sense, because of our language. But we have to be careful that when we say we are Spanish, we are not trying to deny our mestizo origins and culture.

A trip to Spain, for those who can afford it, is enough to convince those "Spanish" Chicanos about their real origins. One very surprised Raza made such a trip and when he came back, he said: "Man, I thought I was Spanish but they don't even know what tortillas and chile are. I found out that I am a Mexican."

Then we have the Chicana who is a gung-ho "American." She thinks that being an American means that you have to shed everything that isn't Anglo. You have to wipe out your culture and your history to be a real, red-blooded American. But then this American finds out that no matter how hard she tries, she is considered "different." She can't get a job, or she can get only certain kinds of jobs. After a while, she may be ready to recognize what she really is: a Chicana and brown.

> Can't you hear it?
> that I feel ugly . . .
> to discover after all these years . . .
> That I don't love myself
> That all these years I've been looking
> at myself through gavacho eyes . . .
> Judging, condemning.
>
> Damn! I was a racist
>   against myself.
> I hated myself because I'm me???
> No more, white man, no more
> Gavacho, Gavacha . . .
> I'm brown, I'm beautiful
> I'm a Chicana
> Y sabes que, white man, pig, educator
> No chingas conmigo mas! ! !
>
> From a poem by
Olivia de San Diego

A Chicano or Chicana is simply a person who does not identify with the Anglo society. Not all of our people call themselves Chicanos today but many Raza— especially the youth—are thinking that way. Today many young Raza are saying that they do NOT want to be red-white-and-blue imitation Anglos. They are refusing to submit any longer to the torture of trying to be something they are not. Our people are refusing to be what we sometimes call coconuts—brown on the outside, white inside. We are rejecting the big brainwash, once and for all.

Many Raza parents are also saying: we don't want to lose our children to the so-called "American dream." We think it's a nightmare, with its emphasis on making money and buying things. We want our children to know the warmth, love, richness, and individuality of our own life and culture. Nothing is more important than saving our youth from what we see as a sick society. Is it asking too much to want our own kind of joy and happiness?

Our people can see that the problem of cultural genocide, the identity question, has produced some great evils. It has given rise to drug addiction, alcoholism, and sometimes serious mental disorders among our people. It is a major reason why today there are more Chicanos in prison than in college. So when we speak of saving our youth, we are not just talking about wanting them to speak Spanish. We are talking about matters of life and death, of enslavement and liberation.

Today, we have learned that a basic tool for winning that liberation is our *real* identity. It is the very weapon that has been used against us: our peoplehood, our Chicanismo. We could not see this for a long time. Like the air we breathe, its importance was invisible to us. But more and more Raza are opening their eyes today.

This weapon is often called nationalism. It doesn't

mean the kind of nationalism that is used as an excuse for making war or invading other people's countries. For us, nationalism or Chicanismo means having a feeling of group pride instead of self-hatred—unity instead of division. It means that we will build upon the history and culture that are ours. It means that instead of being a curse, our brownness will be a source of dignity.

Our new nationalism means that we pay tribute to our ties with Mexico and recognize that we were once Mexico. It does not mean that we feel allegiance to the Mexican Government as such. But we do look upon the people of Mexico as our brothers and sisters. We do recognize our cultural roots. And beyond Mexico, we see all of our Raza in Latin America as brothers and sisters. We appreciate the differences between these nations but we believe that we must avoid petty divisions. They only serve to keep all of us down.

One of the best symbols that has been found to express this new nationalism is the mestizo head. It is an emblem of a head with three faces. One is the face of the Indio, representing the indigenous people of America. The second face is that of the Spaniard. And the third is us, as we are today—a mixture called the mestizo. The mestizo head doesn't just represent a racial mixture but a mixing of cultures and histories too. It is a mixture of East and West, of ancient and modern, of spirit and technology.

This idea can be taken even further. Sometimes you hear the words "La Raza Cósmica"—the Cosmic People (or Race). These words come from a Mexican thinker named José Vasconcelos. He used the word cosmic because La Raza represents not only the blending of the red man and the white man, but the other symbolic colors of humanity too. The history of America includes the Black (the Africans imported as slaves by the Spaniards) and the "yellow" or Asian.

To us, La Raza Cósmica means an absolute rejection of racism. For if we are all races, then none can be called superior. This is not at all the same as the so-called American "melting pot." That phrase only makes us think of culturally different peoples dissolving into a faceless, tasteless mass. Anglos who talk about the wonderful melting pot don't see it as we do. To us, the real purpose of the "melting" is to create a white-dominated pot.

Some of us can remember our parents telling us about "El Gringo," about how we are oppressed as a people. But if we asked, "When do we fight back?" they said, "not now, it is not the time." But surely now it is the time. When a family is evicted from its home or land, it is the time to help that person and be committed to all our people. When farmworkers protest starvation wages, it is the time. When a Chicano is beaten in jail, it is the time. When our children are pushed out of school, it is the time. Now is the time to take care of our people, to commit ourselves in the new spirit of *carnalismo*.

It is the feeling of "now is the time for action," and "now is the time for change," which best explains what is termed as the movimiento or movement. We use this term quite often, and perhaps that is what this book is about. Movement is learning and growing; it is the refusal to sit back in apathy. For Raza, it is the end of the era of "Now is *not* the time," or "*sea por Dios*" (it is the will of God) in defeat. It is the beginning of the era of change, the beginning of the fight for justice and freedom. Chicanismo is being free *to be what we are*. It is the native roots of the American coming to light again. And as we free our minds, we find hope—hope for our people, hope for all of America, for all humanity.

The Chicano today is saying to all of our people who still try to be white: COME HOME, BE YOURSELF. Your brothers and sisters are waiting and need you. We want all of you with us, as one. Together we will win back our identity and break down the divisions among ourselves. Together we will fight racism and oppression. Together we will cease to be a colonized people.

The nationalism that we seek to develop today is like creating a giant family. It means working not for our individual self-interest, not just for our immediate families, but for the good of the entire Familia de La Raza. It means living for each other, not for money and not for personal success. The time of just thinking about ME and MY must end. We have to think about US and WE. This is why we see Chicanismo as a road to world humanism. To us, it is the first step toward a revolution that is needed by oppressed and colonized people all over the world.

8

Tierra o Muerte!

The land, it is everything. My wife and I, we have grown twenty-eight crops on this land. How can I say what the land means to me? Some people used to criticize me. I would be somewhere and I would kneel down and take some of the rich black earth in my hands. It would break in my hand, it was rich. "Estoy encantado con esta tierra," I would say—I am enchanted by this land. A man said, "Sevedeo, he's a little crazy." But this man, he came and worked one day with me and my wife. He put his hands in the earth and he told me, "Sevedeo, maybe you're not so crazy, maybe you're right to love the land."

Yes, I love the land. The land is in my blood, in my heart. The land it is everything.

Sevedeo Martinez of Monero, N.M.

IN SPANISH, the word for land is *tierra* and it rolls on your tongue with all the richness and sweep of la tierra itself. For La Raza, the land is part of one's family and does not exist to be bought or sold. We do not see it only as "real estate" or "property," but as the source of food and therefore, life. For us, the land is our mother and without her we are orphans.

Our people have lived and died for that idea, crying *"Tierra o Muerte!"*—Land or Death. Our long struggle began when the Anglo came West to begin the great land robbery that we described in Chapter 4. That struggle never stopped. It was because of the land that, on June 5, 1967, twenty armed Chicanos took over the courthouse in a New Mexico mountain village called Tierra Amarilla—Yellow Land. Their action shocked the white society of the United States into realizing that the Mexican-American existed.

That day, June 5, Cinco de Junio, has since been recognized as a national Chicano holiday and it is a very important landmark in our liberation struggle. The leader of the men who went to the courthouse that day was Reies López Tijerina (RAY-es LO-pez Tee-heh-REE-nah).

Tijerina knew about gringo oppression and our struggle for the land from an early age. He was born in a share-cropper's shack in Texas. His father supported the family by growing a crop and then, at the end of the season, he was supposed to receive payment for his share from the landowner. But twice the gringo landowner came and told the father, after he had brought in the crop, that he had nothing coming to him. The owner said that the father owed him all the money for supposed debts. All they could do was pack up and leave; few Mexicans would argue with a gringo boss. The third time this happened, the father finally protested—and the whole family was driven from their home at gunpoint.

Reies' great-grandfather had been a land grant heir. When some gringos wanted the land, they pulled an old trick: they drove their cattle into one of his corrals—then accused him of stealing the animals. Six Texas Rangers came and hanged the man from a tree in his own yard. One of his sons, Reies' grandfather, saw that hanging as a child and became a fighter for the land.

Hearing these stories made a deep impression on Reies. As a small child, he had a certain dream over and over again. In the dream, he saw a fine new car drive up to his family's shack. As it came closer and closer, he realized that the car had no driver. He woke up trembling, terrified with fear that if an Anglo saw the car the Tijerinas would be accused of stealing it— and probably be lynched. It was like the story of his great-grandfather all over again.

Reies' mother, Herlinda, was a strong woman. When her family had no food in the house, she made a bow out of an automobile spring and shot a jackrabbit for the children to eat. She worked hard in the fields too, and was a very religious woman. Her strong spirit helped the family to endure as migrant farmworkers, after the father stopped share-cropping.

While the family followed the migrant trail up from Texas to the Midwest, Reies went to twenty different schools. When he grew older, Reies decided to become an Assembly of God minister. He would work as a migrant and preach from the Bible, moving from one place to another. During this time, he married another young worker named Maria Escobar.

In 1956, Reies and sixteen other migrant families put their earnings together and bought a small piece of land in Arizona. They built houses and a little church, and worked the land communally. They called their new home "Valle de la Paz"—Valley of Peace— and hoped to create a community of poor people living in harmony. They would try to bring back some of the spirit of sharing, of living in a co-operative way, that had existed among our people before the Anglo invasion. But the local whites didn't want this. They called the Valley of Peace a gypsy camp and began to drive out the Raza families by falsely accusing them of various crimes and "Communist activities." The homes were burned down. A girl was raped. Tijerina and the others finally had to leave.

What should they do now? Reies had always been interested in the old land grants and our struggle to win back the land. He had often asked himself, why are the Spanish-speaking people in such a miserable situation? Now he felt that he might have the answer: *la tierra.*

Reies went to Mexico, to study the old documents about land rights. He discovered how the Treaty of Guadalupe Hidalgo had promised protection for our land rights. He also traveled a lot in New Mexico, looking at many of the old land grant documents that Raza still had, packed away in old chests or under mattresses. He talked with many people who had lost their land and become terribly poor. They didn't receive any help from the government except some powdered milk and other "surplus" foods that nobody else wanted.

The more that Reies saw and heard, the more he believed that the land was the right problem to focus on. The treaty had guaranteed our rights, hadn't it? And if we could win back the land, then we would have the basis of life—the "mother" that our people talk about.

By 1963, Reies and others felt ready to form an organization. It was called the Alianza Federal de Mercedes (Federated Alliance of Land Grants) and is usually known just as the Alianza. At the founding convention of the Alianza in Albuquerque, New Mexico, there were eight hundred people representing some fifty land grants. Their main goal was to organize land grant heirs so as to make the authorities respect the Treaty of Guadalupe Hidalgo. They wanted to recover both the lands and culture which had been lost as a result of the treaty being violated.

The lands that the Alianza wanted to recover were the ones that used to be communally owned—the *ejido* lands. These were now in the hands of the government, especially the U. S. Forest Service. To our people, the Forest Service did not mean that friendly-looking fellow, Smokey the Bear. To us, the Forest Service is an army of occupation. It puts up signs that mean our people cannot use the land to produce food for our people. It doesn't let our people cut wood where they once could, for centuries. It doesn't let our people graze their animals in the fields as they once could, communally. Instead, we have to pay fees for permission to do this. These government agencies were the target of the Alianza.

A year after it was founded, the Alianza claimed six thousand members (to be a member, you had to be a land grant heir). Many members were attracted by Tijerina's power as a speaker. Although he had great knowledge of land grant law and history, he didn't use a lot of big words when he talked. Instead he would tell stories, such as the fable of the lion and the cricket.

In that story, Tijerina said that the government is very powerful—very powerful, like a lion. And we are like a little cricket. "The lion," said Tijerina, "he's big and powerful—what can the cricket do against the lion? But the cricket, he sneaks up and gets into the lion's ear and gives him a little tickle. Then another, and another. The lion begins to scratch at his ear with his big claw, then scratches harder and harder until he bleeds. Soon he grows weak, but he keeps on scratching with his big claw. He grows weaker and weaker, while the cricket sits inside—smiling and chirping!" Tijerina's voice would rise dramatically as he told that story, and each time he told it the people would laugh loud and hard.

Reies and the Alianza gave us a new hope. They rekindled the fire of resistance that had never died. They helped us to realize that we did not have to accept defeat and injustice. We could do something, we could fight back. This was the message that the Alianza spread, from the city to the smallest village at the end of a dirt road. Alianza members talked to small farmers, families living on welfare, construction workers, old people, and the young. They would talk in the kitchens of poor homes and in big auditoriums. Tijerina expressed our anger and our thirst for justice in words like these:

"They took your land away and gave you powdered milk! They took your trees and grazing away from you and gave you Smokey the Bear! They took your language away and gave you lies in theirs. They took your manhood away and asked you to lie down and be a Good Mexican. They told you you were lazy and cowardly and backward, and you believed them . . . ."

But our people were not so ready to believe the lies any more.

The Alianza continued to grow and it drew members from many places. From the beginning, one of its main strongholds was northern New Mexico—especially the country of Rio Arriba. About the size of Connecticut, Rio Arriba is a land of many small villages set down among low mountains covered with pine trees, winding rivers, and fantastic formations of reddish rock. The U. S. Forest Service now owns 70 per cent of the land here. It was once communal land owned by the people who lived from it. Today the people of Rio Arriba—who are about 80 per cent Raza—have an average income of less than a thousand dollars a year. There are many "ghost towns" in this county, villages where the people had to leave and go to the city in search of work.

Rio Arriba has a long history of resistance to the

gringo invader. Right up to today, it has been the scene of many acts of resistance such as cutting the fences and burning the barns of big Anglo ranchers. The Raza of Rio Arriba have also held fast to their culture: the traditional fiestas for different saints' days, horse racing and rodeos, much singing of the ballads called *corridos*, and big wedding dances.

The county has long been a stronghold of the Hermandad—the religious brotherhood known as the Penitentes. A semisecret organization, the Penitentes have enjoyed wide respect in the Raza community. They not only hold their religious rituals but also take care of the needy and settle disputes between neighbors. They are like village elders and have played an important part in keeping up the resistance of our people to the invading culture.

The county seat of Rio Arriba is the village of Tierra Amarilla, with about five hundred people today. It is part of a land grant of 595,515 acres, a grant that was recognized by an act of Congress in 1860. This grant was later lost in the big land grab carried out by the Santa Fe Ring of lawyers, businessmen, and politicians. Today one of the heirs to the grant works as a janitor in the local high school. Many have no work at all.

A few miles from Tierra Amarilla is Canjilón, almost 100 per cent Raza. Its people have endured a long history of conflict with the U. S. Government—especially the Forest Rangers. For a century, the people depended on grazing and timber-cutting for survival. But the Forest Service has taken away a thousand cattle permits along with all free horse permits. While cutting down on the people's rights, the Forest Service has leased land to private timber companies that come into the area with their expensive equipment and trailer homes. They come, grab the timber, and leave poverty behind them.

The people of villages like Tierra Amarilla and Canjilón had good reason to welcome the forming of Alianza. It was no surprise when, in July of 1964, the Raza of this area began "to treat foreigners as foreigners"—meaning the Anglos. Heirs of the Tierra Amarillo grant began sending eviction notices to the "foreigners." When an Anglo rancher found that one of his cows had wandered away, he was told by a land heir that he could have it back only if he paid seven dollars— the regular grazing fee of the Forest Service. The tables were being turned on the master. But all of this action was stopped by a court injunction, and the people's rule was short-lived.

The eviction notices were a way of saying to the United States: you must live up to the Treaty of Guadalupe Hidalgo. The Alianza tried other ways too. That same year, a caravan of land grant heirs went to Mexico with the idea of getting support from there for the treaty. But Tijerina was arrested and deported by order of Díaz Ordaz, who later became President of Mexico.

The Alianza also sent a delegation to Washington, D.C., that year. They asked for congressmen to support the Alianza's demand for an investigation of the land claims. This, too, led nowhere. The U. S. Department of Justice refused to consider the claims at all. What the Alianza asked in Washington, as in Mexico, was said to be "not in the best interest" of either government.

But Reies and the Alianza were feared by the gringos in New Mexico. They called Tijerina "King Tiger" (Reies or *reyes* means kings in Spanish, and the name Tijerina looks a little like the name tiger). People in the power structure were afraid of the rising militancy among Raza in New Mexico and other areas. The non-white peoples of the United States, especially Black people, were in a mood of revolt. So it was decided that steps should be taken to crush both Reies and the Alianza.

A campaign began to make the Alianza look bad. The government tried to frame up two of Reies' brothers, and charged them with robbing a general store in Rio Arriba. The first brother, Anselmo, a man who worked closely with Reies for years, could clearly prove that he was not in the area at the time and he was released. The other brother, Margarito, was also far away at the time but still the court convicted him. He was sent to the state penitentiary and remains there today.

Still the Alianza continued to grow, and still it tried to make its demands in a polite way. On the weekend of July 4, 1966, a big delegation of Alianzistas marched from Albuquerque to Santa Fe to see the governor and ask him to support a congressional investigation into the land grants. They walked sixty miles and presented the governor with a petition. The governor did nothing, Raza was left with nothing except a strong sense of unity and pride in their march. The U. S. Government, the Mexican Government, and the government of New Mexico had all turned their backs on the land struggle.

It was clear by now that the people had to *force* the government to consider the land issue. There were two ways to do this. One would be to bring some kind of suit—but this was very expensive for an organization of poor people. The other was to take some action that would make the government have to prove in court that the United States had a right to the land. That way, the burden of proof would be on the government, not on the people. Also, the publicity from such an action would inform many people, and it couldn't be filed away so easily as a court suit.

This second tactic was the one that the Alianza chose. They would make a direct, open challenge to U.S. laws.

On October 15, 1966, a hundred Alianza families moved into a campground of the Kit Carson National Forest in Rio Arriba county. The spot they chose was Echo Amphitheater, a giant amphitheater naturally formed from reddish rock. It is a popular attraction for tourists run by the U. S. Forest Service, but to our people it is part of the big San Joaquín del Río de Chama land grant.

The people declared the area to be the San Joaquín Pueblo Republic, and they elected their own mayor and council. They did not buy camping permits, and put up their own armed guards. They announced that the United States had been evicted and sent a message saying so to the President of the United States. The people took over, and then they settled down to building fires, cooking their food, and enjoying each other's company. The old ways of sharing and living together, which the gringo had almost destroyed, now came back to life.

The people expected to be arrested, but nothing happened that weekend. The next weekend, the second "camp-in" began. This was a different story.

As some fifty carloads of Alianza members and supporters arrived, they found state police, FBI, and Rangers waiting. They were told by two Rangers to pay the camping fees or get out. An argument began between the Rangers and the people, and one Ranger ran to get a loaded revolver from his pick-up truck. The angry crowd closed in and began shouting. Reies Tijerina and other Alianza members quickly moved the Ranger away from the crowd. This man and another Ranger were then brought before Raza justice: they were placed on trial before the officials of the San Joaquín Republic. They were not lynched by the crowd, as the gringos have lynched our people so often, but just found guilty of trespassing and given suspended sentences, released unharmed.

The "camp-ins" at Echo were meant to bring the land struggle before the courts. But instead the U. S. Government turned the whole thing into a criminal case. The men who probably saved the Ranger's life were accused of "assault." Reies López Tijerina, who hadn't even touched the Rangers, was one of those accused this way. It was the beginning of the long persecution of the Alianza and its leaders.

Many Raza came to visit Reies and the Alianza, to show their support. Rodolfo "Corky" Gonzales of the Crusade for Justice in Denver, Colorado, was one of these. Black and Indian leaders from many tribes also came. The Alianza was gaining support from many parts of the country.

In New Mexico, our people grew more impatient. In the spring of 1967, the Alianza held a protest march in Albuquerque. They called it "the last human warning" to the U. S. Government. In Santa Fe, Alianza people waited five hours to meet with the governor—only to come face to face with a man who had nothing to say. The people realized once again that the politicians, the Establishment, did not represent them or care about them. As this realization grew, there were more and more protest actions. U. S. Forest Service signs were damaged; a mysterious fire broke out near the town of Los Alamos, home of the atomic bomb.

The Alianza announced that it would hold a big meeting on June 3, 1967, at the village of Coyote—in Rio Arriba. There were rumors that the Alianza would attempt a takeover of the land that day, that a showdown with the government was about to happen. The state authorities now decided that it must crush the Alianza once and for all. The Coyote meeting must be stopped at any price—immediately.

They began by demanding that the Alianza turn over its list of members. This was refused, and the Alianza was taken to court. Then the district attorney, a man named Alfonso Sánchez, went on the radio and attacked the Alianza as "Communists." The police put up roadblocks and began making arrests of Alianzistas —Alianza people. Often they refused to tell people what crime they were supposed to have committed. Sometimes they accused the people of *planning* to go to a meeting. Eleven persons were arrested altogether.

All this happened on the day before the June 3 meeting, and for many of our people it was a day of horror that they have never forgotten. Police burst into people's homes without warrants, threatening women and children. A sixty-eight-year-old man later told how police came into his home after he had gone to bed, pushed his daughter aside, refused to show a warrant, and jailed him for three days. He lost his job as a result of this incident. While all this was going on, the governor of New Mexico said he *thought* some civil rights were being violated—but there was nothing that could be done about it then. Then he got on a plane and went to a fund-raising dinner for his political party in Michigan.

The people were furious. The police were brutally preventing people from going to a meeting, and the people knew that the U. S. Constitution promised us "freedom of assembly." The next day, June 3, the meeting never took place but it was decided that something must be done. The people felt that District Attorney Sánchez had "sold out" his own people and must be brought to justice for his violation of the people's rights.

Twenty men were deputized to perform a citizen's arrest on Sánchez and to free the eleven men arrested. The right of citizens to arrest wrongdoers is part of U.S. law and in some states, such as New Mexico, the law says that such arrests can be carried out by force of arms. The twenty men would carry out the people's justice on Monday, June 5, at the courthouse in Tierra Amarilla. Sánchez was expected there for a hearing on the eleven arrested men.

The group of twenty included rancheros, loggers, disabled veterans, a migrant worker. They ranged from a man aged seventy-two to a teen-ager. Some knew the whole history of events and exactly why they were going to the courthouse, while others only knew what Sánchez had done. But they all had three things in common: they were poor, they were angry, and they were armed.

It was three o'clock when the people's deputies drove up to the rundown, pink and blue courthouse of Tierra Amarilla. With them came Rose Tijerina, the daughter of Reies. One group began walking up the front steps. A state patrolman, who stood near the entrance, was told to drop his gun. He reached for it, and was shot in the chest. In a few seconds, gunfire echoed throughout the courthouse.

The jailer jumped out a window to escape and was shot twice. The judge locked himself in the toilet. A sheriff, the county commissioners, and some office personnel were subdued and led into an office by the people's deputies. They were kept under guard while others searched the courthouse looking for Sánchez. Then they learned that he was not there, and had never been there. The eleven men had already been released on bond.

The deputies held the courthouse and the town for about two hours. They released the prisoners in the jails. A state cop came on the scene, took one look, turned white, and ran. Other state police who drove into the village were met by rifle fire and Alianzistas with fists in the air. *"Ya no están tan bravos!"* cried one of the people's deputies, as the police fled. "They're not so tough now!" Another man looked sadly at the courthouse officials, all Raza, and exclaimed: "*Vendidos!*" He felt the pain of seeing his own people used to carry out the purposes of our enemy.

The people's deputies allowed an ambulance to come and take the state patrolman to the hospital. Then, about five o'clock, the deputies decided Sánchez was definitely not coming so they began to leave. Their mission could not be carried out that day.

The last two men to leave the courthouse were twenty-two-year-old Baltazar Martínez from Canjilón and his seventy-two-year-old companion. They got into the sheriff's patrol car, taking the sheriff and a white reporter with them, and headed for Canjilón. The police did not interfere on the highway. But they were waiting in droves at Canjilón.

Baltazar confronted the police, holding a cocked pistol at the sheriff's head and what looked like a stick of dynamite in his belt. It seemed as though the whole village was holding its breath. Then, in the middle of all the tension, a tiny and very spirited woman walked out between the heavily armed police and Baltazar. It was Baltazar's mother, and she was trying to negotiate a settlement between the two. But her efforts did not succeed. Baltazar led the sheriff toward the hills, then suddenly released him and ran toward the mountains. The old man was captured and the white reporter released, while Baltazar became a Chicano guerrilla disappearing into the twilight.

Within hours, a thousand National Guardsmen, state police, mounted patrol, and other "lawmen" began moving into the little villages of Rio Arriba. They brought guns, horses, a spotter plane, and even tanks. A reign of terror began. The man in charge of it was General John Pershing Jolly—named after the gringo who had volunteered to capture Pancho Villa. General Jolly set up his headquarters at the U. S. Forest Service station in Canjilón and gave his orders: "Shoot to kill."

That same day, June 5, about forty Raza were having a picnic in the field of a private home in Canjilón. They were mostly old men, women, teen-agers, and small children. The police descended on them with guns drawn and rounded them up. The people were forced to sit down in mud that even the police chief said was up to the knees. They were marched up a hill to the house to be searched, with their hands folded on top of their heads like captured Viet Cong. Even though not a single gun was found on the people, they were jailed in a sheep corral. National Guardsmen watched them, and occasionally fixed bayonets on their rifles.

The people were kept there that night and all the next day, without drinking water and without food. Then they were released without being accused of any crimes or given any explanation as to why they had been locked up like animals.

In Rio Arriba and three other counties, people were not only threatened and abused but many also lost their jobs. To this day, some people have not been able to get a job since then. Sánchez and the police invented fantastic stories of a "Castro-ite conspiracy" to take over the state. An all-out manhunt began to find Tijerina. One of the authors of this book, Enriqueta Vásquez, remembers arriving in the state at that time and finding the gringo society of New Mexico almost hysterical. Among Raza, some felt that all the events were like a terrible dream—while others wanted to go help the courthouse "raiders."

One by one, the courthouse "raiders" either turned themselves in or were captured. Tijerina's second wife, Patricia, and daughter, Rose, were also arrested. Dozens of charges were filed against these people. But Baltazar Martínez remained free for over a month.

The newspapers called Baltazar "the most dangerous man in the North" and the police hunted him everywhere. But he was hiding in the woods that he knew so well, and he had the people's support. "That boy could live under a rock," the police chief admitted. Then Baltazar heard that the governor had posted a personal reward of five hundred dollars for his capture. At that time, Baltazar wanted to get married and have a big party. Also, his mother needed medical treatment. So Baltazar had his mother turn him in. She collected the governor's reward, and Baltazar got married with a fine fiesta.

The Tierra Amarilla courthouse rebellion was followed by many struggles in the courts. The state tried to punish the Alianza as hard as it could for daring to protest injustice. After many months, the number of defendants was reduced from twenty-one persons to ten Raza and one Anglo supporter, Jerry Noll.

We should remember their names: Esequiel Dominquez, Tobias Lebya, José Madril, Baltazar Martínez, Moises Morales, Reies Hugh Tijerina, Jr. (son of Reies), Reies López Tijerina, Juan Valdez and Salomon Velasquez. All of the "T.A. Ten," as they became known, were released on bond until they would be brought to trial. Two years later, another name would be added—the mystery man known only as "Indio" to most people.

These defendants were not only charged with dozens of supposed crimes but a judge also put them under a gag order—meaning they could not write or say anything in public about the whole case. Because of this order, the men have not been allowed to publish their own story of Tierra Amarilla and June 5, 1967. Perhaps they will someday. It will surely be a better story than the books and articles by many Anglo writers who have exploited the courthouse story for their own fame and profit, for it will be Raza history seen through Raza eyes.

While the police and the courts were reacting in fear to the courthouse rebellion, the official Right Wing was also working to crush the Alianza. In the fall of 1967, the John Birch Society published a pamphlet called "Reies Tijerina—the Communist Plan to Grab the Southwest." Some fifty thousand free copies of this pamphlet were distributed in southern New Mexico which we call "Little Texas." The pamphlet is full of gossip, sensation, and just plain lies, but many people who had never heard of the John Birch Society took it seriously.

The next month, the trial of Tijerina and others on the Echo "camp-in" charges began—right in "Little Texas." Most of the people on the jury had probably read the pamphlet, but the judge refused to let the trial be moved to another place where there might be less prejudice. The Alianza people were all found guilty, and the long process of appeal began that would go all the way to the U. S. Supreme Court.

A few months after the trial, in January 1968, the Tierra Amarilla courthouse jailer Eulogio Salazar was murdered. Since he would have been a key witness against the "T.A. Ten," the Alianzistas were blamed for the murder and all put back in jail. There was no evidence that they had killed Salazar, but several of them had to spend more than a month in prison before they finally got out again. The murder of Salazar is still officially unsolved. But the Alianza has revealed some important information. For example, a man who confessed to the killing was kept hidden by police for months and then tucked away in a mental hospital as "insane." Yet this same man had recently been used by the police as their star witness in another case. How could the police do that, if the man was really insane? It seems as though the police don't want the murder to be solved—and many of our people suspect that the police themselves were involved in it.

The white-dominated news media tried hard to blame the Salazar murder on the Alianza. Again and again, they tried to build up an evil image of the Alianza. In 1968, when Dr. Martin Luther King, Jr., announced that Tijerina should organize the New Mexico section of the Poor People's March to Washington, D.C., the press yelled "the wrong choice." Reies went to Washington anyway with many other Raza.

When Tijerina returned from Washington, he announced that he would run for state governor on the ballot of a new party—the People's Constitutional Party. There would be other candidates for other offices. It was no surprise when the New Mexico Supreme Court ruled that he could not run for governor because he was a "convicted criminal" (from the Echo camp-in). They had to shut him up.

A week after the election, Reies went on trial for the first three out of fifty-four charges brought against him from the Tierra Amarilla rebellion. The charges were: assault on a jail; false imprisonment of a deputy sheriff; kidnaping a deputy sheriff. At that time, you could get the death penalty for kidnaping. Reies suddenly announced that he would defend himself. He would have three lawyers to consult, but he would do the job himself. Our people heard this, and they were a little nervous—Reies had no formal legal training—but they were also very proud. We can defend ourselves, Reies was saying.

Many Raza sat through every day of the month-long trial and one of the authors of this book, Elizabeth Martínez, was also there. Reies presented a brilliant defense in the Anglo-dominated courtroom, in the Anglo's language and on the Anglo's terms. He called many Raza citizens to testify—poor people who sat in the witness stand, proud and unafraid. They told about the terrible night of June 2 and why the people had decided to make a citizen's arrest on Sánchez. Reies even got a deputy sheriff to say in court, "I don't blame you for anything, sir."

On December 13, 1968, after many days in court, the jury brought back its verdict: NOT GUILTY on all three counts. There was an explosion of feelings. The people burst into tears of joy, while the faces of the district attorney and other officials fell miserably to the floor. Everybody was taken by surprise.

The joy that followed the trial was short-lived. The next year, 1969, brought an all-out war to destroy the Alianza. It was a war led by the legal system, the news media, and violent Right Wing groups like the John Birchers and Minutemen. It was a war that made a mockery of the U. S. Constitution, with its promises of free speech, fair and speedy trial, the right to appeal, protection of life and property. The Constitution just didn't work for our people and our land rights (it never has).

Here are just a few of the major events in that 1969 war on Tijerina and the Alianza:

JANUARY 23: The Alianza headquarters building in Albuquerque is bombed with dynamite for the second time in two months. The windows are smashed and Mrs. Tijerina with her baby son narrowly escape serious injury or death. Before that, rocks were thrown through Alianza windows at least ten times. On April 16, 1968, a former sheriff's deputy named William Fellion was about to throw a stick of dynamite through a window when it exploded in his own hand. Police followed and arrested him, but he served only sixteen hours of "hospital duty" (while he recovered from injuries) as punishment.

FEBRUARY 2: The main building of a large ranch in San Cristóbal, New Mexico, is totally destroyed by fire just a few hours after Tijerina announced that it would be used as a cultural center by different Raza groups. Footprints and tire tracks of "unknown persons" are found in the snow.

MARCH 15: A powerful bomb explodes just outside the Alianza building, totally wrecking the car of its vice-president and damaging three others. About an hour and a half later, a bomb explodes at the home of Alianza member Tomas Gallegos, blowing out the doors and windows; fortunately none of the family are injured. These bombings, like the others, are never solved and it is obvious that the police do not want to hurt the bombers. The police officer assigned to investigate the attacks on the Alianza is a man who later openly admits in court, "I hate Tijerina."

MAY 6: NBC television carries a racist documentary on Tijerina and the land struggle called "The Most Hated Man in New Mexico." (Hated by whom?)

JUNE 8: This is the final day of an Alianza gathering in Rio Arriba. The day before, Tijerina and other Alianza members tried to carry out a citizen's arrest on the governor (who fled in a state plane) and on a nuclear scientist for crimes against the people (he hid). Now Patricia Tijerina sets fire to a U. S. Forest Service sign at the village of Gallina. She does this after announcing to the public that she will burn the sign as a symbolic protest against the U.S. occupation of Raza lands. It is broad daylight and hundreds of people watch—including state police, who do nothing.

Mrs. Tijerina then sets fire to a second sign, at Coyote. This time, some twenty Forest Rangers come swarming down from the hills with their rifles—threatening unarmed men, women, and children. An armed man named James Evans who is a Forest Service official but wearing no uniform comes up and tells Reies Tijerina that he is under arrest. Reies objects while

Evans lets his special, semiautomatic rifle point in all directions. The people shout protests and move to protect Tijerina.

The two-year-old daughter of the Tijerinas is crying in their parked car and the arrested mother asks Reies to look after her. He walks to the car, only to see a state police agent standing beside it with a gun pointed straight at his head. Reies hears the firing pin click and waits to be killed. But apparently the gun misfired. After a few minutes, Reies lets himself be arrested along with six other people. He is rushed off to jail in Albuquerque. The police also arrest Mrs. Tijerina, but she is not the one they really want. Later, charges are dropped against the other six—but not against Reies. He is put in jail indefinitely.

JUNE 12: Thirteen Raza men, women, and children had filed charges saying their civil rights were violated just before and after the 1967 courthouse "raid." These charges are against District Attorney Alfonso Sanchez, General Jolly, and the state police. A nine-day trial is held, ending June 12. The all-gringo jury decides that none of the people had their rights violated except one man, who is awarded some damage money. But his case was only against the police; none of the high-ranking officials are found guilty.

JUNE 24: Shots fired into the Alianza building.

JUNE 30: Juan Valdéz, one of the "T.A. Ten," is convicted of assaulting (shooting) the state policeman and another crime at the courthouse "raid." During the trial, the state cop says that the man who shot him definitely had a beard yet all the other witnesses say Juan Valdéz did not have a beard that day. In the middle of the trial, another man comes and says that he—not Juan—shot the state cop. This is the mysterious "Indio"—Geronimo Borunda. But in spite of the weak case against Juan, the jury convicts him. Two weeks later, he is sentenced to two to ten years. He files an appeal and is freed on bond. (A year later, Geronimo Borunda is accused of "perjury." The state says that Geronimo lied when he said that he, not Juan, had shot the policeman. Despite a lie detector test proving that he was not lying, Geronimo is convicted and sentenced to prison.)

SEPTEMBER 4: The Rio Arriba People's Clinic is half destroyed when several men break in at night and set it on fire. La Clinica is a project begun by poor people—including several from the Alianza—to provide medical and dental care in a ninety-mile area without any doctor or dentist.

SEPTEMBER 27: Reies Tijerina, who has been in jail all this time, is found guilty of helping in the burning of the two U. S. Forest Service signs. His wife and others say that she burned the signs, not Reies, but the state is interested in locking up Reies—not his wife. On the witness stand, two state police agents admit that they "hate Tijerina" and wanted to kill him at Coyote. Reies goes back to jail after this trial and is kept in solitary confinement—for seven months.

OCTOBER 10: Reies is sentenced to three years in prison for the false sign-burning charges. A year later, two Anglos confess to stealing two Forest Service signs and are fined twenty-five dollars each. "A double standard of justice," the Alianza tells President Nixon—but the words fall on deaf ears.

OCTOBER 13: The U. S. Supreme Court upholds the convictions of Tijerina on the old Echo "camp-in" charges. His two-year sentence for that goes into effect right away. The Alianza elects Ramón Tijerina, a brother of Reies, as its new president.

OCTOBER 18: Powdered tear-gas is put into the ventilation system of several Alianza cars, for the fifth time since June. This makes the drivers and passengers sick.

NOVEMBER 26: Reies Tijerina is found guilty on two or more charges from the Tierra Amarilla rebellion. He attends this trial from jail, and goes back to jail afterward. His sentence on this conviction is a total of two to ten years. (Of the other courthouse "raid" defendants, only one—Baltazar Martínez—was ever brought to trial and he was found innocent.)

That was only one year in the life of the Alianza—one year of jailing, bombing, and suppression of our struggle. Our enemies were getting more and more worried as the Chicano struggle grew stronger and stronger. Not only in New Mexico but all over the Southwest, Raza were becoming more aware and more unified. Thousands of families were marching in California and students were protesting everywhere. Chicanos were demonstrating, we were making demands, we were speaking without fear.

Reies was kept in prison. In January of 1971, when he finished serving one prison term, the government did not release him. Instead, it made him start serving time for the burning of those forest signs. Even though that conviction was still being appealed—still going through the legal process—he had to stay in prison. We all knew by then that Reies was a political prisoner.

The years of deporting our leaders, as in the 1930s, had ended. The years of imprisoning our leaders had begun. History was repeating itself; and nothing had changed except on the surface. Reies was in prison for all of us. He was in prison for doing what had to be done, for exposing the truth about the gringo system. It was as if every one of us had been judged and sent to prison. This is what we mean by "political prisoner."

On July 26, 1971, Tijerina was finally freed on parole—after 775 days in prison. The Chicano world that Reies came back to from prison was different from when he left. For one thing, the land struggle had been recognized even in the halls of Congress. A few weeks before Reies was released, a congressman from California introduced a bill prepared by the Alianza that called for recognition of the Treaty of Guadalupe Hidalgo and an investigation of the community land grants. Lands should be given back to the people where found proper, the bill said. The expenses of this large operation would be paid by the federal government at a cost of $12,500,000. This bill has not passed.

There is a different spirit among our people today from 1969. There are new organizations of Raza in New Mexico. They are fighting on many fronts: against racism in the school system, against exploitation and racism on the job, against poor health and medical facilities, against the welfare system and police brutality. Organizations like the Black Berets, La Gente and the Chicano Youth Association have not only struggled to change existing institutions but also started new ones that are of, for, and by the people. These include people's clinics, cultural centers, schools, libraries.

The attitude of many Raza has changed. For example, at one time it was hard to make people believe that the police really would abuse people and lie about it. Then two young Chicanos were killed by police in 1971, within a month of each other: Felipe Mares in Taos and Roy Gallegos in Santa Fe. The police said the two had committed petty crimes and were trying to escape. But according to Raza witnesses, Roy was shot while handcuffed. Felipe had reportedly escaped from jail and was being chased; there were several police on the scene, he had no gun and there was no need to kill him.

Then came the Albuquerque rebellion of June 1971. Police abused some young people sitting peacefully in a park on a Sunday afternoon, and the community was angered. That night, a thousand people stormed through the streets of downtown Albuquerque, breaking windows and setting fires in the big stores, finance companies, and other places. Although Anglo businessmen fumed over their losses, most of the Chicano community knew that some kind of protest against the powers of Albuquerque was long overdue.

Not long after that, on January 29, 1972, two young Chicanos were shot and killed by police in Albuquerque. Their names are Antonio Cordova and Rito Canales, and they had both been working with a militant Chicano organization called Las Gorras Negras—The Black Berets. They were both known for their work in exposing police brutality and the brutal condition in

New Mexico's state prison. They became martyrs of our *movimiento*.

Police said they caught Antonio and Rito trying to steal dynamite from a construction site in an isolated area, outside the city. But the police never explained why they had to pump nine or ten bullets into Antonio and six bullets into Rito—most of them in his back. Many people also thought it was too big a coincidence that the police killed these two Chicanos the night before they were to appear on a television program talking about police brutality and prison brutality.

Another Chicano as well as a Black man and an Anglo youth were also killed by police in early 1972—making a total of seven victims within a twelve-month period. The situation became so bad that the U. S. Civil Rights Commission called for a special federal investigation of four of the killings. Fatal police shootings stopped for a while but then on July 28, 1973, an eighteen-year-old Chicano named Melvin Ortiz was killed in Grants. A fight was going on between a group of Raza and some whites; police say they opened fire with a "stun-gun," a special weapon for crowd control which was not supposed to be fatal. But it killed Melvin.

All the killings helped to unite our people. Others were frightened by the murders, of course. The struggle in New Mexico as everywhere is still very young; it takes many people, many martyrs and many leaders to bring about change. There are many ups and downs. Organizations are born and sometimes fail. Leaders emerge and play an important role for a while, then sometimes take another direction—and are no longer leaders. But we know that a new period of history has begun, a new spirit of rebellion has been born. The cry for Tierra o Muerte! helped to begin it, and that cry will always stir our Raza wherever they may be.

9

Huelga!

When we are really honest with ourselves, we must admit that our lives are all that really belong to us. So it is how we use our lives that determines what kind of men we are. It is my deepest belief that only by giving our lives do we truly find life. I am convinced that the truest act of courage, the strongest act of manliness . . . is to sacrifice ourselves for others . . .

César Chávez

THESE WORDS of César Chávez were spoken in March 1968 when he ended a twenty-five-day fast. César was too weak to speak himself, so he prepared a message to be read in Spanish and English to the many people who had come to celebrate the end of his fast. But they are not just words for a special occasion. They are the basic spirit of César—the essence of his life as leader of the farmworkers' struggle.

Like the struggle for the land, the struggle of La Raza for rights as workers is a long, long story. Our workers have suffered much of the same racism and exploitation as other workers in the Southwest—especially the Chinese, Japanese, and Filipinos. But the labor struggle of Chicanos also reflects the conflict that developed when a people with ties to their own land and culture *within their own country* suddenly found themselves reduced to a landless, "alien" labor force working for the same group that took away their land and culture. So we have a special anger.

For years, the gringo exploited both the Chicanos born here who had been robbed of their land and the Mexican nationals who came here looking for work. The bracero program, which had been started during World War II, was continued after the war at the request of the big growers. The growers liked Mexican labor. They could always get Raza hands to do the dirtiest kind of work under the worst possible conditions—feeding them the worst kind of food, paying them the lowest wages—and receive the least complaints. The workers themselves, facing land problems and low living standards in Mexico, had no choice but to welcome the chance of making a few dollars up north. More than 3,300,000 came between 1950 and 1960, to climb, bend, stoop, and squat in the production of every fruit and vegetable.

Along with the braceros came thousands of so-called

"illegals," who lived and worked with the braceros, under the same miserable conditions. They, too, helped to build the great wealth of the gringo agri-business.

The bracero program was ended by law in 1965, but the next year a new law was passed that served the growers almost as well. Under that law, Mexicanos could enter with a special, green permit and become U.S. citizens after five years (if they paid Social Security, taxes, and served in the Armed Forces). Many Green Carders do not want to give up their citizenship and prefer to come across the border to work during the day and go home again at night.

There have been many protests against the bracero program and working conditions, in general. But the situation of the Raza farmworkers—both those born here and those who came as citizens of Mexico— seemed almost hopeless for years. How could they organize to fight for their rights? If the worker was not a U.S. citizen, and complained about conditions, he or she could be deported immediately. Even if the worker *was* a citizen, he felt this fear. Most farmworkers could not stay in any one place long enough to get organized—they had to follow the seasons of the different crops in different areas. The farmworkers' lack of schooling also made it hard to organize against oppression. And finally, the National Labor Relations Act—which established the right of workers to organize into unions that could then negotiate with bosses—did not include farmworkers. They had no legal right to organize, no legal way of making demands for better pay and working conditions.

The campesinos had sometimes gone on strike and

won a few temporary improvements. But they had never been able to build a lasting organization. Gringo terrorism stopped them every time. Organized labor was white-dominated, and neglected the campesino. Many people believed it was "impossible" to organize seasonal farm labor, until a small, quiet Indio came along named César Chávez.

César Chávez (pronounced SAY-sar CHAH-vez) was born on March 31, 1927, near Yuma, Arizona. His family had a big house on about 160 acres that had been acquired by his Mexican grandfather as a homestead. The land produced fine grapes as well as other fruits and vegetables, which César's father sold in town. Everyone in the family worked. During harvest time, they sometimes hired extra workers, whom they paid well and provided with decent conditions. "My father did not act like a boss man," César says. His mother had made a pledge never to turn away anyone who came for food, and she fed many people even when there was not much in the house.

In 1937 the farm fell into serious debt. A local banker refused to make a loan to the family, although such loans were then guaranteed by the federal government. When the farm was seized by the county to pay off taxes, guess who bought it for almost nothing? The same banker who had refused to make the loan.

With the farm gone, the Chávez family set out to do what they knew best: to work the land. They became migrant farmworkers in California, sleeping in their car the first night. César was only ten at the time and his brother Richard was eight, but they worked beside their parents up and down the state for wages of fifteen to forty cents an hour. Three years later, César took part in his first strike when the family was working at a farm where the owners demanded five cents for a dipper of water. His father organized the strike, which was quickly crushed. But César had learned something about strikes. As he grew up, still working in the fields and sometimes at part-time jobs, he learned about many other things.

He learned that the average life of the campesino is forty-nine years, in comparison with the life expectancy of the white majority—which is seventy years.

He learned that the possibility of a migrant baby dying as an infant is twice that of the average baby in the United States. Farmworkers are three times as likely to get tuberculosis as the average person. They are twice as likely to get flu or pneumonia. And they are three times as likely to get injured at work.

He learned that the two million farmworkers in this country earn less that two thousand dollars a year each on the average. Before César began organizing, they had no paid vacations, no holiday pay, no overtime, no health insurance or pension plans, no unemployment benefits, and accident compensation in only a few states.

He learned that living conditions in the many migrant labor camps have not changed much since the days when, in one camp, there were seven toilets provided for twenty-eight hundred people, and even state authorities said the ranches were "devoid of the accommodations given horses."

He learned about the short hoe: a back-breaking

tool that forces the worker to bend over close to the ground or work on his knees—a tool of torture.

He learned that workers were still being transported in old, broken-down, unsafe trucks. Workers were still dying inside those trucks. In 1968, for example, a labor contractor drove a group of Mexicanos to San Antonio illegally. There he parked the truck and went inside a house to sleep. The truck was completely closed and the people locked inside could get no air. Hours passed while they screamed for help and pounded on the walls. Three men suffocated to death before help came.

He learned that the children of migrant farm-workers' families never have a chance at schooling. Over half never get past the eighth grade. César himself did not get beyond the seventh grade.

He learned that the laws to protect workers are openly violated by growers.

He learned that a farmworker can't get welfare if he is working at all—even if it is only a few days out of the month.

Much of this César learned after meeting a man named Fred Ross, who came to see him one day in 1952. Ross worked for the Community Service Organization and wanted César to help him organize people for the CSO. At first César was suspicious of this gringo, but after several talks he agreed to serve as a CSO volunteer worker and later became a full-time organizer.

At that time, César lived in a barrio of San Jose called Sal Si Puedes—Get Out If You Can—because it was such a trap of poverty from which few escaped. He was working part-time in a lumberyard and married with several children already. Many of his friends were men who in their younger days had belonged to pachuco groups—neighborhood "gangs." They had some experience in communication systems and organizing chains of command. César was able to draw upon that past experience of Chicano organizing in his new work. He also learned that organizing was like digging a hole—nothing secret about it, just a lot of hard work and persistence.

For ten years, he continued learning to be an organizer. But when the CSO would not accept his proposal for CSO to organize farmworkers, he quit. Two Chicano friends from the CSO liked César's proposal and soon joined him: Dolores Huerta and Gilberto Padilla.

With his wife, their eight children and twelve hundred dollars in personal savings from the past ten years, César moved to Delano. He had lived there as a young boy, and knew it was an area where the campesinos stayed most of the year—they were not constantly migrating—so they might be easier to organize. But he also knew that just twenty-five miles from Delano, a massacre of striking cotton pickers had taken place in 1933.

César went to work the way he had learned: talking with people in their kitchens, on the street, in the barber shops, stores, and poolrooms. He wanted first to learn exactly what the campesinos wanted, so he handed out eighty thousand postcards with very simple questions: how much do you earn now, and how much do you think you should earn? César didn't try to call big organizing meetings right away. Instead he held dozens of "house meetings," with just a few people at a time. That way, there was real and personal contact with the people and everyone's questions could be answered.

The first real meeting of the National Farm Workers Association took place in September 1962. Its now-famous flag was revealed at that meeting: the black eagle in a white circle against the red background, designed by Manuel Chávez, a cousin of César's. Probably nobody had any idea then that this flag would someday wave above thousands of heads, from one end of the country to the other.

The organizing went very slowly at first. César's family spent all its savings and had no food at times. But even in this penniless period he turned down a twenty-one-thousand-dollar-a-year job with the Peace Corps. César was lucky to have a wife—Helen Fabela, daughter of a colonel in Pancho Villa's army—who agreed with him that organizing the farmworkers was more important than money.

César did not have an impressive personality or speaking style, at first sight. He wasn't very big—only five feet six inches tall—and many people called him quiet. But maybe that quietness helped him to organize. The campesinos could see that he and his family were like themselves: poor, dark-skinned, not well-educated. Slowly the organization grew and by 1964 the NFWA had over a thousand members. It started a newspaper called *El Malcriado* (The Unruly Child), a credit union, and a burial society to assist with funeral costs—always an important concern to poor people.

The NFWA helped in a strike of rose workers in early 1965, and later that year won a pay raise for some grape pickers. But César believed in building slowly; he knew that a strike against a big enemy without a strong organization to back up the strike could at best win only small short-term victories. If the growers were not forced to sign contracts with a workers' organization, they could always break promises they made during a strike. A new season, a new group of workers, and the victory had to be won again.

In September 1965, Filipino grape workers—who were exploited and oppressed in the same way as Raza workers—went on strike in Delano, California. They asked César to have his people support them. At first César said his organization wasn't strong enough yet. Then he asked the membership to decide. A big meeting took place and the question was put to vote by secret ballot. The campesinos' decision was one loud cry of HUELGA! HUELGA! HUELGA!

On September 16, Mexican Independence Day, the Delano Grape Strike began. For the first time the NFWA called itself a union—it had not done so before, because the campesinos knew that word would seem threatening to the growers and it could bring down terrible repression even before they were organized. Within a few days, eleven hundred harvest workers walked out of the fields and then began picketing at the fields to bring out more workers. Ranch foremen with shotguns destroyed picket signs and car windows, beat and kicked the picketers, tried to run them down with speeding trucks. The police watched all this with broad smiles, and if they arrested anybody it was always the strikers. Forty-four picketers including Helen Chávez were jailed just for shouting "Huelga!" Still the picketers kept on marching up and down, shouting to other workers to join them: *"Vénganse, señores! Huelga! Para su respeto y dignidad! Compañeros! Huelga! Huelga!"*

The cry of Huelga! grew from what seemed like a mere whisper in Delano to a rumbling echo that fired the blood of Chicanos across the nation. Soon there were thirty-five hundred union members on strike. Many supporters came to help. There were Blacks and whites from SNCC and CORE, who had experience in non-violent picketing; white clergymen and nuns, some of whom were so stirred by what they saw that they left the church; and hundreds of students. Many stores and companies donated food to help provide three hundred strikers and their families with three meals a day in Filipino Hall, the union's dining room. The strike was soon costing forty thousand dollars a month in all kinds of expenses, and many donations of money also flowed into the union's office.

But the growers would not budge. They hired scab workers by the dozen, many of them "Green Carders" from Mexico. This forced the campesinos to find a new tactic: the boycott.

In that first year of the strike, the main boycott target was wine—not table grapes, the kind you eat. César sent hundreds of students out all over the country to work on the boycott of Schenley, which was making wine from scab grapes. The boycott, too, went slowly at first. It wasn't easy to organize a consumer's boycott in the United States—the land of consumerism.

Meanwhile, in Delano, there came the exciting moment when a priest got hold of a small airplane and took César up over the fields where scabs were at work in an area far from the road, hard to reach. They flew high up, to avoid any legal problems about violating air traffic regulations. The plane had a loud-speaker attached to the bottom, and César would call out "Huelga!" from the plane. Some of the campesinos below must have thought it was God himself telling them to strike. The priest was later arrested for this action.

The union also had the Teatro Campesino, a farm-workers' theater organized by Luis Valdéz. It had come into being in late 1965, when Luis tried to convince the strikers that a theater group would be a good thing. He made cardboard signs with names on them like HUELGUISTA (striker), PATRONCITO (Boss), and ESQUIRÓL (Scab). One evening, he asked a campesino to put on the ESQUIRÓL sign and begin to act like one. Slowly other workers began to join in, until everyone was shouting, screaming, jumping, and laughing. The campesinos acted out their own story, poured out their feelings about La Huelga. The Teatro Campesino was born that night. It performed on picket lines, in labor camps, and at events to raise funds for the strike. It took the spirit of Huelga! everywhere.

The same kind of creative spark and imagination that produced the Teatro gave birth to the famous *peregrinación*—pilgrimage—of 1966. This was a three-hundred-mile-long walk from Delano to the capital of California in Sacramento. Its purposes were to call the nation's attention to the campesino's struggle, to show the strike had wide support, to lift the strikers' spirit and to awaken other campesinos. In our Raza culture, the peregrinación is a very meaningful and honorable thing to do in times of stress—times when people want to demonstrate their sincerity. Now the California strikers, with many supporters, would walk three hundred miles to the land of the governor during Lent.

Some called it a pilgrimage, some a march, some a demonstration—but whatever it was called, this event clearly showed the campesino's determination. It also showed what the campesinos' struggle was all about: not just a labor issue but basic social change, La Causa (The Cause). The themes of the pilgrimage were *penitencia*, pilgrimage, and revolution. At the head of the procession went the patron saint of the Mexicano—our own Virgen de Guadalupe, the *virgen morena*. Behind her came the farmworkers' flag with its black eagle and bright red background. Then came the people of music—the guitars, the voices that sang beautifully. Other marchers followed. At the back came the nurse's car, a truck with a portable altar, and a car to carry urgent messages. On the sides of the road, people lined up to watch the peregrinos pass. Many brought food and water, offers of help and love, and quite a few joined the pilgrimage.

The peregrinación was also an organizing expedition. The union distributed its Plan de Delano—inspired by Zapata's Plan de Ayala—all along the line of march. It explained the reasons for the pilgrimage to Sacramento, and the campesinos' goals in general. "We have suffered unnumbered ills and crimes," said the Plan de Delano. And then it continued:

> Now we will suffer for the purpose of ending the poverty, the misery, and the injustice . . . This Pilgrimage is a witness to the suffering we have seen for

generations. The Penance we accept symbolizes the suffering we shall have in order to bring justice to these same towns, to this same valley . . .

Across the San Joaquín Valley, across California, across the entire Southwest of the United States, wherever there are Mexican people, wherever there are farm workers, our movement is spreading like flames across a dry plain. Our Pilgrimage is the match that will light our cause for all farm workers to see what is happening here, so that they may do as we have done.

Almost every night, the marchers would stop in a small town or village along the way and hold a meeting with the Raza who lived there. People talked, sang, and grew closer. Many of them had not heard about the Huelga and the union before; now they signed up with the union. The local people would find food and places to sleep for the pilgrims. Often they would be entertained by El Teatro Campesino.

About eighty people marched all the way from Delano to Sacramento, in temperatures that sometimes went over a hundred degrees. And always they went singing the songs of the struggle, like "Viva la Huelga en General." Its chorus says:

> Viva la huelga en el fil!
> Viva la causa en la historia!
> La raza llena de gloria!
> La victoria va cumplir!

(Long live the farm strike, long live our cause in history! Our people full of glory will achieve victory!)

The people—thousands of them by now—arrived in Sacramento on Easter Sunday, April 10. For a while it looked as though the campesinos would get lost in the shuffle of dignitaries. But then someone called for the eighty people who had walked all the way—*los origi-nales*—to come up to the speakers' platform. They were the real heroes and deserved the cheers. Governor Pat Brown was not there to receive the marchers (he had left town to spend the weekend with Frank Sinatra) and hear their story.

On the steps of the capitol, it was announced that the farmworkers had won their first victory. Under the pressure of the march, Schenley had agreed to recognize the NFWA as a union—as having the right to represent Schenley grape workers—and to negotiate. The contract later signed with Schenley provided a raise in pay from $1.10 to $1.85 an hour; holidays and vacations with pay for workers who put in a certain number of hours each year; agreement to replace the hated labor contractors with a hiring hall, run by the union. Except for contracts won on behalf of pineapple workers in Hawaii, this was the first farm labor contract ever negotiated in the United States.

Not only the growers but also the old labor unions had to take the farmworkers more seriously now. The Teamsters, who had supported Chávez at first, began to compete with him by trying to sign the farmworkers up with the Teamsters instead of César's union. They said *they* would represent the campesinos.

This made people very worried. The white-dominated Teamsters had supported the bracero program in the past and often acted in favor of the bosses more than the workers. It was also a very powerful union, and had the means to take over many farmworkers. César saw that his people needed help. The only way out, it seemed, was to merge with the Filipino group under the big AFL-CIO. César knew that the AFL-CIO is part of the Establishment. But it would be a powerful protector. So the campesinos voted to join the AFL-CIO and to change their name to the United Farm Workers Organizing Committee (UFWOC).

The boycott on Schenley had been called off but there were many other opponents left—like Di Giorgio, the biggest of them all. That summer of 1966, César together with a minister, a priest and six campesinos, were arrested for supposedly "trespassing" at a ranch. They were all stripped naked, then chained together by sheriff's deputies. But this only won more support for the campesinos. The next year, the false arrests and acts of violence increased against the campesinos. They had to fight not only the growers and their supporters, who included the police, but also the Teamsters—who were calling the United Farm Workers "Communists" and trying to sabotage their work in many ways.

False arrests and violence against the farmworkers were not limited to California. In Starr County, Texas, right near the Rio Grande, melon pickers organized a branch of the UFWOC with important help from Gilberto Padilla and other California organizers. The story of the Starr County strike and how it was repressed became one of the most important, most brutal chapters in the history of the campesinos' struggle.

Starr County is the poorest county in Texas and one of the poorest in the United States. Thousands of migrant workers are based there. In 1966, the highest wage for farmwork was one dollar an hour—and sometimes it went as low as forty cents an hour or less.

Even Anglos from Texas have said that the campesino's life there is no different from slavery, except that slavery was legal in its time.

When the 1966 melon-picking season rolled around, some of the slaves decided they had had enough. Although very little organizing had been done, seven hundred melon pickers walked out of the fields on June 4, the first day of the strike. Texas gringos and vendidos moved to crush the campesinos using every means. Trains bringing in scab workers were guarded by men armed with machine guns. Union organizers were shot at. Over 125 organizers and sympathizers were arrested on false charges. In one incident, fifteen persons—including a minister, Reverend Ed Krueger—were arrested while picketing a train loaded with scab melons. Texas Rangers and deputies slapped them, broke cameras, cursed the people, and held their faces within inches of the passing train.

One night, several carloads of Texas Rangers pulled up at a building where the strikers often gathered. They were looking for Magdaleno Dimas, a young *huelguista* who was not afraid of talking back to the Rangers. Without a search warrant or an arrest warrant, they smashed down the front door and broke into the house with their shotguns leveled. According to the men inside, they all raised their hands but the Rangers found Magdaleno there and proceeded to pistol-whip him in what the local doctor called "the worst beating I have ever seen given by the police." They smashed the back of his head and left him near death.

After this incident, the farmworkers brought a suit against the Texas Rangers for harassment of its members. In a hearing before the federal judges, Captain Allee of the Rangers claimed that Magdaleno Dimas had had a gun and so he (Allee) was really quite lenient. "I could have broken his neck if I wanted to," said Allee. "I could have killed him if I wanted to, and maybe I should have." Captain Allee was chief of a Ranger company for forty years; his grandfather and great-grandfather were also Rangers and so is his son. To Chicanos in Texas, he is a symbol of the Ranger spirit. (Six long years later, the suit against the Rangers was won.)

This kind of brutality, together with the fact that the growers could easily hire new workers from Mexico, broke the effectiveness of the Starr County strike. But the struggle to organize in that part of the Rio Grande Valley did not end.

Back in Delano, the strike and boycott grew stronger every month. So did the struggle against the Teamsters. Finally Di Giorgio gave up and in August 1966, for the first time in U.S. history, farmworkers voted for the union of their choice. Many people predicted that they would vote to join the Teamsters but instead the campesinos gave a huge vote to the UFWOC. After that, a new boycott began against another company. When it surrendered, other companies folded one after the other like dominoes. Christian Brothers and Gallo didn't wait to be boycotted; they signed up soon to avoid bad publicity.

But some of the grape growers held out stubbornly. These companies felt strong. Thirty of them handled 85 per cent of all the table grapes grown in California, while the California and Arizona growers together raised 98 per cent of the U.S. grape supply. They had a monopoly, and were sure they couldn't be beaten by a bunch of "dumb Mexicans."

One big company that was struck tried to get around the boycott by putting false labels on its grapes, so that people wouldn't see the company name. This led the UFWOC to call for an International Table Grape Boycott against *all* grapes. The message began going out around the world in late 1967:

DON'T BUY GRAPES! DON'T SHOP AT STORES THAT SELL GRAPES!

The boycott was not just a tactic used to force the growers to negotiate. It was also a campaign to educate people about the conditions of farmwork. At first it aimed to educate people in the United States. Now it was educating people all over the world.

As the new boycott grew in strength, so did the growers' violence against the workers. The farmworkers' union always had a policy of non-violence because of César Chávez, whose ideas were much influenced by Gandhi and Dr. Martin Luther King. César is the one Raza leader who has taken a firm stand in favor of non-violence. But the violence of the growers made it hard for many people to believe in that policy at times. As 1968 began, several incidents of violent resistance took place and there were many rumors of more violent resistance by union people that summer. This deeply troubled César, as did the war in Vietnam. His heart was also heavy for the strike-drained workers, who had been through a hard winter on top of two hungry years. He decided to go on a fast, as a sign of his commitment to non-violence and as an act of prayer and love for the campesinos. He stopped eating on February 14.

César had been on short, private fasts before and he did not announce this new fast at first. He did not even know how long he would stay on it. But when people learned that he was not eating, and became upset because the fast was indefinite, he called a meeting.

First he talked for an hour and a half about non-violence. On other occasions, he had said that non-violence was best because it won lasting respect—not just short-term victories. It made the man with the gun have to decide whether to be violent, instead of the huelguista. Now, at the meeting, César said that people were falling into violence because they were not being creative enough. Violence was a sign of failure to win by other means. It was above all a loss of the will to win, he said.

César also said that proving *machismo*—manliness—through violence was a mistake. Finally, he talked about his fast. It was a strictly personal decision, he explained, and there would be no vote on it. He would keep up his work as best he could, and he did not know how long the fast would last. He did not want others to try a fast of sympathy.

César's speech did not convince everyone, but most of the campesinos accepted the fast—although they worried about their leader. It went on for weeks, and during that time about ten thousand people came to the building where César was resting in a tiny, sound-proof room. Some talked with him, some just gathered quietly outside his doorway, many played music—all kinds, from soft mariachi to spirituals of the Black people to folk songs. So many people came that no one could say the UFWOC did not have widespread support.

Still the campesinos and many others worried. In one incident, which César describes with great humor, a group of campesinos decided that their leader must be *made* to eat—at any price. They sent one man to carry out the job. The man went to see César in his little room, taking with him some big, juicy, warm tacos and a lot of determination. César refused, trying to explain why he had decided to fast, but the man became desperate. He knew the others would be angry if he did not carry out his mission. So he jumped up on the bed and tried to force the taco into César's mouth. There was our leader, squirming away from that taco as if it were poisoned and hollering for help. But since the room was soundproof, help didn't come right away. The Battle of the Taco went on until finally a group of men heard César's cries and burst into the room.

That man and many others must have been very happy when César decided to end the fast after twenty-five days. Chávez did this mainly because of the deep concern it was causing people. But he has often spoken about the good effects of that fast, and fasting in general: how it clears the eyes, the mind, and opens all the senses. It makes people better able to concentrate. For example, after a conversation he could repeat word for word all he had heard. With music, he could hear every separate sound. Of course we must remember that not all people are physically able to fast, or to fast for such long periods. It can hurt your health and should be done only under a doctor's care.

Some people might not understand the point of a twenty-five-day fast. But they fail to understand that César's spiritual life is not that of the institutional churches. His religion comes from within, it lives and breathes. It is the *Indionismo* that forms the basis of our spiritual heritage, the heritage of Las Americas. Like the Virgen de Guadalupe, it is older than the Catholic Church and goes far beyond it.

César is El Indio in many ways. His high cheek bones, black hair, and arched nose all speak of his Indian heritage. Like the Indio, he believes that suffering brings strength—not death—and this is the idea behind such actions as the peregrinación and the fasts. He has a deep kind of strength that comes from being in harmony with the big life forces and with oneself *as part of nature*. To hear César speak in his gentle voice is to feel his strength. With just a glance, he seems to communicate. When César is communicating with *hermanos*, friends, he communicates the feeling of a common bond and quick warmth. He can also communicate anger quickly, and he does become angry— especially about cowardice and sneakiness and racism.

In the United States, we see Indionismo most clearly in the strong, enduring campesino. Despite all the skills and knowledge that César has acquired, despite his ability to debate with congressmen or growers or college professors, he will not let himself be separated from the campesino. He, his wife, and children have no new car, no fancy clothes, and no big savings account hidden away. César has always refused personal awards, and becomes truly upset when he feels that people are giving him too much personal attention. He doesn't *pretend* to be modest; he *is*. And if he has to assert leadership, he does.

He has directed the union in the same spirit. No big salaries and Cadillacs for the officials—a policy which the big Establishment unions cannot understand. He recognized from the beginning that if people started working for the union because of the money it offered, the union would soon be like any other U.S. business. La Causa would be lost in the grab for dollars. Also, if the union paid big salaries, then only a few people could work for La Causa. But if it paid just enough for people to live on, then many people could work for it. A month's salary for one big union official can feed twenty volunteer workers for that same period.

César recognized the best and truest qualities of the campesino, then built on them. In the union, César often spoke about the great endurance of women— their ability to stick with a job and keep on struggling, when men would want to finish it up in a hurry or else get discouraged. This strength has been shown by many active union women including Dolores Huerta— the union's top negotiator, which is usually called "a man's job."

This was the kind of leader and the kind of union that had taken on the grape industry, with its millions of dollars and many powerful friends—including the governor of California himself, Ronald Reagan. He called the strikers "barbarians," and threw all his power on the side of the growers. How could the "barbarians" possibly win?

But the strike and boycott against grapes grew stronger every month. By May 1968 it was reported 95 per cent effective in New York City—one of the biggest shipping points for grapes—and growing in other big cities. By the end of the year, the boycott was spreading in England and Scandinavia. At the same time, campesinos were on the move all over the country. In Wautoma, Wisconsin, Chicanos began organizing cucumber workers into the Obreros Unidos (United Workers); onion pickers in Ohio started an organization of the UFWOC; a campaign began to organize fruit and hops pickers in Washington state.

In Arizona, the other big grape-producing state, UFWOC organizers met with even worse resistance than in California. Arizona has never had a victorious farmworker strike, and its labor laws are even worse than those of California. The foreman for a grape grower on one Arizona ranch said: "Don't worry, we had a meeting with the sheriff. They said that as soon as the union organizers come in, they'll get a paddy wagon and extra help, and put them all in jail, and run them out of town."

Threats like that did not stop 150 grape workers from striking in June 1969. The Arizona growers fought back at the strike with a new tactic. They got high school coaches to convince teen-agers that they should help break the strike by going to work in the fields. The coaches didn't tell those Anglo boys how tough it was to bend and stoop all day in 110-degree heat, and the boys just couldn't work as fast or well as the Mexicanos. That harvest must have cost the growers a lot of extra money and headaches.

The Arizona growers also brought in Green Carders to break the strike. This tactic continued to be one of the union's biggest problems. César made a trip to Mexico to ask that government for help in stopping the illegal use of Green Carders as scabs, but it was a failure. In May 1969, four thousand UFWOC members and supporters marched a hundred miles in broiling heat to Calexico, at the Mexican border, to show international solidarity between the farmworkers of the two nations. Many Mexicanos came to meet them at Calexico; others were frightened away by threats that they would lose their Green Cards if they went.

But the biggest strikebreaker of all was not the Mexicanos. The biggest strikebreaker turned out to be Uncle Sam—the U. S. Government itself.

In 1969, the UFWOC revealed that in the four years since the grape strike began, the Department of Defense had increased its purchase of grapes *by* 700 *per cent*. In 1967, the Pentagon bought 7.5 million pounds of grapes—but in 1969 it bought more than 16 million pounds. "If it hadn't been for these huge purchases of grapes," said César Chávez, "this strike would have been settled by now."

The Pentagon gave all kinds of excuses like "increased troop acceptance" of grapes in Vietnam and other places. They insisted they were "neutral" in labor disputes. But a Department of Defense official admitted to a U. S. Senate investigating committee that the department had "advised" military commanders and purchasing departments to order table grapes. The order came from high up. All this meant that the U. S. Government itself was using the people's money— taxes—to help the rich growers beat a strike of poor people.

Why did the Pentagon do this?

And why did Vice-President Spiro Agnew serve grapes at his inaugural ball in early 1969, when everybody knew there was a grape boycott?

And why did President Nixon announce that he had every intention of eating California grapes "whenever I can" and laughingly eat grapes for a news photograph?

The farmworkers raised another big question in 1969. The nation's largest buyer of California table grapes was the Safeway food market chain—it bought $1,500,-000 in grapes a year. When many other stores had agreed not to buy grapes, Safeway held out. They held out even when they were given a petition signed by 140,000 people just in the San Francisco Bay area saying they would not shop at Safeway unless it stopped buying grapes. Like the Pentagon, Safeway said it was "neutral"—but then it arrested six persons who came to talk with the management about the boycott. Why did Safeway act like this?

To answer all these questions, we must first realize that Anglo farming in California has almost no connection with our picture of the little house in the country where a family raises one or two crops on a few acres, keeps some chickens and pigs and perhaps a cow, and lives there all year around working hard. Farming is Big Business in California—the biggest of them all, worth five billion dollars in 1969. Seventy-nine per cent of the farmland is owned by 7 per cent of the farm owners. The trend is toward bigger and fewer farms— what Carey McWilliams called "factories in the field." By big, we mean from ten thousand acres on up. One of the richest is Christian Brothers, owned by the Catholic Church. Few of the growers actually live on their farms.

These big growers receive federal assistance in many forms: irrigation water, farm labor recruitment, university research to find new improved farming methods, technical assistance of various types. All this is financed by the federal government—meaning the taxpayer. The growers also get subsidies, direct grants of money from the federal government for *not* growing certain crops. This is what some people call "welfare for the rich." The growers in one California county received over three million dollars in subsidies in 1966. (Yet 81 per cent of these growers said, in a poll, that they did not approve of federal aid to the poor—it would take away their "incentive," said the growers.)

All these facts were revealed by the farmworkers' union, especially in its newspaper *El Malcriado*. It also revealed that Safeway has very close connections with agri-business. The chairman of the board of Safeway in 1969 was a director of J. G. Boswell, Inc., one of the largest cotton growers in California and the largest grape grower in Arizona. One of the directors of Safeway was J. G. Boswell himself. In 1968, he received over $4,000,000 from the federal government for NOT growing cotton—the biggest subsidy paid to any rancher in the nation. Still another Safeway director ran a 168,000-acre ranch in California that was irrigated by a federal government project and he also received a subsidy.

These men had high-level connections with many other areas of big business such as Del Monte, Macy's department stores, Southern Pacific Company, the Spreckel's Sugar Company, Caterpillar Tractor Company, and the Times-Mirror Company, a powerful chain of newspapers.

From all these facts brought out by the farmworkers, it was clear that the huelga wasn't just a strike against some grape ranches in California, but against a whole, national power structure directed by Big Business. Agribusiness and the government were partners. Together they moved to keep the poor down and profits up—all at the expense of the taxpayer. You could even say that agri-business *was* the government, or an important part of it. It said "eat grapes" and the President ate grapes. It said "buy grapes" and the Pentagon bought grapes. The farmworkers had begun with a little strike in a small town called Delano, and they ended up exposing the reality of the whole nation.

Of all the truths that the campesinos exposed, none was more shocking than what they revealed about the poisons used by agri-business.

César Chávez had known for a long time that growers used chemical sprays on the crops to get rid of insects, parasites, and certain diseases, and that these sprays caused illness among the farmworkers. But when many workers and children began coming to the clinic of the UFWOC, he realized that this problem was extremely serious. The campesinos and their supporters began looking into this problem with more attention than ever before.

Until ten years ago, DDT was almost the only pesticide being used. But when the use of DDT was restricted by law because of its bad effects on people, the growers began to use new pesticides—which are just as bad or worse. Several of the chemicals are similar to those developed by Nazi Germany to exterminate human beings. Among our workers, they have caused loss of vision, loss of hair and fingernails, convulsions, rashes, birth deformities, leukemia, cancer, and death. Minor symptoms are nausea, headache, dizziness, and muscle weakness. César Chávez calls these minor symptoms the "Walking Death," because they are not bad enough to put a person in the hospital right away but by the time a worker gets there it may be too late—the person has a fatal illness or is going blind.

César's study shows that between 1951 and 1961, there were 3,040 workers poisoned by the pesticides; 23 adults and 63 children died. Many more suffered from the "minor symptoms." The conditions under which a campesino works are very dangerous, yet one common result—blindness—is not recognized as a work accident under the law, and compensation is not paid. All over the nation more farmworkers are hurt every year by pesticides than industrial workers are hurt in the big city plants.

There is another kind of victim too: the consumer, anybody who eats food. Fruits like the grape, which are not peeled before being eaten, have been sold in grocery stores with some of those deadly sprays still on them. Even if the fruit is peeled, it may have been penetrated by pesticides which cannot be washed off or cooked out.

The farmworkers' newspaper, *El Malcriado*, charged that in August 1969, a test was made on California table grapes bought at a Safeway store in Washington, D.C.—and they contained 180 times the safe limit of a pesticide called Aldrin. According to *El Malcriado*, Safeway stopped buying grapes for a while, but then they began again. Dolores Huerta, chief contract negotiator for the UFW, said angrily: "As long as selling grapes makes a few lousy dollars' profit . . . they will sell the poisoned fruit to anyone that will buy it."

The reaction of the growers and their friends to the facts brought out by the campesinos was what you could expect: they said it wasn't true. The companies that manufactured the pesticides went right on doing so, and often did not label their products honestly. "They have no responsibility to the public," said a Los Angeles doctor, "except to collect the money, and they've done a lot of that!"

This same attitude showed in another practice exposed by the farmworkers: pumping a plant hormone into fruit to make it look fat and solid. This is just for looks, because it also makes the fruit tasteless. The growers don't care if the buyer ends up with fruit that is no good to eat: all they care about is selling it.

The growers have made food—a source of life for all people—into nothing but a profit-making business. We realize this even more clearly when we learn that two chemical sprays (defoliants) known as 2-4-D and 2-45-T, which growers have used, are made by Dow

Chemical Company—producers of napalm. The sprays were found to cause birth defects and banned, but growers reportedly continued to use them. In 1972, a pesticide spray used on lettuce, known as Monitor 4, was found to cause cancer and other illnesses, even death. Yet the growers reportedly went on using it for months afterward. This is called "free enterprise," and the growers, the pesticide companies, and the war-makers are all in it together.

The union was so worried about the poisoning of workers that César said his people would even accept a lower wage if the grape growers would agree to regulate their use of pesticides. But the growers stubbornly refused. Ten of them were willing to sit down and bargain with the UFWOC about all its demands—but they would not agree to control their use of pesticides in any way. So the boycott went on.

Then came the first breakthrough: one major grape grower signed a contract with the UFWOC on April 1, 1970. The others soon were ready to do the same. At 11:10 A.M. on July 29, 1970, the Delano grape strike ended.

Five hundred farmworkers and boycott supporters filled the room where the contracts would be signed. They sang "Nosotros Venceremos" and shouted "Viva la huelga!" When the twenty-six grape growers walked in, the strikers joyously began singing one of the most popular songs of their long struggle—"De Colores." The growers had sworn that this moment would never happen, but it was about to happen.

César then spoke: "The strikers sacrificed all of their worldly possessions. Ninety-five per cent of the strikers lost their homes and cars. But I think that in losing their worldly possessions, they found themselves . . ."

Then, one by one, the growers signed, while the news cameras rolled and clicked and reporters strained at attention. All the new contracts placed strict control on the use of pesticides, as well as providing wage increases. They said it would never happen, but it happened.

Forty thousand grape workers were covered by the contracts begun at Delano. The California victory helped grape workers in Arizona to get the first union contract for campesinos ever signed there. Then, only a few days after the Delano victory, the cry of Huelga! sang out once again. This time the location was Salinas, the town where César and Helen Chávez had spent their honeymoon picking lettuce many years before. And the new target of the campesinos was . . . lettuce.

The Teamsters had made a promise to leave the UFWOC a free hand in organizing farmworkers. But then they began signing up workers again and making sweetheart contracts with the growers. The campesinos were angered by these backdoor deals, and many lettuce workers went on strike in protest. The Teamsters then made a new promise—and broke that one too. So on August 25, ten thousand angry farmworkers walked out of the fields.

The strike swept across two valleys faster than the union could organize it. In one place, people said that a car drove by a field where a group of campesinos were at work and someone in the car shouted, "Viva la huelga!" A few seconds after the car had passed, the workers just left the field—on strike. The surprised boss called up the UFWOC office to ask what the workers' demands were. But even the union didn't know yet. Soon there were not only lettuce but also broccoli, cauliflower, garlic, and strawberry workers striking, all in the area around Salinas which is often called "the nation's salad bowl."

A UFWOC office was dynamited, and one of its lawyers was viciously assaulted. Two cars of huelguistas were attacked by a foreman on a bulldozer. The town of Salinas is located in what people call "John Birch territory," and has always repressed Raza struggles violently. The average Anglo there wants to keep things that way, and during the strike many of them put U.S. flags on their new cars to show what good Americans they were. "Go back to Mexico!" they screamed when the huelguistas drove by in their battered old trucks with the red and black huelga flag flying.

In mid-September, the UFWOC started its second big boycott—against scab lettuce. The grape boycott machinery was oiled up and put back into action. Right away, several of the biggest companies were ready to negotiate. César Chávez said, "After three weeks we are at the same stage in the lettuce as we were in the grapes after three years." Things had changed a great deal for the campesino since 1965.

But the U. S. Government had not changed. One of the big companies that held out against the farmworkers was Bud Antle, Inc. The Department of Defense stepped up its purchases of lettuce from Bud Antle—just as it had once increased its purchase of scab grapes. It bought more lettuce from Antle in three months after the boycott began than it had in the previous two years. The Pentagon also paid Antle at prices far above the prices of other lettuce growers although it was government policy to buy from the lowest bidder. And at the same time, the Pentagon cut off its purchases from companies that had signed with the UFWOC.

Bud Antle is partly controlled by Dow Chemical, the napalm makers. This connection led to many protests and demonstrations at Dow Chemical offices by campesinos and their supporters—including GIs at bases from coast to coast. More than thirty were arrested in one protest. The GIs also refused to eat scab lettuce.

But Antle and Dow were so determined to break the strike that they had César Chávez sent to prison. Antle got the court in Salinas to order the UFWOC to call off the boycott against Bud Antle and also to put up a $2,750,000 bond while the matter was being settled. The union hardly had that much money, and César certainly would not call off the boycott. So on December 4, 1970, he went to jail in Salinas for refusing to obey the court's order. It was a cold, rainy morning but thousands of campesinos from all over the area came out to march with César and his wife. They heard César's last cry as he walked into jail: "Boycott Antle! Boycott Dow! Boycott the hell out of them!"

Two days before Christmas, the California Supreme Court finally ordered César released without bond. When he came out, people asked what he was going to do now. César gave a typical answer: "Back to the grind." Back to the day-to-day struggle that consumes his life.

By that time, the union had fifty thousand members. Sixty per cent of them were Mexicanos, about 20 per cent Filipinos, and the rest Blacks, Arabs, whites. The union had many programs to benefit the workers including a health insurance plan, a credit union to make loans to workers, and a retirement village for older workers. The union had its own center, a stretch of land outside Delano called Forty Acres, where there was a clinic, a co-operative gas station, and other services. All the services, by the way, were named after campesinos who had been in the struggle and died.

Most of that next year, 1971, and all of 1972 were devoted to fighting a new tactic of the campesino's enemies. In many states, the big growers and their friends tried to pass laws that would make it illegal to strike during harvest time, and to boycott. These laws would take away the campesino's only weapons, their only source of power. At the same time, the farmworkers' union was still struggling to get contracts for the lettuce workers. Most of these workers had been signed up by the Teamsters—the little union's big enemy.

In the November 1972 elections, one of those laws against the campesinos—"Proposition 22"—was defeated by a huge vote in California. And the next month, the California Supreme Court said that the Teamsters did not rightly represent the lettuce workers; that the Teamsters and the growers had forced the campesinos to join the Teamsters. Both the defeat of Proposition

22 and the Supreme Court decision were victories for the little union.

But in that same 1972 election, Richard Nixon was re-elected President—with heavy support from the Teamsters. Frank Fitzsimmons, president of the Teamsters, knew that he could count on help from the man in the White House, whom he had helped to get elected. He announced in January 1973 that the Teamsters had declared war on the UFW and the lettuce boycott. And 1973 became the year of the war against the Teamsters.

The first big blow fell in April. The three-year contracts, which the little union had signed for the grape workers in 1970, ended—they expired. The grape growers began announcing that their workers were not going to sign up again with the UFW but with the Teamsters. These new contracts were called "sweetheart contracts," because the Teamsters union—which was supposed to defend the workers—made contracts to please the bosses. In other words, the Teamsters and the growers were like sweethearts.

It seemed as if the grape workers were headed right back to where they had been eight years before. Once again, they had to strike. Sixteen hundred out of two thousand went on strike in the Coachella Valley, to protest the Teamster contracts. Then, on July 29, twenty-nine growers in Delano also broke off with the UFW and signed with the Teamsters. Out of 180 contracts that the UFW once had, it now held less than twenty. As a result, the number of official UFW members had fallen from forty thousand to six and a half thousand.

The little union now faced a life-or-death situation. The campesinos and their supporters strongly believe that this situation was caused by a conspiracy to destroy the union—a conspiracy of the Teamsters, the growers, and Nixon—with even the Mafia and Watergate involved. Here are some of the reasons given for that belief:

Way back in 1949, when Nixon was a member of Congress from his home state of California, he was known to be anti-labor. There was a strike then of farmworkers, led by another union. Nixon took part in some hearings on the strike and signed a report which killed that union. Also, as a politician Nixon always depended a lot on support from California agri-businessmen to advance his career.

The support given to Nixon by Teamster officials in the 1972 elections is no secret. Teamster President Fitzsimmons has been called Nixon's strongest supporter in organized labor and he was a national vice-chairman of "Democrats for Nixon." But on top of that, it has been reported that Fitzsimmons gave $175,-000 in Teamster pension fund money—money that rightfully belongs to the workers. He gave this to one of the men, Murray Chotiner, who was deeply involved in the Watergate affair. This money wasn't listed with other Nixon campaign contributions, according to the article, but kept in a secret fund—a fund used to finance Watergate spying activities.

Millions of dollars from that same Teamster pension fund have, according to another newspaper (The Los Angeles Times), been lent to the Mafia to help build gambling casinos and country clubs in Las Vegas, Ne-

vada. Money from Las Vegas gambling operations reportedly helped to finance Watergate.

According to the UFW, lettuce growers paid thousands of dollars to Teamster officials in 1970 for the
Teamsters to destroy the little union. It was a Teamster
man himself who testified to seeing the money pass
hands. The Department of Justice said they indeed had
evidence of this and an investigation was begun but
then dropped.

The owner of one of the ranches struck by the campesinos in 1973 is, according to the California newspaper *People's World*, a close business partner of a
multimillionaire who personally raised over one million
dollars for Nixon's 1968 campaign.

These are just a few of the reasons why César accused Nixon of being responsible for a plot to destroy
his union that was being carried out by Teamster boss,
Fitzsimmons, and the grape growers. César also charged
that the Teamsters and Safeway stores have had a close
relation since the mid-1930s.

With such powerful enemies, the farmworkers faced
a grim fight for life in 1973. The Teamsters had the
contracts and officially they had the members. However,
as César said, "the Teamsters may have the contracts
but we have the people." So César called a general
strike against the table grape growers.

Repression came fast and hard. During just nine days
in late July, almost twenty-seven hundred people were
arrested. Nuns, priests, and ministers were jailed. The
arrests were made on the basis of a court order that
limited picketing at the fields. The order said, for example, that there could not be more than one or two

people picketing every hundred feet. César said the court order was against the U. S. Constitution, and people went on challenging the order. By the end of the summer, a total of five thousand people had been arrested. There wasn't enough room for them in the jails so law officers began trying to arrest only picket leaders and not so many women and children. But, as one sheriff complained, this was hard to do. "They all insist on being arrested," he said. That was the kind of courage and solidarity you could see in the campesino families.

The arrests were only part of the repression. Violent attacks by Teamsters left a trail of blood across California worse than anything seen since the 1930s. The UFW and many witnesses charged that Goons—strongmen hired by Teamster officials for $50 a day plus expenses—viciously attacked men, women, and children. They attacked them not only on the picket line but also in motels, at bars, wherever they found them. There were fifteen shootings, many beatings, fire-bombings, at least one kidnaping and one union family's house was burned to the ground. A Catholic priest working with the UFW had his nose broken by a Teamster. Strikers and their supporters were also attacked with clubs and tear gas by law officers, who made no secret of which side they were on.

On the night of August 14, a young Arab farmworker named Nagi Daifullah was fatally injured by a deputy sheriff in Lamont, California. Police said he died from a fall suffered after he threw a bottle at the deputy sheriff. But campesinos said the sheriff hit the young Arab on the head during an argument, and clubbed him to death. Ten thousand people marched in the funeral procession for Nagi, to protest his death.

Later that day, August 15, six shots were fired at Fernando Chávez, son of César, while he was at a picket line. He dived behind a car and wasn't hurt. But the next day, another farmworker was killed. Juan de la Cruz, a sixty-year-old campesino who had been one of the first UFW members, was shot to death at the Guimarra Ranch by a strike-breaker who drove by and fired a gun at him.

It was four months of organized terror. It was an all-out war to destroy the little union once and for all. It was a war in which one side was armed and the other was not. The union asked the U. S. Government for federal protection and didn't get it. But the union had other kinds of weapons. It had the support of other unions, and many members of the Teamsters—ordinary workers—supported the union because they, too, were struggling against the Teamster bosses. The little union had the support of millions of students, housewives, church people, and Raza everywhere.

So César called off the picketing, because of the lack of federal protection against violence, and went back to that tried-and-true tactic: the boycott. Once again the call went out across the nation: BOYCOTT GRAPES AND LETTUCE. Also, BOYCOTT SAFEWAY, A&P, and other big stores that sold grapes and lettuce produced by scabs or were under Teamster contracts.

Five hundred striking farmworkers left California in late August to push the boycott in over sixty cities. Now it was the workers themselves who were doing that job. A National Student Boycott was called against all

Gallo products. Across the country, people picketed supermarkets—sometimes getting arrested—and carrying the cry of "Huelga!"

On the weekend of September 22, the campesinos' union held its first convention—the first convention of any farmworkers in almost forty years—hundreds came together in Fresno, California, to adopt a constitution and elect officers. To nobody's surprise, César was elected president; also, the union changed its name slightly, to the United Farm Workers of America. The convention was "a harvest of unity," as one reporter said, in which a spirit of self-confidence and determination filled the meeting halls.

A few days after the convention, it was announced that the Teamsters had agreed to give up the grape contracts they took over and to let the UFW organize the field workers—campesinos. But this didn't mean that the little union's struggles were over. They still had to fight the growers—but at least now they were fighting only one giant instead of two. And so the struggle went on.

The desire to destroy the UFW was never just a matter of money. The big growers and their friends are afraid of a successful Raza movement. They are also afraid of any successful *rural* movement. For many years, the rural areas have been a comfortable power base for conservative politicians. They counted on the "Messicans" and other "ignorant" people not to give them any trouble. But César and the campesinos have rocked their base and set that prairie fire going where it was least expected. As for the Teamsters, they are sitting on a powder keg. They have many Raza and

Black members who are fed up with racism and boss-ism, who want to make big changes inside the Teamsters and give the union back to the workers. Everywhere, the "little people" are shaking things up for those who have taken their power for granted so long.

The cry of Huelga! has been heard from farmworkers in Oregon, Idaho, Colorado, and other states. In Florida, the United Farm Workers was formed to fight some of the worst conditions in the nation. Three children burned to death in a shack at one of the migrant camps. A camp in a Minute Maid orange grove (owned by Coca-Cola) has been called the worst in the United States by farmworkers. In early 1972, the new union won the first farm labor contract in the history of Florida.

Campesinos are not the only Chicano workers who have begun to unite and show their new strength. There are many Chicanos working in factories, mines, steel mills, the garment industry, packing houses, canneries, construction, and the service industries—hospitals, restaurants, garbage-collecting, gas companies, and so forth. Anglos get promoted while Chicanos with the same or more experience and qualifications stay in the same jobs for years. In many areas, Chicanos are last to be hired and first to be fired. They get the worst jobs and worst wages. The established unions have generally sold-out Chicano workers and treated them in the same racist way as the bosses. But the workers are no longer accepting this situation so obediently.

In Austin, Texas, Chicano upholstery workers at the Economy Furniture Company carried out a two-and-a-half year strike that began in November 1968. In Silver

City, New Mexico, Chicana hospital workers struck with the same determined spirit that we can see in the movie, *Salt of the Earth*, which is about a Silver City miners' strike of the early 1950s.

It was also our women who played a leading role in the long strike of workers at Farah pants factories, which are found in Texas and New Mexico. This struggle goes back to 1969, when Farah workers tried to join a union—the Amalgamated Clothing Workers of America (ACWA). They were still trying three years later to fight extremely low wages, no job security, poor treatment of women workers, and so forth. In early 1972, twenty-five Chicanas working in the sewing room walked out when Farah management refused to meet with them. Then Farah fired seven union organizers in San Antonio, Texas. Over five hundred workers walked out of that plant—on May 9, 1972. The same day, workers at the El Paso plant also went on strike. More and more workers struck, until two to three thousand were out.

Boss Willie Farah answered by having mass arrests of picketers—over seven hundred in all—and by trying to scare picketers with police dogs. The "legal system" worked hand-in-hand with Farah; a local justice of the peace reportedly got $4.00 for each arrest warrant. Finally the National Labor Relations Board said that Farah was guilty of unfair labor practices. But Willie, who has called union organizers "filth," went on resisting the workers. Finally the Farah huelguistas began to use the nationwide boycott as a weapon—DON'T BUY FARAH PANTS, they told shoppers. Soon the boycott was hurting Farah's profits, and there seemed to be hope for the workers.

Another long strike was that of Chicano blue-collar workers for the city of Artesia in the southern part of New Mexico often called "Little Texas." They walked off the job in September 1972, making some modest demands for union recognition and a few benefits. The city refused and tried to repress the strike with laws against the Constitution saying, for example, that the mayor's house could not be picketed. Strikers and supporters were arrested under these laws and physically attacked. As the strike went on into 1973, it became clear that the workers were not just waging an ordinary labor struggle for higher wages or more benefits for themselves. They were challenging the racist power structure of "Little Texas"—the same kind of power structure that now rules over all Aztlán. They were fighting for all of us. This understanding led to state-wide support for the Artesia city workers.

Although there have been many strikes by Chicano workers in the last few years, none have exposed that power structure more than the Artesia and Farah strikes. We can expect to see still more movimiento by Chicano workers in the future. They will be fighting not only the bosses but also the established unions, whose leaders go around in Cadillacs and seem to be closer to the bosses than to the workers. Raza workers in the cities are now recognized as an important element in *la lucha*—our struggle.

The truth is that the worker's or campesino's struggle does not stop with winning higher wages and better working conditions from the present bosses of the land.

It leads further—to the question of who has a right to the land itself and all its riches. If and when the campesinos and workers begin that struggle, we wonder if it can remain non-violent.

It is the campesinos who have caused us to ask those questions. Their struggle has confronted us with bitter truths about our double-standard democracy. We see it clearer and clearer, and it seems more and more to be like an octopus with many tentacles that intertwine. Business, the government, the military, and the courts are all tied together in impossible knots, and together they try to smother us.

But as we learn more about the monster, we become stronger. We become more involved. Slowly we realize how we have been held in the grip of that monster until we were almost lifeless. Our city people can no longer look down on those who work with their hands in the earth. We all have acquired a great and special respect for the campesinos, because it is their endurance and sweat that helps put the food on our plates for every meal, every day. We have come to see that the worker of the earth is a little piece of the sun, a little bit of the whole planet—and the conscience of humanity. That is why the red flag of the United Farm Workers with the black eagle on it has become a symbol of the movimiento everywhere. It flies proudly above the heads of Raza on the march, not only campesinos but also city people—Chicanos across the nation.

10

Crusaders for Justice

I am Joaquín,
Lost in a world of confusion,
Caught up in a whirl of a
    gringo society,
Confused by the rules
Scorned by attitudes
Suppressed by manipulations,
And destroyed by modern society . . .
And now!
  I must choose
      Between
  the paradox of
Victory of the spirit,
despite physical hunger

                    Or
                to exist in the grasp
            of American social neurosis,
            sterilization of the soul
                and a full stomach.
            (*From "I Am Joaquín/Yo Soy Joaquín"
            by Rodolfo Gonzales*)

I MUST CHOOSE, wrote Rodolfo Gonzales—and he did choose. In doing so, he set an example for many other Raza who are caught up in that "whirl of a gringo society." The story of Rodolfo Gonzales is the story of how a Chicano who "made it" became committed to serving his people. It is also the story of how an organization was born and developed—the Crusade for Justice in Denver, the strongest urban organization of Raza today, an organization with special appeal to barrio youth.

Rodolfo Gonzales, known to most people as Corky, was born in a Denver barrio on June 18, 1928, the son of a migrant worker from Mexico. He was the youngest among four sons and two daughters. Corky's mother died when he was two years old and his father never remarried but somehow managed to keep the family together. As the youngest, Corky received much love, care—and, of course, scolding—from everyone else in the home. The entire family had to keep an eye on Corky, for if he was after an animal (chasing a squirrel, for example) he never thought of the city and its hazards. He set out to do many things in his own world. He was a creative child of nature.

His father often spoke to him about the Mexican Revolution, about Mexican history in general, and there was no doubt in Corky's mind as to who he was or who his people were. But then the gringo's system went to work: on his first day of school, Corky was told by the teacher that his name wasn't Rodolfo but Rudolph. He was introduced to the rules forbidding him and his Raza friends to speak· Spanish in school. Like so many other Chicanitos, he was forced to forget much of his own language.

Corky's father worked as a campesino in southern Colorado, and Corky went with him to the fields every spring and summer—often to work the sugar beets. During the fall and winter he was back in the barrio, going to four grade schools, three junior highs, and two high schools. He worked in a slaughterhouse at night and on weekends. He became as tough as the barrio itself—and a very fine boxer.

Before he was twenty years old, Corky won the National Amateur Championship and the International Championship as a featherweight. Boxing writers praised his quick, catlike movements and rated him the the third-ranking contender for the World Featherweight title. He was a hero to young Chicanos of the barrios and traveled to many places to fight. Once, in New Orleans, Louisiana, Corky was standing on the sidewalk outside the building where he would be boxing that night. An Immigration Department officer came up to him and began asking many questions. Corky had to produce his identification, to show the official that he was a U.S. citizen and not a Mexican here "illegally." The official went on with his questions, until finally Corky pointed out the picture of himself on the poster announcing that evening's fight.

This and other experiences showed him the bitter fact that he was a stranger in his own land. They also made him want to read, to learn more. Corky read much Spanish poetry in many different dressing rooms and went through an intense self-education. The more he traveled and studied, the more he learned about the U.S.A.—and about himself, his people. The seeds were planted that would one day produce a great poet and Chicano leader.

After seventy-five professional fights, Corky quit. He had gone into the ring mostly to escape the slaughter-house, but it wasn't for him. He knew now that he wanted a different life.

Corky became a dozen different kinds of men: lumberjack, field laborer, big-city politician, insurance salesman, businessman, poet, and playwright. His fame as a boxer opened the way to politics and he became the first Chicano district captain in the Denver Democratic Party at the age of twenty-nine. In the 1960 presidential election he was Colorado co-ordinator of the Viva Kennedy campaign; his district brought in Denver's biggest Democratic vote. Meanwhile, he had become owner of an automobile insurance agency and of a bail and bond business. He soon had a yearly income of eighty thousand dollars, owned several buildings, and had large investments. Corky had "made it," and his people loved him for it.

He not only made it financially; he was also honored by the system with many appointments to agencies that were supposed to help the people. He became chairman of the board of Denver's War on Poverty, president of the National Citizens Committee for

Community Relations, a member of the National Board of Jobs for Progress, and so forth. He ran around the country to all kinds of meetings about "poverty" and "the Mexican-American." The Anglos were predicting a tremendous future for Corky, and his own people were proud because Corky had licked the gringo system on its own terms.

Even in those years of wealth and what the Anglo calls "success," Corky did not forget his own people. Soon after he entered politics, he opened a free boxing gym for poor youth. He gave a lot of money to poor people and lent money as well—more than seventy thousand dollars—which he has never collected. He spoke up for Raza, and as a district captain he talked about the problems of La Raza. He never accepted any of the payoffs offered him. He helped to set up the Denver chapter of the G-I Forum, and a political action group called Los Voluntarios.

But it wasn't enough for him. A complete break between Corky and the system had to come. He had seen firsthand that politics was a mass of corruption and payoffs. He had also seen firsthand that the poverty programs did nothing to improve the day-to-day lives of poor people; they were designed to pacify people and to provide fat salaries for a few administrators. Chicanos who worked for either ended up betraying their people and selling themselves.

Corky knew he had to make that choice, he had to reject "sterilization of the soul and a full stomach."

He resigned from the Democratic Party, then from the other appointments. In 1965, he was employed directly by the mayor of Denver as head of a program that he had started called the Neighborhood Youth Corps. His skill in communicating and working with youth gave the program real meaning, and it served as a pilot program for other youth programs in the country which are still operating today. That same year, an incident took place that gave birth to the Crusade for Justice.

Corky was chairman of Los Voluntarios when a split occurred in the organization over the question of running its meetings according to parliamentary procedure —called Robert's Rules of Order. This is a very formal, English-language set of rules that tell you when to speak at meetings, who can speak, what the chairman can do, how to vote, and so forth. For poor people, parliamentary procedure has always been a source of confusion and frustration. Following the rules becomes more important than the problem being discussed. Instead of solutions to a problem, one hears "Point of order!" People who have been to college and know Robert's Rules can manipulate a meeting by using the rules to their advantage. These rules are the opposite of the way people make decisions in a communal structure: reaching basic agreement in an atmosphere of mutual respect—often without voting.

Corky and others wanted an organization that anyone could relate to and participate in, a grass-roots organization with a grass-roots kind of structure and procedures. This would be the Cruzada para la Justicia— the Crusade for Justice. It would keep voting to a minimum, and only on major issues. Basic goals would be clear, with justice being the end result.

The Crusade, founded in 1965, is based in a large

city and its founder is mostly a city man. Today 80 per cent of our people live in the cities. Most of them either grew up in a rural area or are the children of parents who did. There is no greater shock for our people than that of going from the land, where we live close to natural forces and work in growing much of our own food, to the unplowable concrete of big cities. Where we once saw rows of beets, onions, tomatoes, green beans, and trees as we worked under the hot sun, we now see rows of streets and sidewalks filled with strangers who are often cold, friendless, alien. Where once we met people and stopped to talk casually with everyone, we now find ourselves in crowds of shoving, rushing robots that seem to look at you with cold steel eyes—and yet not see you.

Facing this alien new world, often separated from friends and family, it is only natural that the new Chicano arrival looks for a home in the barrio where he will find a few relatives and friends from his home area, and small stores, restaurants, barbershops run by his own people in which he will hear his own language and familiar music, eat his own kind of food. A city can consist of many barrios, each with a name of its own, usually Spanish names like El Rebote, Penjamo, or Barelas. One of the most famous barrios was Chávez Ravine in Los Angeles, which existed for many years until Raza were forced out in order to make a home there for the Los Angeles Dodgers. We remember old people who refused to move and were carried out sitting in their rocking chairs; this makes some Chicanos spit as they walk past Chávez Ravine today.

The close-knit barrio is today being broken down in

many places by a process called urban renewal, which usually amounts to Chicano removal. Poor people are forced out—sometimes with compensation for the homes they have built, but never with enough to build or buy a new home of the same quality, free of any mortgage. In place of the old homes of poor Chicanos, new housing for the middle class or new offices for big business rise up.

Once the new arrival solves the difficult problem of finding a cheap home, he or she has to find a job. The Chicano is asked, "Are you QUALIFIED?" and usually told that he is not. Rarely has he had the chance to get the higher education that would QUALIFY him, because of the racist school system and the racist cycle of poverty that makes him have to leave school to work. Often that word QUALIFIED is just an excuse used by Anglo bosses who prefer to hire other Anglos. One way or another, the Chicano looking for a job gets hit by racism. If he does find a job, it will probably be something like washing dishes or working on a construction project. And even then he will often find himself the first laid off during the "slow season."

The woman can find work more easily—she can be hired for less wages. If both parents are working, the job of keeping the family intact becomes harder and harder. The older children stay out late at night with friends whom the parents don't know; the younger children seem to have trouble in school; and usually there is one member of the family with a serious health problem that drains the family budget.

All of these problems lead people to one institution or another. The Raza family that once had friends and family to help them now seems to face nothing but agencies and offices—usually full of Anglos who can't understand our problems. In rural life, our people make many decisions about their lives: when they go to work, what their work produces, what they do with it. The power to make these decisions provides a kind of dignity. But in the city, a paycheck is supposed to be the purpose and reward of living and decisions about work are imposed from unknown outside forces.

As this urban life pattern unfolds, it tends to make the family disintegrate more and more. The man, not able to get work regularly, may find it easier to leave home. The mother faces an impossible burden of support and care of the family, so she and the children end up at the mercy of the welfare department. In Denver, at least half of the people on welfare have Spanish names. To get welfare, the woman must press charges against her husband for child support and face a continuous court battle.

Meanwhile, our youth are also paying a heavy price for living in the gringo-controlled, smog-filled jungle. They seek protection and status within a circle of barrio friends, often getting involved with drugs or petty stealing. Many of them end up in juvenile court—with no decent legal defense available, their relatives not knowing the legal system and scared to fight a strange enemy. In Denver, over half of the youth in reform school are from broken homes. The label of troublemaker has been fixed on those youth by the courts and by the press; their criminal records have begun, which will follow them everywhere they turn. For his attempts to survive in the city, the young Chicano is destroyed.

The young Chicana also learns about life, and often the hard way. She learns through being used and abused by the young Chicano, who is himself trapped by oppressive forces. The price of this learning can often be a child, which leaves her on the same dead-end streets that her mother may have traveled: the welfare roles or prostitution or a poorly paid job with help from relatives if she is lucky. While the young Chicano is killed and beaten by cops, the Chicana is raped by cops. *Sal si puedes!*

This is the destiny of Raza in the city again and again. All institutions seem oppressive and racist: the schools, the police, the courts, the social agencies, the industries, the press, even the Church. The city is one big conspiracy to destroy the creativity of Raza and breed defeatism, to take away our sense of dignity and encourage self-hatred. It was all those institutions, that whole conspiracy, that became the target of the Crusade for Justice when it began its work in 1965.

Shortly after the Crusade opened its first headquarters, a Denver newspaper called *The Rocky Mountain News* published a series of articles about "the Mexican-American." The articles were considered insulting and untrue by many Raza in Denver. Again it was a case of the Establishment press analyzing and studying an ethnic group—our Raza—as it has done all over the country. We were tired of being insulted and lied about. We knew that the only way to end those practices was to get out and challenge the newspaper itself.

The Crusade for Justice organized a boycott of *The Rocky Mountain News*. People were asked not to buy the paper and to cancel their subscriptions, as a sign of protest. Over a thousand subscriptions were canceled and newsstand sales also dropped. Corky Gonzales, people from the Crusade, G-I Forum, and others picketed the main office of the paper during lunch hour and for two hours in the evening, five days a week, for about four months. The picketing was ended only after a million-dollar lawsuit was filed against the *News*, charging libel and slander against Mexican-Americans.

During the boycott and picketing, the mayor of Denver sent a telegram to Corky Gonzales firing him from his position as director of the Neighborhood Youth Corps. The mayor said it was "deplorable" for a city employee—Corky—to be involved in the picketing. So Corky lost a job and Raza gained a full-time leader.

In the 1967 elections, Corky himself ran for mayor and other Crusaders ran for other offices. To get Corky's name on the ballot, many signatures on petitions had to be obtained. This meant door-to-door campaigning by many Crusaders. Among them was Enriqueta Vasquez, one of the authors of this book, who was a notary public and helped out by notarizing signatures on the petitions. The whole election process created a new political awareness among our people.

Corky's election platform called for many reforms that would improve life for the sick, the aged, the youth, and all poor people. He also exposed many kinds of corruption in the city. When the election was over, Corky came in third out of five candidates. He did not win, but the most important action was yet to come.

According to the Denver City Charter, the mayoral election is non-partisan and a candidate can spend no more than one thousand dollars on his campaign. This law had never been enforced. But when the Crusaders got involved in the campaign and became aware of the law, they started keeping track of just how much the man expected to win—Tom Currigan—was spending on his campaign. People kept track of all advertising—radio and TV spot announcements, neon signs, billboard ads, newspaper ads. Photographs were taken all over town as proof, and records dug up. It was a big job.

The Crusade declared the election a fraud and filed a lawsuit against Mayor Tom Currigan. At a hearing in court, the mayor swore under oath that he had spent only seventy-five dollars on his campaign (Corky, by the way, spent twenty-three dollars). But the Crusade showed that Currigan and his machine had spent well over one hundred thousand. Representatives of a billboard company, TV and radio stations, and other businesses testified, or else their records were brought into court by force of a subpoena. All this showed that the businesses were either directly paid by the mayor or expected to be paid in the form of contracts and political favors.

The courts never decided in favor of either side. But the Crusade had done what it set out to do: expose the political machinery of the city for what it was. It had brought the mayor, the city, and county of Denver to answer for their actions. A "bunch of Mexicans" had shaken up the smug power structure. The Crusade had taken on a powerful newspaper, then a powerful official, and exposed the truth about both.

The city welfare department soon became another

area of Crusade activity. Poor Raza were left out in the street, desperate for low-cost homes, while project houses sat vacant because those who needed them didn't have a deposit and the first month's rent. The Crusaders helped people to find homes and to move, but soon realized that they could not handle the thousands of cases that existed. They were actually doing free what the welfare department rightfully should have been doing. So the Crusade began working on the basis of test cases. A Crusader would go to the welfare office with a family that had been denied its welfare rights, and see to it that the office did what it should have done in the first place. Slowly but surely, the welfare office was forced to improve some of its policies.

In those early years, the Crusade also began to reveal many of the injustices in the so-called legal system. Corky's past experience in the bail and bond business gave him useful background for this struggle, and the Crusade was soon confronting the racist courts of Denver.

Many people came to the Crusade with reports of family or friends having been brutalized on the street or in jail. Crusaders investigated, using police records and court records which are public information that anyone has the right to see. The Crusaders would check on the time an incident took place, get the names of the police involved, collect eyewitness accounts and then write up a full report exposing all the facts—including the contradictions between what the police said and what the people said. These reports were put together for a Chicano police review board established by the Crusade, and were also presented to the mayor, the police chief, and other officials. Although the Establishment did not often take action on the Crusade's accusations of brutality, they never disproved them either.

Through the efforts of the Crusade, an official charge of murder was brought against a police officer who had killed a seventeen-year-old youth named Louis Pinedo in July 1967. Police claimed the youth had injured the cop with a knife (a one-half inch wound in the upper arm) and so the officer shot in self-defense. A Crusade investigator, after a thorough investigation of the incident and search of medical records as well as an interview with the coroner, said he proved beyond a doubt that Louis had been shot in the back. The policeman's alibi of being attacked did not agree with the statements of eyewitnesses whom the Crusade found. The officer was charged with murder by the state but the case didn't even go to the jury; it was dismissed by the judge. From the Crusade's point of view, the trial turned out to be a mockery of justice in which another public servant turned killer received the blessings of a decadent society.

In another case, a Raza man aged sixty-seven had been hospitalized with broken ribs, a broken arm, and head cuts after a beating in jail. His family came to the Crusade and described the case. Before the arrest, he had been in good physical condition, they said. Photos were taken of the man in the hospital, hospital records were checked, jail inmates were interviewed—all of which confirmed that he had been beaten. This case and many others like it soon filled the files of the Crusade. They help to explain the statement of one Crusader: "And they ask us why we are militant, why we are angry! It's because we are no longer blind, and in our farsightedness we have developed a protective love for our people, a love for justice."

The Crusade also began to fight the racist school system of Denver. Corky Gonzales, backed by cheers from youths and adults, took over the speaker's stand at a Board of Education meeting in late 1968 to present Chicano demands. They included the teaching of Raza history, culture, language, and contribution to the nation; bilingual teaching, free education for Chicanos from preschool through college as a form of compensation for the psychological destruction of our people in the past; neighborhood school boards, and so forth. Corky also told the board that it could not represent Chicanos: "There is not one of you who lives in our barrios," he said, "there is not one of you who looks like us."

The Crusade did not limit its activities to Denver. In 1968, a strike began of workers—mostly Chicana women—at the Weld County ranch of the largest carnation grower in Colorado. Ricardo Romero of the Crusade and others organized several demonstrations to support the strikers. The strike lasted more than seven months and became very bitter. According to eyewitness reports in *El Gallo* newspaper, once a scab worker drove into the picketers, running down the fourteen-year-old daughter of Corky Gonzales. Twelve patrol cars of police came in, and also a goon squad of deputized men on horseback—looking a lot like Texas Rangers. The women workers were badly tear-gassed.

The strike was called off because of the police repression.

Outside the state, the Crusade showed its support for the land struggle in New Mexico by making several trips there in 1967 and again in 1968. Corky Gonzales joined the Alianza protest march in Albuquerque just before the 1967 "courthouse raid" and returned with a caravan of Crusaders who went to Santa Fe and talked with the governor on behalf of Reies. Corky and his people also went to Washington, D.C., for the Poor People's Campaign of 1968.

By that time, people were coming to the Crusade for help from all parts of Denver—all parts of the country. The Crusade's headquarters, a converted apartment with five bedrooms and a kitchen, had become an oasis for the tired, hungry, and thirsty. No one was turned away and many spent the night there. César Chávez's boycott organizers came here, as did hundreds of other people.

Somehow everyone was helped, yet the Crusade itself remained self-supporting and non-profit. Workers were volunteers—as many still are today. From time to time, a drive would be made to raise urgently needed funds but the Crusade never depended on the power structure for survival. It always followed one very simple but important principle: the secret of helping our people when they are in need is to be one of them, to suffer with them.

The time came when the Crusade had to move to a larger building, but it still followed this principle. For its new home, it bought a huge building that had for-

merly been a church. The building was bought with
donations, loans, and pledges from the community—
"no government money, no grants, no rich angels, no
hypocrisy, no begging, no handouts," as Corky said.

On September 13–15, 1969, the Crusade's new center formally opened. The date was chosen in honor of
Mexico's September 16 Independence Day, and the
center opened in a strong spirit of *Mexicanismo, Chicanismo.* There was singing by the Los Niños de la
Cruzada, a choir of sixty children from five to thirteen
years of age, performances of Mexican folk dancing; a
mass with mariachi music, in which the priest dedicated the mass to justice and men of justice—like
Zapata, Villa, Fidel Castro, Che Guevara.

The new center had a five-hundred-seat auditorium
for plays, theater, and meetings; a huge ballroom for
dances; a Mexican gift shop and art exhibit; a dance
instruction hall, a gym, nursery, a library of books and
one for tapes, lounges, classrooms, offices. Young Chicanitos were already learning to box at the new center,
to encourage physical fitness. There were plans to hold
workshops to develop organizers and speakers—called
Fishermen. These Fishermen's meetings have become
a very important part of the Crusade's work and philosophy, and are still held weekly.

At Christmas time that year, the Crusade held Las
Posadas—the traditional Mexican pilgrimage in which
our people act out the search of Joseph and Mary for
shelter before the Christ child was born. Homes, yards,
and sometimes the streets are lit with *luminarias,*
covered candles, to guide the pilgrims. Nine nights

in a row, they go to different homes asking for shelter with a certain song. The host answers with a song, then lets them in and a fiesta follows with tamales and other delicious foods. For the children, the highlight of the night's events comes with the breaking of the piñatas: huge animals, usually made out of papier-mâché and stuffed with goodies. The piñata is hung up high and the children, blindfolded, strike at it with sticks until it breaks and the presents fall out.

Chicanos in Denver and everywhere were very proud of the new Crusade building with its tremendous facilities. But from the beginning, it has always been much more than a building. It is a unique cultural center for La Raza, a place where our new spirit can come to full flower. It is not just a building, it is a movement in itself. Above all, it is people: a segment of La Familia de La Raza.

The Crusade does not only organize individuals; it organizes families. This is another way of returning to our roots, to our tribal or communal origins. It is another blow against the corruption of life by gringo values—a corruption which has produced the "generation gap" as well as a cultural gap. Of course, different age groups have different interests. But at the Crusade they have a basic unity of purpose in life: to live selflessly for the good of our people.

At the Crusade, decisions are made by consensus—not by parliamentary procedure. Meetings are like big family gatherings with people coming together to present a united front on an issue. Another example of the spirit of unity is the Chicano clap. When we clap

Chicano style, the whole audience begins in a slow, steady rhythm and then claps faster and faster until there is a tremendous, final burst of applause. Clapping this way feels communal, like one body of people united in showing their enthusiasm. It is also exciting and full of emotion. The Crusade was one of the first places where our people clapped Chicano style; today, the Chicano clap is heard all over the country.

All these ideas did not come at once at the Crusade. They developed over the years and they will continue to develop. Many people helped to develop them, but there can be no doubt about the importance of Corky Gonzales as the leader in this process. In looking for his own roots, he looked on behalf of all La Raza. In his personal pilgrimage to find himself, he searched for all of us. And what he found, he shared with everyone.

Corky did this in actions and also in words. His poem *I Am Joaquín—Yo Soy Joaquín*, published in 1967, is considered the finest Chicano epic poem to date. He also has many other poems yet to be published. His play *The Revolutionist*, one of several he has written, became well-known in 1966 after thirty-five performances in various Denver churches. The play moved every Chicano who saw it and enlightened many Anglos about their society, for it told *our* story— it grew out of our lives and history. Both the play and *I Am Joaquín* (a fine film has been made of that poem) became ways of waking up our people everywhere.

Ever since the formation of the Crusade, Corky has devoted all his life, his time, his energy to La Causa.

His wife, Geraldine Romero Gonzales, and their eight children do the same—performing dances, teaching classes, picketing, cooking, cleaning, organizing, leading workshops, working with other groups.

Corky represents many different things to different people. To many friends and co-workers, he is "El Jefe"—the name used for chiefs and leaders throughout our history. By tradition this is a term used to honor a leader who will not ask his people to do something he would not do himself. We speak of "El Jefe" Pancho Villa, and "El Jefe" Emiliano Zapata. Like them, Corky is a *jefe* not because he aspired to be a leader but because he *is*. He accepted a responsibility assigned to him by people who had found good reason to respect and love him. He accepted leadership without fear for self or thought of personal consequence.

Corky Gonzales is like a mirror. A reflection that makes you face up to yourself. Some people may look in that mirror and like what they see; others may not. But he forces people to look, evaluate, and recognize the truth. One cannot avoid issues with Corky present. He compels people to confront themselves and society, to recognize a responsibility to help make the revolution. And once a person has accepted that responsibility, the person is never the same again. Pride has replaced fear and a freedom has been won that nobody can take away.

This is the legacy of all true leaders. This is the legacy that has been disclosed to the Mestizo by the leadership of Raza in the Southwest. This legacy was always ours for the asking, ours for the taking. It is our strength—the strength described by Corky in *I Am Joaquín*:

I am the masses of my people and
I refuse to be absorbed.
        I am Joaquín
  The odds are great
  But my spirit is strong
        My faith unbreakable
        My blood is pure
I am Aztec Prince and Christian Christ
        I SHALL ENDURE!
        I WILL ENDURE!

For many years, Corky Gonzales had dreamed of a meeting that would bring together Chicano youth from all over the country for an exchange of ideas and the building of unity. In the spring of 1969 the dream was going to come true. The word went out that the first National Chicano Youth Conference would be held from March 27 to 31 at the Crusade for Justice's new center in Denver. As the date approached, it seemed as though all roads led to Denver for Raza throughout the country.

A few days before the meeting was scheduled to begin, a different kind of Chicano youth event took place in Denver. Students at West High School had complained about the racist attitude of one of the Anglo teachers. They demanded that the teacher be fired, but the school administration and school board refused to fire or transfer him. Some of the students came to a weekly Fishermen's meeting at the Crusade to ask help in planning a walk-out. They said that perhaps fifty to seventy-five students would walk out. But the next morning, hundreds joined in the protest.

Police moved violently against the students and supporters, swinging their clubs and shooting their Mace. Corky Gonzales was nabbed by five policemen and Maced, then charged with resisting arrest and assaulting an officer. Over twenty people were arrested and jailed. Police planned to hold them seventy-two hours for "investigation," but soon changed their minds.

In the jail, the people arrested and other inmates were shouting "Viva La Raza" and "We want Corky" so loudly that they could be heard more than a block away. Then an angry crowd marched on the police building, stopping traffic and setting up a picket line. Police quickly agreed to release Corky, but he refused to go until all the other arrested persons were bailed out. Money for this had been collected from over six hundred people at a community meeting that night. The police finally agreed and everyone was released. (Months later, Corky was acquitted of the charges against him in an exciting trial where the defense showed movies proving that it was the police who had rioted—not the people.)

The next day, March 21, a crowd of close to fifteen hundred gathered at West High School where school officials listened to student demands. The crowd marched to a park, where a rally was held, and then back to West High. People were still angry about the police riot the day before, and the windows of several police cars were broken. Out came the Mace again, and another battle of The People vs. The Police began. When it was over, many police cars and several officers had been put out of commission. Crusaders met with the governor and mayor, and the police were ordered out of the community. The students' boycott of West High ended only after the school agreed not to punish any of those who had walked out, and promised to meet the demands for change.

The National Chicano Youth Conference opened at the Crusade building a few days later in an atmosphere of confusion and excitement. More than fifteen hundred youth came from all over the country, representing over one hundred organizations. Both authors of this book were also present. Because so many Crusade people had been arrested, the conference was not tightly planned—which in the end worked out for the best. The youth had to create their own discussion groups and workshops, develop their own topics. And they did.

Everywhere that you walked in the Crusade building, there were young people discussing politics, art, newspapers, theater, writing, and many other topics. When the people were not in different workshops, they were gathered together in the large auditorium to see Chicano theater or listen to readings of Chicano poetry, Chicano music, and Chicanos expressing their ideas. The theme song of the conference became "Bella Ciao," an Italian song rewritten by Che Guevara. The whole gathering was not so much a conference as a fiesta to celebrate the new spirit of Chicanismo. Our once secret whisper of "We are proud to be brown, we are beautiful," grew into a grito—a roar—that rocked the Crusade building and would one day rock the nation.

At the end of the meeting, a historic idea and document was presented: El Plan Espiritual de Aztlán—the Spiritual Plan of Aztlán. Its introduction is a new declaration of independence:

"Brotherhood unites us, and love for our brothers makes us a people whose time has come and who struggles against the foreigner 'Gabacho' who exploits our riches and destroys our culture. With our heart in our hands and our hand in the soil, we declare the independence of our Mestizo Nation. We are a bronze people with a bronze culture. Before the world, before all of North America, before all our brothers in the Bronze continent, we are a nation, we are a Union of free pueblos, WE ARE AZTLÁN. March 1969.

When many of us first saw the plan, we had not heard of Aztlán and we ran back to our books to learn the meaning of this word. What we found was a mystery. Historians say that Aztlán was the land from which the Aztecs began the long wandering that finally led them to Mexico City. According to some, this land was located in the northwestern part of Mexico—today, the Southwest of the United States. Others say that Aztlán may well have been "the place of the reeds," an ancient marsh—now desert—near Kanab, Utah. And according to still others, the word "Aztlán" in the Náhuatl language simply means *el lugar mas allá*—"the place beyond." This of course could mean almost any place and that is very appropriate to our new concept of Aztlán. It means that Aztlán may be a myth or it may be a real place, but always it stands for the idea of a homeland, of freedom from that which we are not, of reclaiming what we are.

At the second annual National Chicano Youth Conference the plan was discussed further and ratified. This meeting, also organized by the Crusade for Justice, saw over thirty-two hundred youth from all over the nation gather in Denver. That meant thirty-two hundred people to house, feed, and transport around the city. Plans were made months in advance and hundreds of people helped.

For five days—from March 25 to 29, 1970—our people met and spoke of our experiences in many parts of the nation. We shared ideas on how to turn talk into action, how to create a program that would work and that we could live every day. In this spirit, El Plan was adopted. Its basic goals are to build Chicano strength and unity and to win CHICANO CONTROL OF CHICANO COMMUNITIES. The following guidelines were set up:

POLITICAL ORGANIZATION: El Plan announced the birth of the nation of Aztlán. The congress of the nation of Aztlán would be its governing body—not a Congress like the one in Washington, D.C., but a congress like the tribal councils of our Indio ancestors. El Plan also called for the creation of an independent political party, called La Raza Unida, with the plan as its basic platform. (We will talk more about this new party in the next chapter.)

ECONOMIC CONTROL: El Plan recognized that we must be economically free. We must drive the exploiter out of our communities and build an economic base for our people. We must develop our talents, our labor, our own resources to this end. A chain of co-operatives should be established for the purchase and exchange of goods. We must work co-operatively, not in the spirit of materialism, and educate our people against becoming consumer slaves.

Land banks should be set up for the purpose of holding land by and for Chicanos. We must make every effort to see that our people do not continue to lose land. All land shall be held retroactive to the native Indian, and the land question shall not be viewed with the Chicano as the new oppressor but in the knowledge that the Indian and the mestizo have the same oppressor. The conference called for the homeland of Aztlán to be in southern Colorado and northern New Mexico, where 54 per cent of the land is now controlled by the U. S. Forest Service, and no one would be displaced if it were taken over for use by our people. This area is already heavily populated by Raza.

OTHER KINDS OF COMMUNITY CONTROL: We will move to take absolute control of all existing institutions in our communities, including the church, the so-called "anti-poverty programs," and community services like parks, swimming pools, recreation centers. At the same time, we will try to develop our own services and centers wherever possible.

The POLICE in our communities must also be controlled by us. Those who serve as police must live among us and be responsible to us. The people of the community will decide what is a delinquent act and what is a revolutionary act performed in defense of the people. For example, since the police are not interested in ridding our neighborhoods of the real sources of drugs,

our defense units will have to do this. We will defend
Raza communities ourselves whenever necessary.

In the area of EDUCATION, we know that the present
school system has played a big role in teaching us to
see ourselves through racist eyes and thus wiping us
out as a people. So we must bring out the truth
about our people, develop the creativity of our people,
and bring the "drop-outs" into the colleges and universities.

We will work to take community control of the
existing schools so that they will serve our people, and
at the same time establish our own Chicano school
system. We will write our own books and our own
histories. We will demand compensation from the Catholic Church for the psychological and educational genocide inflicted on our people.

THE ARTS: Art and writing will be an expression of
Aztlán—of who we were, who we are, what we feel.
Art is seen as a weapon to strengthen the spirit and
unity of La Raza. The suppressed creative powers of
Raza will be released. The artists of Aztlán will serve
La Raza and humanity first, and themselves last. Work
will be shown for and to our people, not as com-
modities for tourists or for exhibit in gringo galleries.
It will bring the message of liberation to our people,
it will bring awareness of our history and struggle.

The conference also drew up important ideas about
the woman of Aztlán, which we will talk about in
another chapter. It adopted resolutions against the war
in Indochina. Support for all political prisoners in
Aztlán was declared, and our people took the position
that ALL Chicanos in prison are in fact political pris-

oners because they were arrested, tried, and sentenced under a racist system.

The political prisoners of Mexico and all other nations of Las Americas were also supported. The conference protested the use of our tax dollars to support dictators in Latin America, and demanded U.S. withdrawal of military missions, troops, and other aid to those dictators.

These were the basic guidelines set up for the nation of Aztlán. Everyone understood that the plan would be applied differently in different areas, according to local circumstances. El Plan is not meant to be a rigid blueprint with every line drawn in. It is alive, growing, and changing all the time. At the third National Chicano Youth Conference in Denver, more plans were made for the building of Aztlán. These included setting up a national chicano welfare rights organization; the decision to provide legal advice to draft-age youth and support to draft resisters; and plans to step up the war on drugs in our communities.

Since the time that El Plan first appeared, people have raised several basic questions about it. First, they ask if El Plan means that we want to be returned to the nation of Mexico today. The answer to this question is no; we are a new nation and want to be recognized as such. But our awareness of Mexico gives us spiritual strength. The Mexicano in us has been ridiculed, portrayed as inferior and foreign. This we now reject. To be Mexicano is to be mestizo.

Other people ask, what about the relation of Indian and Chicano under El Plan de Aztlán? The relationship between our two peoples under the plan has yet to be discussed in full, but we do not see any great problems in this area. Chicanos recognize that the Indian is the original inhabitant, and has the oldest claims to the land. The cultural heritage of the Southwest is based on the Mexican and Indian heritages. Our peoples have mixed a great deal and we are not far apart in culture and values—we recognize our alikeness and know we are both far from the white society.

Some ask, what of the Chicanos who do not live in the Southwest—can they belong to Aztlán? The Raza can be all over the world, they may live wherever they choose, but they will always know that home is where the spirit is. Even if they do not live here, they can always relate to Aztlán; they can live in the spirit of Aztlán wherever they may be. And Aztlán waits for them, if and when they choose to come home in body as well as spirit. Although the homeland of Aztlán is in the Southwest, the spirit of our people has no borders.

Some people say they fear Aztlán means armed revolution, violence, bloodshed, blind destruction. El Plan is a very constructive program and the whole idea of it is to begin *building*—not destroying, which seems to be the goal of gringo society. As for violence, the smell of blood on this land is still fresh. There has been a continual flood of our blood over the Southwest. The gringo took the Southwest by bloody force and keeps his power here by force. It is his violence that creates fear, not ours.

Some people say that Aztlán means separatism—that we secede from the United States. In a sense, this is true. We are a nation within the belly of the monster, but we are now refusing to raise and feed our children to the monster. Separation from the majority society means the end of separation among ourselves. It means that our brothers and sisters who "made it" are coming back to the people, coming home to the service of La Raza. Nothing is more important than this: winning Chicanos away from the materialist, competitive gringo society and bringing them home to themselves. For years a success symbol was somebody who had managed to get out of the barrio. Today we are creating a different kind of "success symbol": the Chicano who goes back to the barrio and serves the people.

There are those among us who will remain interested only in themselves, in competing, in material goods, and we will not be able to change them. But Chicanos still believe that we can build upon El Plan. Already we have begun to feel freedom of the mind and the body. Already we have begun to love ourselves again—not as an "I" but as "we," a people.

The endurance of Raza cannot come to an end so long as the promise of Aztlán exists. It is the next, natural step in the evolution of the corn people of Las Americas. El Plan de Aztlán says: the conquest of the Southwest has failed because an insane, sick society has not been able to impose its way of life on us. El Plan is a plan of survival, a plan of life, a plan of freedom.

How has El Plan de Aztlán been put into effect? One of the best examples is in education, as applied in Denver. First of all, the West High School "blow-out" of 1969 brought about some important changes in the existing school system. Fifty new Raza teachers and six administrators were placed in the schools; for the first time in the history of Denver, there was a Chicano principal in the school system. But Crusade people always knew that this wasn't enough; that we needed our own schools, schools that would be controlled by the community.

In 1970, our own Chicano school system was born. The Crusade had been holding liberation summer classes for several years (that summer, 325 pupils attended). Then, at the September 16 celebration, Corky Gonzales announced before a crowd of ten thousand Raza that a year-round Chicano school would open during the next month. It would cover the years from kindergarten through college, and it was accredited. The school would be named Tlatelolco, after the famous town of ancient Mexico and the present-day plaza in Mexico City (also called Plaza de las Tres Culturas), where one thousand innocent citizens became martyrs of justice when they were massacred by government forces in 1968.

The new school, housed in the Crusade building, is a bilingual, bicultural school and unlike any other school in the country today. Its whole purpose is, in Corky's words, to offer "education that opens your eyes, not washes your brain." The first seven years of the school represent the seven cultures of Mexico. Instead of passing from one *grade* to the next, children move from one *tribe* to another and learn the culture of that tribe.

The teachers not only teach the students but also

learn from them. This is one of the most important principles of the Crusade school, and one of the things that makes it very different from the regular school system. Under this principle, everybody is both a teacher and a student—and the teacher isn't there for the money or professional status, but out of love for La Raza and especially the youth.

That first year, one of the best loved teachers was Ricardo Romero. Ricardo is the toughest of men, and the most gentle. He knows his history by memory, inside and out, and he also takes his classes on field trips where they can relate what they learn from him to the real situation—today for example, a trip to a courthouse where they see with their own eyes how the U.S. legal system operates. Ricardo, by the way, did not go beyond the sixth grade of school. Other classes went to visit Raza businesses, to see other schools so they could compare, to look at the rich section of town and learn what causes the differences in the public schools. In one trip, the class visited the welfare office and learned what a person goes through when applying for welfare.

That first year, the Tlatelolco school had 130 students at all levels. The next year it took twice as many, and there are still hundreds on the waiting list. As Corky Gonzales stated in an interview published in the Chicano newspaper *La Voz del Pueblo*: "Tlatelolco is a model for schools across the country. We're getting people from all over the country now, coming to see how we're doing it . . . The schools want to send what they consider problem kids to us . . . We feel that in-

dependent schools for Chicanos will be starting to develop all over the country."

To visit Tlatelolco and see the faces of the children
is to know that this school is giving a real education.
Their faces tell us that these young people are growing
in knowledge, free to express that growth, and happy in
the discovery and development of what they are.
Tlatelolco is meeting the real educational needs of our
people, and only we ourselves can do that. No one else
can do it for us.

One of the best examples of what will be coming out
of the Chicano school system is the Ballet Chicano de
Aztlán. At one time, Mexican folk dancing was something that only a select few could learn because you had
to pay for lessons, and more Anglos were studying it
than Chicanos. Then the Crusade sent fourteen young
people to Mexico City where they spent six weeks of
dedicated and concentrated study. When they returned,
they taught all the young people—down to the age of
three—how to dance. Out of this learning and teaching
came the Ballet Chicano, under the direction of Enrique Montoya, which gave its first performance on
September 16, 1970. Since then, the ballet has performed at many schools and colleges.

One of the most popular dances of the Ballet Chicano is the dance of Adelita. This famous figure of the
Mexican Revolution is represented by twenty girls in
modern dress, wearing black and red, with black boots
to the knee, their hair sleek, packs and rifles on their
backs. They move in a combination of dancing and
marching, often aiming the rifles in different directions.
The new Adelita is a good example of how the Cru-

sade school draws upon our heritage and adapts it to to-day's struggle. There is no separation of "the arts" from the revolution.

That night, a birthday party was taking place at one of the apartments in a building next door to the Cru-sade, where Tlatelolco teachers—including Luis Mar-tinez—lived. Around midnight, a police car parked across the street. An unidentified youth went up to the car and asked the officers inside what they were doing there. They asked him for identification and put him in the car for "jaywalking" when he couldn't pro-duce it. Luis Martinez and several other Chicanos then went over to the car from the apartments. While they tried to convince the police to free the youth, the boy ran out of the car and escaped.

According to police, Officer Stephen Snyder then tried to get out of the car and Luis kicked the door against him. Then Luis ran to a parking lot with Snyder after him. According to Snyder, he was shot at three times, and then killed Luis. People were sniping at the police from the apartments. More police came, the apartments were searched, and many people were ar-rested. About 2:00 A.M. a huge explosion blew apart a section of the apartment building. Police said it was caused by dynamite inside. They also claimed to have found many guns there.

But our people did not believe this story. The Cru-sade stated that it had witnesses and evidence proving Luis was executed in cold blood. Corky Gonzales said Luis was shot in the back, not from the front as police claimed. According to Ernesto Vigil, Luis didn't run away. When last seen, he was walking backward, away from Snyder, without a gun and with his hands up, saying, "Leave me alone, man, I don't want no hassle." There is also the fact that Snyder was suspended three years earlier for hitting a sixteen year old whom he had arrested. Chicanos know how rarely an officer is suspended for brutality, so it must have been serious.

As for the explosion, Crusaders said it was caused by something fired at or thrown into the building by police. Why would Crusaders blow up their own building? And if there was sniper fire from the Chicanos, why hadn't officials mentioned bullet holes in any of the police cars? Crusaders also pointed out that the police had changed their story of what happened several times.

But even the police didn't deny that there was police brutality that night. The chief just wouldn't answer questions about it. Almost a hundred people were arrested in connection with the incident, including juveniles in their homes who said they were just watching TV. Many violations of civil rights were reported by Chicanos and many Crusaders said they were beaten for no reason.

> today,
> history and time
> as we have known it,
> came to an end.   today
>   is the birth of
>   a new history of man,
>   AZTLAN.

11

La Raza Unida: Our Own Kind of Politics

OF ALL THE TRUTHS exposed by Chicanos in the recent years, none is clearer than this: the two-party system in the United States is a total failure as far as serving the needs of our people. That is why many Raza see the creation of our own political party as a very important step in building Aztlán.

It took many of us a long time to realize the truth about the two-party system. For years, when we spoke out about the injustice against our people, we were told: "Get some representatives into the political system, let them speak for you, make your grievances known." So we tried it. Many Chicanos believed that the Republican Party was the party of the rich, the big business interests, while the Democratic Party cared about the working class and the poor—the Democrats would help us. Out of this belief, most Chicanos voted Democrat in one election after another. But nothing changed. Maybe a few of us got jobs, as a reward for bringing in votes, but that didn't help our people as a whole. We found that even if we joined the Democratic Party, we weren't really *in* it—except one day out of every four years. The rest of the time we were humiliated or ignored.

We also tried forming our own political organizations in the past. There was the Congreso de los Pueblos de Habla Español of the 1930s and 1940s; more recently, the Mexican-American Political Association (MAPA) in California, the Political Association of Spanish-speaking Organizations (PASO) in Texas, and others. But these failed to unite the people despite much good work of certain types. In any case, none of them was a political party—they were more like big civic clubs with middle-class aspirations.

We also tried getting some of our own people into office. Many of us worked hard, rounding up votes and holding enchilada suppers to raise campaign funds for Mr. Montoya against Mr. Smith, Mr. Pacheco against Mr. Jones, or whatever the names were. But once these people with Spanish names got in office, we discovered that they no longer related to us. They didn't even talk like us. They didn't care about our problems and if we complained about this, they said, "Well, I have to represent *all* of the people"—meaning the already controlling white majority. We began to call them *vendi-*

dos, sellouts; they were lost to us, they were Raza only in name and perhaps color of skin.

For Raza, a leader is someone who suffers with us, who lives among us as well as speaks for us, who shares our life style and our feelings. Those Spanish-surnamed politicians could not be leaders to us. They had been chosen *for* us by the gringo politicians. The majority society did not understand our objection to this; it thought we should be happy with these "success symbols." But we were not happy; we suffered as we saw our brothers and sisters "make it," then turn their backs on us. It hurt for us to see them begin their deceptions and insincerity, their smiles turning from real warmth to a "vote for me" twist of the mouth. It hurt to hear them say "I am one of you" when we knew that was no longer true. It hurt to see them building personal kingdoms of power while the poor they were supposed to represent struggled to get food stamps.

From this kind of bitter experience, we came to realize that it didn't matter if we elected a Montoya or a Pacheco—they all became puppets and parrots of the party they represented. We began to see that the Democrats and the Republicans were not different after all. Both were controlled by money and racism—the Business Establishment. They might sometimes act or sound different on certain kinds of issues but on important basic questions like the war in Indochina it didn't matter. Whether a Democrat or a Republican was President, the war went on. It went on because the real powers in this country wanted the war, and they control both parties.

More and more Chicanos began speaking out these

truths. "The two-party system is one animal with two heads eating out of the same trough," said Corky Gonzales in 1970. Still another Chicano, Frobén Lozada of California, described the process like this: "We don't get better deals from these two parties, we only get more promises. Promises that are never kept . . . The ruling class of this country uses the two parties to deceive us into believing that we have a choice. It is like two baseball teams disguised in different uniforms and pretending to be enemies, but all along being owned by the same man. In this ball park, we Chicanos are relegated to the role of water boys, with no voice, no decision-making power."

As for the long-time popularity of the Democratic Party among Chicanos, this was ending too. José Ángel Gutiérrez of Crystal City, Texas, has told us: "Everybody said, 'We can't get out of the Democratic Party. Why bite the hand that feeds you?' Well, you bite it because it feeds you slop."

Corky Gonzales had much to add to this, since he was once an organizer for the Democratic Party. "I learned the hard way that I was a stooge for the party, delivering my people's vote . . . when I asked for social change, when I demanded jobs for people, they winked and I could have gotten a liquor license under the table or a political job that was equipped with a gag to keep your mouth shut."

The party of La Raza Unida was born in Texas in 1969, in Colorado in 1970, in California and Arizona in 1971, in New Mexico in 1972, and now exists in many states. The party has been organized differently in different areas. During its early days, the idea was that in areas where Raza form the majority of the population, the partido would aim to win elections and actually put its people in office. In areas where Chicanos form a small minority, the partido would concentrate more on educating Raza and acting as a pressure group. But whatever the population, people agreed that La Raza Unida should not be concerned just with elections. It should work 365 days a year for the good of our people.

Of the areas where Chicanos are in the minority, Colorado was the first place that La Raza Unida party began to organize. The new party was announced during the second annual National Chicano Youth Conference of March 1970, held at the Crusade for Justice in Denver. Almost immediately, twenty Democratic Party officials sent a letter of resignation to the Democratic Party chairman. Their letter, dated March 29, said that the two-party system "has been a double-standard party system as far as the Chicano community is concerned. We are tired of your digging up of old políticos every election, and your telling us who our leaders are or will be . . ."

In May of that year, at the town of Pueblo, the party held its first state convention. It adopted a state platform that called for many important reforms in the areas of education, housing, job development, law enforcement, land ownership, farm labor—and also condemned the war in Southeast Asia while calling for a redistribution of the wealth in the United States. In many ways, the platform was like El Plan de Aztlán—but with lots of hard-hitting points that were specific to

Colorado. The convention made several nominations for state offices.

The Raza Unida candidates were not "políticos." They were mostly young and all had been activists. They had given years of service to the people—in the struggle for welfare rights, for education that truly serves Chicanos, and against the racism of employers like Coors (manufacturers of beer and other products). On the other hand, many of the people working on their campaigns had experience as political organizers. They had left one of the regular parties or had served on committees; they knew how politics works, and they would not be tricked or cheated.

None of the candidates won in the election that year, but this had not been their main goal. As Jorge García, candidate for lieutenant governor, said, they had two objectives: the main one was "to educate our people": informing the Chicano about the reasons for our oppression, how the system works, and how to overcome it. In other words, to expose the system and start people thinking about how to change it—a process that is often called *politicizing*. The second goal was to meet the state requirement of winning 10 per cent of the vote, so that Raza Unida candidates could automatically be put on the ballot in future years without going through a long, complicated process.

La Raza Unida of Colorado ran still more candidates in 1971, this time for city offices in Denver—mayor, the School Board, the City Council. They also did not win (Denver is 10 per cent Chicano), but again the goal was *to educate and unite* our people rather than to win seats. The Raza Unida candidates talked about issues and took positions that the regular party candidates wouldn't touch or dare to express. The Raza Unida offices did not just open for the election campaign and then close again afterward. The party saw itself as an ongoing thing, another aspect of the movement, not a separate force. In Pueblo, for example, the party kept its office open year round and it became a service agency like the Crusade—helping people with legal problems, food, clothing, housing.

Corky Gonzales himself did not run for office in the 1970 or 1971 elections because he felt that the youth should be emphasized. But he contributed his organizer's experience, and he always had good answers for the critics of La Raza Unida. To those who said, "We must work within the two-party system," Corky answered: "You can't walk into a house full of disease with a bottle of mercurochrome and cure the disease. You end up sick yourself." To those who said, "The best thing is to vote for the lesser of two evils," Corky answered: "There is no lesser of two evils. If four grains of arsenic will kill you, and eight grains of arsenic will kill, which is the lesser of two evils? You're dead either way . . . remember the lesser of two evils, Johnson vs. Goldwater? They equaled war either way."

In Oakland, California, the Raza Unida also made a very good showing from the viewpoint of votes. In the 1971 city elections, for example, Florencio Medina —a candidate for the Board of Education—won almost twenty-seven thousand or 33 per cent of the votes against the Anglo in that office, while Trinidad Lopez, running for the Board of Trustees, received twenty-five thousand or more than 25 per cent of the votes. Both men were advanced students at Merritt College.

La Raza Unida has continued to grow in northern and also southern California. In Los Angeles, Raul Ruiz—who had previously worked with *La Raza* magazine—ran for Congress. He lost, but his campaign showed that the Democratic Party could no longer be quite so sure of having the Chicano vote tucked into its hip pocket. Chicanos were thinking and organizing for themselves.

In Los Angeles, a labor committee of La Raza Unida was formed and has done intensive organizing with Chicano workers in the area. The labor committee's activities are an example of the partido's intention to be active 365 days a year—not just at election time. This committee also reflected the growing awareness of the importance of organizing the Chicano working class in the cities.

In areas where Chicanos are in the majority, La Raza Unida party has won some election victories. The best-known example of this is Cristal—Crystal City —in southwest Texas.

The town of Crystal (pronounced kree-STAHL) is located in the so-called Winter Garden, an area known for its production of vegetables and fruits all year round. Anglos like to call Crystal "the spinach capital of the world," and there is a statue of Popeye in front of City Hall. But most of the ten thousand people who live and work here don't look like Popeye— they are 85 per cent Raza, many of them migrant farmworkers. In the county where Crystal is located, family income runs about $1,750 a year. The average educational level is one of the worst in the country—2.3 grades of school—and there is a 71 per cent drop-out rate. In 1970, gringos owned *all* the farmland and 95 per cent of the small businesses in Crystal.

Ten years ago, Chicanos made a move to win a voice in Crystal, and they took over the City Council as well as other offices. But not long after, these men turned over their power to the Democratic Party. Nothing much changed except that there were brown faces in office instead of white ones.

Then came the student protests in the winter of 1969. They were organized mainly by MAYO, the Mexican-American Youth Organization, which had been founded two years earlier in San Antonio. MAYO became more and more militant as it ran into more and more gringo opposition to any kind of change. People accused MAYO of "racism in reverse" when they said that Chicanos should control areas that were 85 per cent Chicano in population. Gringos and *vendidos* called them "outside agitators," although almost all were from south Texas. The ordinary Chicano wasn't quite sure what to think of MAYO.

But in early 1969, a Chicano couple was beaten by a Texas law officer. MAYO organized a protest at the county courthouse. A number of Chicanos working for a community project under VISTA (Volunteers In Service To America, a federal government operation) were said to have taken part in the protest. So the governor of Texas ordered the VISTA project to be ended and it was. The Chicano workers, mostly people from the town of Del Rio, were fired. This made people really mad—and it united them. They realized that MAYO had been right all along.

On March 30, Palm Sunday, more than two thousand Chicanos from all over Texas gathered in Del Rio for a march to protest what the Texas officials had done. The events in Del Rio increased the popularity of MAYO and helped to create a mood of rebellion all over south Texas. In the spring of 1969, high school students in Crystal protested the fact that for years the high school cheerleaders in this 85 per cent Raza town had consisted of three Anglos and one Mexican-American. The cheerleader situation was a symbol of the gringo's control over Crystal, and young Chicanos were tired of it. The school superintendent thought he would solve the problem by deciding that each racial group could have three cheerleaders. But this didn't end the protests.

On December 9, 1969, the students showed that they had more to complain about than cheerleaders. There was a huge student walkout: about seventeen hundred Chicanos out of twenty-three hundred students from all grades up through high school began to boycott school. They demanded bilingual education, an end to the intelligence tests based on Anglo culture, no more racist teachers, better physical conditions in the schools. The boycott turned into a movement, as the adults got involved through the participation of their children. The Raza community of Crystal rose up to support the students as the struggle became much more than a school issue. Volunteer teachers came in to teach the boycotting students and a truckers' organization provided bus service to liberation classes. When student activists were fired from their jobs in local stores, the people would boycott those stores. The community started its own stores too. And students put a coat of brown paint on that statue of Popeye in front of City Hall.

The boycott lasted until the School Board gave in and met all but two demands. The Raza community had felt its muscle and the obvious next step was to organize on a permanent basis for political control. The leader in this drive was José Ángel Gutiérrez of MAYO, which had been the main force behind the school boycott. They called it the "Winter Garden Project."

Organizing the party was one of those hard, slow jobs like organizing the campesinos' union in California. The whole political system in Crystal was created to make it hard for migrant workers to participate. First of all, it costs hundreds of dollars just to file to run for office. Even more important, the primary elections take place in May—when migrant workers are always out in the fields working. One Chicano candidate lost in a past election by only three hundred votes just because the migrants weren't there. But La Raza Unida got down to work, and it worked hard.

As José Ángel later said, "We didn't just put buttons on people's chests. We created a new kind of feeling and real action. We used what is natural to our culture—the family—to organize. If one person is badly treated by the gringos, everybody is. By moving in this spirit, we can all move together against the ranchers and the *rinches* (Texas Rangers). There is no generation gap in Crystal City."

The results of all this work were that La Raza Unida party won total control of the City Council and majority control of the School Board in the Crystal elections of 1970 and 1971. The party also won important offices in two near-by towns.

Papel Chicano, a Chicano movement paper published in Houston, described the mood of the April 1971 elections in its own, young Raza way:

> Arriving in Cristal . . . we learned that a rally was being held to pick up enthusiasm for the election. We made it to the park and watched as the park became full with Raza. Raza of all ages were there— viejitos, mujeres, niños, young people. It was a gathering of la familia, al estilo raza unida. The music in the background was "La Raza Unida," "El Chicano" and rancheras. The speakers came on with straight barrio talk. They threw no bull quacha at la raza, just saying that if today la raza didn't move up—nobody would move up. The people were really digging it, as the speeches were all informal, without makeup and in Spanish . . . The next evening, the returns came in. La Raza Unida Party had won . . . our people are becoming consciously aware of the power of group dynamics—or, in barrio talk, "una mano no se lava sola [one hand cannot wash itself alone]."

The gringo reaction to the Raza Unida victories was predictable. Over thirty Anglo teachers and administrators resigned from the schools. There were big fights on the School Board, but a fourth Chicano already on the School Board voted with the Raza Unida element and so they won many changes including: complete bilingual, bicultural education from kindergarten through the third grade; free breakfast and lunch programs for all students; banning of the Anglo-oriented IQ tests and English proficiency tests; the use of textbooks that tell the truth about our people and history.

Also, it was decided that Army recruiters could no longer visit the school and that the high school would refuse to give the Draft Board any information about students—which reflected the anti-war feelings of Chicanos in Crystal (eleven have been killed in Vietnam). The high school officially boycotted lettuce that did not carry the United Farmworkers' union emblem. Students were not to be penalized for their political or moral beliefs. The school began ending discrimination on the basis of sex; for example, there is a program encouraging males who show interest to become nurses so as to help meet the serious shortage of nurses.

On the City Council, it was ruled that the state police and Texas Rangers—long famous for their racist "law and order" practices—no longer had authority in Crystal.

Raza Unida candidates have also won in other towns of the Winter Garden area. In 1972, it ran a candidate for governor of Texas. Ramsey Muñiz didn't win but he did get 8 per cent of the total vote—which is a triumph in Texas, where hatred for the Mexican is almost an institution. The partido had to fight all sorts of obstacles during the campaign, from a hostile press that didn't report its activities, to fraud and cheating at the voting booths.

There are twenty-six counties, mostly in southern Texas, where Chicanos form the majority and in theory La Raza Unida could win all of them. There are still more where Raza and Blacks could form a coalition for political power. But political control of Crystal or any other place is not enough. If Anglos still hold the economic power, they will continue to run the show. So La Raza Unida has been seeking ways to take economic control as well. A first step is through taxation, and a major target should be the big growers and packers in the Crystal area, like Del Monte.

Nowhere is Chicano power more needed than in southern Texas, where racism, brutality, and poverty have been giant problems ever since the gringo came. Along the Rio Grande, where the land was once rich and large towns flourished, Chicanos today are poorer than the poorest Blacks of Alabama or Mississippi. No plumbing or hot water is to be found in almost half of the homes in the Rio Grande Valley. In one county just south of Laredo, 75 per cent of the families had less than the official poverty income of three thousand dollars in 1960 and a third earned less than one thousand dollars. In Mercedes, a typical town, 90 per cent of Raza do not finish high school and the average level of education is through fifth grade. To the gringo, the Rio Grande Valley is known as "the Magic Valley." Our people call it "the Tragic Valley."

When Raza has attempted to change conditions, they have been brutally repressed. It is said that the murder of Mexicanos in this valley equaled or even outnumbered the lynching of Black people in the South during the late 1800s and early twentieth century. It was here, in Rio Grande City, that the Rangers crushed the huelga of melon pickers with their brutality and terror in 1967.

When the Rangers are not repressing Mexicanos in southern Texas, the police are happy to do the job. Almost every town has had its share of Chicanos killed by police in a way that the Raza community felt was unjustified. The names of only a few of the victims in recent years are: Mario Benavides, Jose Cedillo, Ignacio Lara, Jorge Licón, Rafael Menchaca López, Victor Nava, and Ernesto Nerios. The victims include a sixteen-year-old youth who died of internal injuries after being arrested for a supposed burglary; he told his girl friend before he died that police had kicked and beat him. Another sixteen-year-old was shot in the back of the head on suspicion of having broken into a store.

In none of these cases were the police in danger of losing their lives. The same is true of the blind, brutal killing of twenty-year-old Alfonso Flores in the town of Pharr on February 6, 1971. That day, a Raza crowd had been picketing against police brutality. At the end of the afternoon, police claim that they ordered the street cleared—but no one heard them. Dozens of Texas Rangers, highway patrolmen, police, and firemen then swept through the streets using tear gas, clubs, guns, and hoses. Alfonso Flores was standing on the street with his hands in his pockets, when a police bullet crashed into his head.

A cry of "Ya basta!" swept the Tragic Valley. Thousands of people came from all over Texas to protest the Flores killing and César Chávez spoke at a rally. More than 150 women, including the widow and mother of Alfonso, held a special March of Women through pouring rain for an hour to protest the low bail put on the officer who had been arrested after killing Flores. Women picketed the police station every day, for twelve hours a day; Raza in Pharr signed a petition to change the law so that a new election could be held for mayor. But the mayor's response to all this was to ignore the petition and carry on business as usual in the Tragic Valley. White racism in this area has not changed much from the days when Juan "Cheno" Cortina became so enraged that he raised an army with the cry of *"Maten los gringos!"*

At Mercedes, Texas—where 90 per cent of Raza do not finish high school—an important step has been taken toward independence from gringo educational control. In 1970, the first Chicano graduate school in the United States opened: the Colegio Jacinto Treviño (Centro Educativo Chicano), named after the hero of the early 1900s who defended his rights against the Texas Rangers. The new college grew out of a MAYO meeting held during the big school boycott in Crystal. Like the school started by the Crusade for Justice, it aimed to create an educational revolution. It is accredited through Antioch College.

The main purpose of the Jacinto Treviño school is to develop Chicano educators who will then teach among La Raza in a way that has meaning to our people. It began with fourteen students, who were to get their masters of arts degrees, then become the teachers for next year's class. Once the school had enough teachers, it would receive undergraduate students. Meanwhile, it set up a special program to tutor Chicanos who had not finished high school.

The colegio ran into a mountain of racist opposition from the beginning. It could not get funds or buildings because of that opposition, which often came from the Church. But the colegio persisted and by spring 1971, it finally had a home and was settled enough to hold a big open house for the public. *Ya Mero*, a Chicano movement newspaper of the Rio Grande Valley, reported that a thousand people attended.

The basic concept of Jacinto Treviño is that there must be a constant learning process—not just reading books with four walls around you and a desk. This process comes about through interpreting work experience. Students achieve both "academic" and "co-operative" education. Co-operative education can mean doing political work, traveling to another area and writing about it, any kind of community involvement. The school now has undergraduate students; during their four years at Jacinto Treviño, they must spend half of the time in co-operative education.

Jacinto Treviño puts much emphasis on co-operative instead of competitive education. This means many things, such as the new kind of student-teacher relationship. The student is not only a student; he is also a teacher—and the teacher not only teaches but also learns from the students. The Raza idea of familia is applied here. Every student has a *padrino* or *madrina* (godfather or godmother) from the teaching staff, who not only advises the student but may even represent the student against the administration.

When the colegio was set up, it was agreed that income earned by faculty or students would go into a common pool. This was one way the colegio aimed to survive in the spirit of Chicanismo. The governing bodies of the colegio were also set up to be truly democratic. Of course, carrying out these ideals is a long, hard process with many experiments and changes in method along the way.

While Raza in the Rio Grande Valley struggle against gringo colonization in its many forms, Chicanos in other parts of Texas face conditions that are not much better. Just a few days after the killing of Alfonso Flores, police in Dallas made a murderous attack on a Raza family. Not in uniform, they burst into the home of Tomás Rodriguez, his wife, and eight children. When Mr. Rodriguez moved to protect his family against these unknown invaders, police shot him down and also wounded his pregnant wife. Later they said it had been the "wrong apartment"; they were looking for someone else (three Anglo police had been killed recently). But still they charged Tomás Rodriguez with assault and kept him chained to his hospital bed.

Dallas police struck again and again, until an extremely shocking incident took place July 24, 1973. That night, at about 3:00 A.M., two officers went to a home in the Dallas barrio called "Little Mexico." They told the eighty-four-year-old grandfather who answered the door that they had come to pick up twelve-year-old Santos Rodriguez and his thirteen-year-old brother, David, who were in bed, for questioning. They were investigating an eight-dollar robbery of a vending machine at a gas station.

The grandfather didn't know the police needed a

warrant, which they did not have, and let the boys go. The police didn't even give them time to dress.

The boys were handcuffed and seated in the patrol car. According to David, Officer Darryl Cain began questioning Santos and trying to make him say that he was involved in the robbery. Cain—who was sitting behind Santos—pointed his gun at Santos' head. He began playing "Russian roulette" with Santos, according to David, to make Santos say he was involved. The first time Cain fired, the gun snapped on an empty chamber. The second time, the bullet blasted into Santos' head. Even Police Chief Frank Dyson called the killing "uncalled for, illegal, and unjustified."

Some two thousand Chicanos, Blacks, and whites marched in protest on City Hall. Their anger was so great that some of the crowd overturned police motorcycles and broke windows. Cain, who had killed a Black man three years before, was charged with murder —one of the few times this has been done when a cop killed a Chicano.

These are only two well-known cases; there are dozens of incidents every day in which Chicanos all over Texas are insulted, abused, falsely jailed, beaten—and almost nobody hears about it. The new party of La Raza Unida offers hope of ending some of this.

On September 1–4, 1972, the new party held its first national convention at El Paso, Texas. Over three thousand people attended from sixteen different states. One of the delegates, young Ricardo Falcón of Greeley, Colorado, never arrived. While driving to the convention, he was shot to death by the owner of a gas station in Orogrande, New Mexico—about seventy miles north of El Paso. Orogrande is a very small, all-white town in an area known for its history of racism against Mexicanos. Ricardo Falcón and a carload of others going to the convention stopped at the gas station when their car overheated. They cooled the engine with water from the gas station but when they asked the attendant to cool it a little more, he objected and said that water was too expensive. An argument began, with the attendant making racist remarks against Chicanos. The attendant shot Ricardo Falcón dead, claiming that Falcón had hit him. Falcón was unarmed. In a trial which took place in December 1972, Chicano witnesses testified that the attendant had pulled out his gun *before* Falcón hit him. But the attendant was found not guilty anyway, which came as no surprise to Chicanos.

At the convention itself, a strong platform was adopted that dealt with all issues facing Chicanos—from jobs to the war, police brutality to housing problems. José Ángel Gutiérrez was elected chairman of the Congreso, the committee that will co-ordinate La Raza Unida party on a national level. "Corky" Gonzales and Reies López Tijerina were among the many speakers, all of whom called for unity.

Of course it is easier to say "unity" than to create it. Also, it is very normal for new organizations and projects to go through many growing pains. Our people are at different levels of awareness. Some still tend to identify with the system or think that you can make basic changes by working with the system. That is just one example of the problems.

As a result, there has been conflict in La Raza Unida. Some elements have acted as though there is nothing wrong with using one of the two Establishment parties to get what they want. They look at Raza Unida as holding the "balance of power" and therefore being in a good position to wheel and deal. Other elements say this is exactly the kind of politics that Raza Unida is supposed to be fighting against. They say that Raza Unida must be a revolutionary party that has nothing to do with the two regular parties, the capitalist system, or oppressive foreign governments. (Some members even say that the goal of Raza Unida should be to create a socialist society.)

At a meeting in Denver in August 1973, that second position was strongly supported. The people adopted a resolution saying: "Because the people of Aztlán are a colonized, third world people, our struggle is part of the common struggle of third world and all progressive peoples against a common enemy—U.S. imperialism."

With all its different approaches, the partido still stands as an effort to organize our people. In one sense, Raza have always been organized. We have what might be called a "communal survival" tradition. This is one of our greatest strengths, and the greatest hero of the Chicanos is the Chicano people themselves. The campesino, the barrio vato, the small ranchero, the woman on welfare, students, and teachers—all are our heroes, the whole Familia. Our hope of victory lies in the people, and in our growing peoplehood.

12

Raza Sí, Guerra No!

IN LATE 1969, Manuel Gomez wrote the following letter to his Draft Board from Temescal, California:

> Today, December 8, 1969, I must refuse induction into the Armed Services of the United States. Please understand it is difficult for me to communicate my feelings through writing, but nevertheless I will try to let you see through my window.
>
> In my veins runs the blood of all the people of all the World. I am a son of La Raza, the universal children, and cannot be trained and ordered to kill my brother . . . For my people, I refuse to respect your induction papers.
>
> It is well known that Mexicans were among the first victims of your empire. The memory of the Mexican-American war is still an open wound in the souls

of my people. The Treaty of Guadalupe Hidalgo is a lie, similar to all the treaties signed with our Indian brothers. The war did not end. It has continued in the minds and the hearts of the people of the Southwest. Strife and bloodshed has never stopped between us. This society with its Texas Rangers and Green Berets has never allowed our people to live in peace. The blood is still moist on the land. Too many of my brothers have been killed fighting for a lie called "American freedom," both in our streets and in foreign lands.

My people have known nothing but racist tyranny and brutal oppression from this society. Your educational system has butchered our minds, strung our hearts, and poisoned our souls. You cut our tongue and castrated our culture, making us strangers in our own land. The sweat of my people watered the fields and their aching bones harvested your food . . .

In the short time that you've held the land, we have felt the pain of seeing beautiful lands turned into parking lots and freeways, of seeing the birds disappear, the fish die and the waters become undrinkable, seeing the sign "Private property" hung on a fence surrounding lands once held in common, and having our mountains become but vague shadows behind a veil of choking smog.

Your judges, armed with the cold sword called law held in the diseased arm of Justice, have frozen the life of my brothers in your barbaric prisons, scarring them deeply. A man steals to live and you call him a criminal and lock him up worse than an animal. A soldier massacres and pillages a village, and he's made a hero, awarded a medal. I believe that if it is wrong to kill within society, then it must also be wrong to kill outside of the society. I am of a peace-loving people.

I see rabid leaders of this land live in luxury and

comfort while they send my poor brothers to kill in a war no one wants or understands. The helpless and the innocent have lost on both sides, as has been the case in all wars. My ears hear the screams of the fatherless children, my heart hurts with the tears of mothers moaning for their sons, my soul shrinks from the knowledge of the unspeakable horrors of Song My and the rest to come. For the Vietnamese people, I refuse to accept your induction papers.

I cannot betray the blood of my brothers. We are all branches of the same tree, flowers of the same garden, waves of the same sea. The Vietnamese people are not my enemy, but brothers involved in the same struggle for justice against a common enemy. We are under the same sky. East and West are one.

My heart is dedicated to seeking justice and peace in this world. My eyes see a new sun, with a far more beautiful horizon, where all the trees can see the sky and share the same water from one river. I cannot fight for the enemy of the spirit of life. For my soul, I refuse to obey your induction orders. PEACE AND JUSTICE.

(Signed) Manuel Gomez

In Manuel's letter, we can see many of the reasons why young Chicanos have been raising their voices against the Indochina war with cries of Raza Sí, Guerra No—Raza Yes, War No. That cry has spread all over Aztlán in the last few years and today forms an important part of our liberation struggle.

One of the first Chicanos to resist the war and the draft was Ernesto Vigil of the Crusade for Justice. He not only refused to go in the Army but also led a demonstration at his induction center. So did Rosalio Muñoz, a former president of the student body at the University of California at Los Angeles. It was on

September 16, 1963—the anniversary of Mexican independence—that Rosalio declared: "Today, the day of independence for all Mexican peoples, I declare my independence of the Selective Service System." Some young Chicanos, such as Ernesto Vigil and Fred Aviles, have been imprisoned for their resistance.

Guy Gabaldon returned to President Nixon the Navy Cross awarded to him for having captured more prisoners singlehandedly (two thousand Japanese) during World War II than anyone in the military history of the United States. He did so because: "I no longer desire to have in my possession an award from your corrupt, immoral, decadent, and bigoted government."

Not only our youth but also parents have been speaking out. In San Jose, California, Army officials tried to present a medal and a U.S. flag to a Raza mother whose son had been killed in Vietnam. The mother threw the flag and the medal on the floor and cried, "Take your damn flag back, I want my son!"

A Raza woman in New Mexico, whose brother was killed in Vietnam and who also had a son there, wrote in a Chicano newspaper: "Our people are taught to hate the Vietnamese for all our boys killed over there. I have to admit I used to feel that way too. But I have come to realize that the blame is not really with the Vietnamese, so now I put the blame where it really belongs—on the U. S. Government. Our war is here, not overseas."

In the past, Chicanos have shed rivers of blood trying to prove that they are first-class citizens and human beings. The Armed Services took advantage of the young Chicano's machismo—his ideas of manhood—and tried to make him believe that he must kill for the Stars and Stripes to prove that he is "a real man." So Raza piled up mountains of medals for bravery in one war after another. The fighting in the Philippines during World War II, for example, was done mostly by Raza, and the men on the Bataan Death March were mostly Chicanos from New Mexico. But the Chicano of today is realizing that he doesn't need to prove his manhood to the United States; he only needs to stay home and serve his people.

The Armed Services were also a solution to the job problem, once. For poor Chicanos as for Blacks and Puerto Ricans, the Army was one of the few places where you could get three meals a day, clothes, and a roof over your head. What this really meant was choosing quick death on the battlefield instead of a slow death in the barrio. But the new Chicano will not accept the idea of dying abroad for a country that treats him like a second-class citizen at home.

The new spirit of resistance came after we took a long, hard look at some facts and figures about the war. A study made by a Chicano college professor showed us that Chicanos have had a higher death rate in Vietnam than all other groups of servicemen—in proportion to our population. In the five southwestern states, we represent 19 per cent of the casualties in all the Armed Services, but about 12 per cent of the official population count. In the Marine Corps, our share of the casualties was 23 per cent. Taking just one state, New Mexico, we have 44.6 per cent of the casualties.

Then we also noticed that something was strange about the economy. Out of every tax dollar, $.66 was being spent on the military and defense-related expenses. Only $.16 went to the Department of Health, Education and Welfare. Why was so much being spent on a faraway war, and so little on the needs of poor people? Who did this war benefit, anyway?

As we looked at the Vietnam war more closely, we also realized that the struggle of La Raza had much in common with the struggle of the Vietnamese people. In Mexico our people had to fight against the Spanish, the French, the British, and the U.S. invasions—much as the Vietnamese had fought for centuries against foreign occupation. The Vietnamese campesinos had a long, hard struggle for their land, just as our people had. And their land—their livelihood—may never recover from the chemical destruction carried out by the United States. All in all, it became clear that we have much more in common with the people of Vietnam than with those who send our young men to kill the Vietnamese.

We have also come to see the connection between the Vietnam war and U.S. foreign policy in Las Americas. On this continent, it is the governments of rich landlords and other big capitalists which the United States supports. This country helps them to oppress the people by providing U.S. military "aid" and loans. It does this because big U.S. companies have made investments in those countries and they want to keep the present governments in power so as to keep on getting big profits from those investments. Bolivia, Uruguay, Brazil, Argentina, and other countries—they are South Vietnam all over again. And those countries may someday become Vietnams.

This picture of U.S. imperialism has made our young people angry. As Rosalio Muñoz said, "Why must we, los Mexicanos, go fight wars to protect the selfish interests of our absentee landlords who stole our forefathers' land?"

In 1969, our people began to hold protests against the Vietnam war, called Chicano Moratoriums. These demonstrations have taken place all over Aztlán—in California, Colorado, Texas, Arizona, and other areas. One of the largest took place in Los Angeles on February 28, 1970, when four thousand people marched for two hours in a heavy rain. Men, women, and children marched with crosses bearing the names of Chicanos who died in the war.

Then it was decided to hold a national Chicano Moratorium—on August 29, 1970, in East Los Angeles. All over the country, Chicanos were making plans to go. Then, on July 16, the moratorium took a new turn.

That day, in an East Los Angeles barrio apartment, police killed two citizens of Mexico with a wild blast of shotgun fire. They had entered the building supposedly looking for a suspect. Beltrán and Guillermo Sánchez, two young cousins from Mexico, were living there and one of them heard some noise. He opened the door to see what was happening, looked out—then closed it. The police claim that the sound of the door closing was like a shot, and they began firing into the apartment. Besides killing the two men, they seriously wounded a third, and police bullets also ripped into the next apartment, almost killing the infant child of another Raza family. Afterward, the police admitted that it was "a tragic mistake." (The four police killers were later tried for violating the civil rights of the two Mexicanos—but not for killing them—and found innocent. At the mayor's request the legal defense expenses were paid with taxpayers' money.)

The community was deeply angered by these insane killings. Already, there had been six deaths in the city that year which the people believed to be police murders. Raul García, Gilbert Hernandez, Richard Hernandez, John Huerta, Sam Kasseroff, and Joe Montano had all died in jail. Police claimed they committed suicide but no one in the barrio believed that. Now, with the open murder of the Sánchez cousins, the people's suspicions turned to rage. The moratorium leaders announced: "The moratorium is not only against the war in Vietnam but against police brutality and against the total repression here at home."

August 29 came, and thousands of Raza from all over the nation marched for several miles to Laguna Park in Los Angeles. People sat on the grass, listening to music and talking, waiting for the program of speakers to begin. Then people in one corner of the park became aware of some disturbance. Suddenly there were five hundred police on the scene with full riot equipment, moving across the park in a "sweep operation." Without any warning, without asking people to leave, they began firing tear gas at all the men, women, and children.

The huge crowd began to run. One of the authors of this book was present and recalls how people desperately tried to escape the gas and clubs. Others resisted the police, throwing the tear-gas cannisters back at them or bottles or rocks. At one point, the police

broke and ran, only to regroup and charge again. On
the edges of the park, people were trying to squeeze
out between the parked buses and cars. Many of us
collapsed from the gas, which not only blinded but
also caused nausea. Hundreds of us took shelter in the
homes of people living around the park, who were
mostly Raza and long aware of police brutality.

Three Raza were killed that afternoon by police:
Ángel Díaz, Lyn Ward (a fifteen-year-old Chicano),
and Rubén Salazar. A well-known newsman from the
Los Angeles *Times* and television, Salazar was standing
quietly in a cafe talking with friends and drinking a
beer when police arrived at the doorway. One of them
fired a tear-gas cannister, about ten inches long and
shaped like a huge bullet, into the cafe. The doorway
was covered only by a cloth curtain, and the cannister
almost blew Salazar's head off. Police later admitted
that this projectile is only for use against "barricaded
criminals" and never in a crowd situation. The killing of
Lyn Ward and Ángel Díaz had no more excuse than
that of Salazar.

How did the whole thing start? No one has said
exactly what happened but some agents working for
the police have admitted that they were paid to provoke
trouble at the moratorium. The newspapers reported
at first that the trouble started when the owner of a
liquor store near the park called the police because his
store had been looted. But later the owner said he had
never called the police or been looted. And in any
case, why would 500 police show up within seconds
for the looting of one store? The community knew
the police had been ready beforehand, hoping for

trouble that would scare our people out of having moratoriums.

But their plan didn't work. Instead, peaceful Raza were horrified and angered as they watched the police with their cold faces, our so-called public servants, making war on innocent people. One man still speaks of how he trembled with anger when he saw a young Chicano from the Crusade for Justice struck in the face with a riot stick as he tried to lift up a child who had fallen on the pavement. The young man was believed to be lost for days, until his family finally located him in the hospital. He had head injuries and lost his sight in one eye.

The police also arrested almost two hundred persons that day. People were scattered and lost all over East Los Angeles, and Chicanos who were not hurt began driving around trying to help them. Among these was Corky Gonzales of the Crusade for Justice, and Al Gurule, La Raza Unida candidate for governor of Colorado. They were riding on a flatbed truck when the police stopped and arrested them for "robbery." (Police later changed that charge to another that was almost as silly. In 1972, Corky served twenty-eight days in jail after being convicted on the second charge.)

The anger of the people rose to a rage. That afternoon and evening, buildings went up in flames all over East Los Angeles. Most of them were banks, finance companies, and stores that had exploited the people for years. Young and old people alike threw stones, bottles, milk crates, whatever they could find, at passing police cars. At least one police car was set on fire. The sky was clouded with smoke all night as the long-suppressed rage of our Raza exploded. The war on the Vietnamese had come home.

In the months after bloody August 29, the police rioted again and again. On September 16, a huge crowd of Raza gathered to celebrate Mexican Independence Day and to remember the moratorium. As before, the police used a small disturbance as an excuse for attacking the people. But this time the people fought back in small scattered "guerrilla groups" and no lives were lost. Two months later, thirty police broke into the Chicano moratorium office with guns and clubs. Three teen-age Chicanos were badly beaten—and then charged with assault on an officer.

On January 31, 1971, eight hundred to a thousand Chicanos came to a rally to protest the brutality. By the time the day was over, the police had attacked again and another young man lay dead in the street while many were wounded. The victim: an Austrian student named Gustave Montag, who looked very Chicano with his dark hair and mustache.

By now much of the truth had come out about the killing of Rubén Salazar. The police had contradicted themselves and changed their story more than once. They claimed that there was a man with a gun reported to be inside the cafe where Salazar was killed. Witnesses in the cafe said no such man was there. The police kept trying to justify the killing but they could not wash away one fact: the "bullet" that killed Salazar was, according to police officials themselves, like a small cannon and never meant to be fired directly at human beings, never meant to be used in a riot control situation. This kind of "bullet" can go through a one-inch thick board at a distance of one hundred yards. It hit Salazar in the head, at a distance of about fifteen feet.

The Raza community also took note of the fact that Salazar had been preparing a series of articles about the Los Angeles police and investigating the six deaths in jail called "suicide." Before that, he had criticized the police killing of the Sánchez cousins. It was never proved, in the investigations that took place, whether Salazar was killed by accident or not. But the community has remained suspicious. According to the general manager of the TV station where Salazar worked, Rubén had been threatened by the police before his death. He had been told, the manager said, that they would get him if he continued to report on police abuses. He didn't stop and then he was killed. As for the deaths of Lyn Ward and Ángel Díaz, they were not even investigated—those two were not well-known reporters like Salazar.

The time had come for another pilgrimage of sorrow and protest, many Raza felt. Rosalio Muñoz of the Chicano Moratorium Committee and others organized a Marcha de la Reconquista, a march to reclaim the right of Chicanos and Mexicanos. People would walk seven hundred miles, from Calexico at the so-called border to Sacramento, the capital of California. They would march to protest against the war, police oppression, the welfare system, the continuing exploitation of el campesino, and the abuses of La Migra—the border patrol.

The long walk began on May 5, 1971—Cinco de Mayo, the anniversary of Mexico's victory over French imperialism. Exactly a week later, the Los Angeles police struck again. Unbelievable as it sounds, they came all the way from their home city to a small village near Coachella, along the line of the Marcha—and murdered a campesino. By mistake. Again.

Young Juanita García witnessed the murder of her father, Francisco. Her account of what happened was published in Mexico—but not in the Establishment press here. She said:

> It was almost 8 o'clock when we saw our father nearing our house in the pickup truck. Our younger sister and I went to greet him and at that very moment I noticed some shadows in the roadway. I thought they were dogs . . . My father got out of the truck and inside the house. Minutes later he came back out accompanied by my mother because they were going into town (to arrange for the christening of their new baby).
>
> He and she got into the pickup and the truck had just begun to move when I heard a shot. Then I heard another and another and another. There were many shots fired. The pickup came to a stop and the motor stopped.
>
> In desperation I ran to the truck but one of those individuals (which she thought earlier was the shadow of a dog) held me back. He held me by the collar and violently forced me back to the house.
>
> I wanted to put up some sort of resistance but was unable to. Then I heard my mother scream in terror as she got down from the pickup and was bathed in blood. The assassins went up to the truck and upon examining the body realized it was not the person they were after.
>
> They came back to where my mother and I were, and all they said is that they were sorry. But the next thing they did was to go into the house and they began to search.

The police, who were disguised as hippies when they killed Francisco García, said they had come investigating a big "marijuana smuggling ring" and thought García was a suspect. But, they admitted, he had no part in any "smuggling ring." It was just "a mistake."

It was out of deep anger and frustration caused by the kinds of injustice described in this chapter that thirty-six-year-old Ricardo Chávez Ortiz hijacked a plane on April 13, 1972. He demanded only to be given radio and television time—so that he could express the grievances of poor Raza to the nation. After the broadcast, Ricardo handed his unloaded pistol to the pilot and said, "Captain, forgive me. I never wanted to hurt anyone." Thousands of Raza rallied to his defense, but Chávez Ortiz was tried and sentenced to life imprisonment.

During his broadcast, Ricardo said: "These wars that have been fought have been a crime . . . because these people have gone to fight with others, and for what reason?" That is the question more and more Raza have been asking. As the Raza mother said, our war is here—not overseas. In the very act of protesting against the war, and in seeing how our protests were treated by the gringo system, we learned the truth of her words. Our enemy was never the Vietnamese, Cambodians, or Laotians, our enemy was and is right here.

13

Viva La Revolución!

ACROSS THE NATION, the cries ring out: "Viva mi Raza!" "Chicano Power!" "Huelga!" "Raza Sí, Guerra No!" Everywhere our people assert their new-found pride and their refusal to accept any longer the oppression of Raza. We hear those cries from small children and grandparents, men and women, and especially from the youth.

The youth is responding to the needs of La Raza in many ways. With fiery enthusiasm and energy, they have helped to organize our communities for action. Again and again, it has been the so-called legal system—the police and the courts—that forced the youth to organize for defense. We could almost say that the police, by their own abuses and brutality, have organized our people.

One of the first youth organizations—the Brown Berets—was born in Los Angeles, where over a million Chicanos make up the nation's biggest barrio. East Los Angeles has long been a Mexican stronghold and the scene of brutal gringo oppression. Much blood was shed in the takeover of California, and again in the "Zoot-Suit Riots" of 1943. Those riots strengthened our awareness of the need for self-defense. The 1940s became the pachuco era—the pachuco being the young man of the barrio who rejects the dominant society and will fight to affirm his identity. The pachuco tradition is very much alive today and we can see it in the pachuco language called Calo—a sort of code that is written on the walls of barrios in Los Angeles, Chicago, and other cities. The pachuco of today is called a *bato loco*—"crazy guy"—but he is the same person in spirit.

It was out of this history and these traditions that the Brown Berets came to be organized in Los Angeles. Their motto was: "To serve, observe, protect"—and this included defending the Raza community against attack by all means necessary, including arms.

The founder and prime minister of the Berets was David Sánchez. In 1966, David was named "outstanding high school student" by the mayor's Advisory Youth Council of Los Angeles. One of his projects was the Young Citizens for Community Action (later Young Chicanos for Community Action), which helped collect food for the striking Delano farmworkers. He and his friends also served the community in other ways that were far from "militant."

But when the young Chicanos decided to open a coffeehouse to provide recreation for teen-agers, the Los Angeles Sheriff's Department felt it was a threat. They didn't want Chicanos getting together that much. The police began to harass the group and the coffeehouse, and finally they beat David Sánchez.

That experience made the group become openly militant. In the fall of 1967, they changed the name of their group to the Brown Berets. Soon there were groups of Berets in many parts of California, and later as far away as Milwaukee and Detroit.

The basic goal of the Los Angeles Brown Berets, they said, was "to unite our people under the flag of independence. By independence we mean the right to self-determination, self-government, freedom, and land." Their program included demands for the return of stolen land, an end to the police occupation of Raza communities, an end to the robbery of our communities by businessmen, an end to the drafting of Chicanos, Chicano control of Chicano education, and housing fit for human beings. They also said that the border lands should be open to La Raza whether they were born north or south of "the fence."

The Los Angeles Brown Berets included both men and women. They began by setting up centers where citizens could bring their complaints of police brutality. They also published a newspaper, *La Causa*, which carried reports on police brutality. The Berets often provided a sense of security to individuals and families, and were often called on to provide security at public demonstrations by Raza.

The beret worn by these young Chicanos became a symbol of help to the community, and a symbol of militant Chicano youth everywhere. For local reasons, some groups call themselves the Black Berets while others are Brown Berets. But the color makes little difference to Chicanos; what counts is their service to the people. What counts is that the youth have started people's clinics, youth centers, anti-drug programs, and many other projects. Beret groups have provided free breakfast-for-children programs much as the Black Panthers and the Young Lords Party (of young Puerto Ricans) have done.

One of the most important targets of the youth groups has been the school system, which has never served the needs of our people. In Los Angeles, one fifth of the city's students are Raza and in 1967 there were seventy-six schools where Chicanos formed the majority of students. But the Anglo school officials never made any allowance for our culture and history. Chicanos in Los Angeles had the highest "dropout rate" of all racial groups. At Garfield High School, 90 per cent Chicano, over half the students did not finish the twelfth grade. To Raza, it was clear that those "dropouts" were really forced out.

In the spring of 1968, the students began pressing the Board of Education for bilingual education, the firing of racist teachers, more emphasis on the Mexican cultural heritage, better school buildings, and many other reforms. The board refused ALL changes. So in March, a school boycott began and soon thousands of students had walked out of five Los Angeles high schools. These protests came to be known as school "blow-outs." Several Black schools supported the Chicanos.

The Board of Education still refused to act on the students' demands. Instead, they had thirteen teachers arrested for supposedly leading the blow-outs. Dozens of barrio organizations as well as teachers' associations and Black groups supported the "East Los Angeles Thirteen," but still they were convicted. One of them, Sal Castro, was suspended from teaching.

Sal Castro was a popular young teacher and his suspension angered the Raza community. The people took over the meeting room of the Board of Education and occupied it for a week. They held meetings of the "Liberated Chicano Board of Education" and planned a new school system. The regular board finally took Sal Castro off suspension.

Two years later, none of the thirty-eight demands made in the blow-outs had been met, and students again boycotted the schools. The police came and beat eight students at Roosevelt High School, and arrested dozens of students as well as adults.

The Los Angeles blow-outs made the Brown Berets a target of police vengeance. Their minister of information was accused of conspiracy to start the blow-outs. Beret headquarters were fire-bombed more than once. Police planted a spy, an undercover agent, in the Berets. Then came the big frame-up at the Biltmore Hotel.

The Biltmore Hotel incident took place in April 1969, when Governor Ronald Reagan spoke at a conference of "Spanish-speaking" people—meaning Mexican-Americans from the Establishment. Several fires broke out at the hotel and Reagan's speech was interrupted by Chicanos protesting Reagan's racism with cries of "*Que viva La Raza!*" and the Chicano handclap. Fourteen people were arrested and charges later brought against six—who became known as the Biltmore Six. Two of these Chicanos were Brown Berets.

In grand jury hearings and two trials held after the incident, it was revealed that a police undercover agent planted in the Berets had helped to buy the flares used in the Biltmore fires and had stood guard while a Beret set one of the fires. The evidence indicated that the agent did not want to prevent the fires, as a policeman should, but instead wanted to help get the Berets arrested. This kind of action, of weakening an organization like the Berets by helping or inciting its members to carry out illegal actions for which they are arrested, has become a common tactic in the repression of our people. Thanks to the exposure of the agent in the Biltmore case, the jury acquitted four of the group and could not reach a verdict on the fifth.

The Los Angeles blow-outs drew much attention to the educational needs of Chicanos and many school protests followed. Denver, Colorado had its West High School blow-out in September 1969—which led to a police riot against the people. Crystal, Texas, had its big walk-out that same year and there have since been Chicano student protests from San Antonio to East Chicago, Indiana; from Albuquerque to Milwaukee, from San Jose, California, to the small towns of Alamosa and Rocky Ford, Colorado. In these demonstrations, the students have had much strong support from their parents.

The spirit of protest and Chicanismo has swept not only the high schools but also the colleges and universities. Many Chicano student organizations have been formed on campus to fight the racism that exists. This racism begins with the fact that so few Chicanos ever get a chance at college. In one county of California, for example, the population in 1968 was more than a third Chicano—but only thirty-five out of over eight thousand students at the state college in that area were Chicano. The racism is even worse when we look at the courses of study offered—which have not taught Raza's history and culture, or told the truth about U.S. history and culture.

Two of the best-known college student organizations have been MECHA (Movimiento Estudiantil Chicano de Aztlán) and UMAS (United Mexican-American Students), both born in California. As a result of efforts made by them and other Chicano groups, a large number of universities now have Chicano studies programs. These programs make college education have much more meaning for our people. There is also a growing number of Chicano students who get involved with problems beyond the campus like the farmworkers' struggle, welfare, food stamps, police, health, and other community issues. But there should be still more.

Students have also taken part in the struggle against racism as we see it in the mass media. Our people have filed lawsuits against TV stations, newspapers, and radio for discrimination at all levels. In many cases, the news media have been forced to hire Chicano reporters to present our side of an issue. We have also got rid of certain degrading commercials. Out of this struggle we have learned that it takes much energy to change these institutions and the mentality behind them.

Our struggles against racism in the existing schools and mass media still go on. But more and more Chicanos today believe that we must create *our own* schools, *our own* cultural centers and institutions, in order to overcome "the big brainwash." We must build our own cultural communities in our own nation of Aztlán.

Steps have been taken toward this goal by the schools in Denver and Mercedes, Texas, that we have already described, as well as others. Creating our own schools also became the goal of Chicanos Unidos para Justicia in Las Vegas, New Mexico. In the spring of 1973, the school board of East Las Vegas appointed a man named Rowland King from Arizona as superintendent. They did this although there was a Chicana candidate for the job who spoke Spanish (King didn't) and was from the area, and who also had higher educational qualifications. They did this although the students in East Las Vegas are 75 per cent Chicano. Junior high and high school students then walked out in protest. For over a month, they held marches and picketed the business places of school board members. King finally resigned.

A person with a Spanish surname was put in his place. But the students knew from previous experience that he would not make the big changes needed. They knew that it was necessary to fight King and expose the racism, but to have the right kind of schools they would have to set up their own. And this is what they began working to accomplish, by taking over an unused church building and starting the Escuela (School) José Antonio Martinez—after the rebellious Taos priest of the 1800s.

A Chicano school might not seem at first like a big thing, a big threat to the Establishment. But that is failing to understand the importance of young people's minds. Our enemies know how important they are. That was shown by what happened to the Escuela Tonantzin, a Chicano school opened in Santa Fe, New Mexico, in June 1973.

Named after a Mexican Indian goddess, the school aimed to teach our language and true culture. Four months after it opened about seventy-five police came one night and shot at people in the school. They said that someone there had shot and wounded an officer; the officer was trying to arrest a hit-and-run driver who had turned into the school driveway. Police claimed that people inside the school building fired at them, and that another officer received a slight wound. According to Chicano witnesses at the school that night, three Raza, including a nineteen-year-old girl named Linda Montoya, tried to come out holding up a white tee-shirt as a surrender sign. Police then opened fire on them and wounded the girl, who died three days later. Other Chicanos were also shot; many were arrested and most of them were beaten, according to Chicano witnesses.

When they had cleared out all the Chicanos, police went on a rampage in the school. They destroyed and scattered Chicano paintings, musical instruments, tapes, and even a clay sculpture made by the school children of a serpent—symbol of the god Quetzalcoatl. They broke furniture and ripped down curtains made for the classrooms by students. They took the school's flag, the flag of Aztlán, and defaced the Mexican flag. Everywhere you could see the results of their hatred for our people and for what Chicano schools try to do.

A few days after the September 3, 1973, events at the Tonantzin school, a Chicano school in Colorado suffered a similar attack. The Academia Ricardo Falcon, named after the young Chicano killed at a gas station in New Mexico while on his way to a Raza Unida convention, had also opened just a few months before. Police swarmed into the academia after reports that persons, possibly from the academia had fired shots at passing motorists—for no apparent reason. They claimed to have found explosives there and arrested six Chicanos, including Ricardo's widow, Priscilla, who helped to start the school. And again Chicanos in the movimiento said, "it was a set-up, to close down the school."

A vital cultural institution of Aztlán has been the Chicano Press Association. The CPA, as it is known, has included about fifty newspapers and ten magazines, published not only in the Southwest but also in such places as Wisconsin and Florida. Some of the papers are published by organizations while some are independent, but all work to give information and a viewpoint that we don't find in the regular mass media. The papers freely share articles, news stories, photos, poems, and drawings in the spirit of sharing that is part of Chicanismo.

Our Chicano press has served the people in important ways. It was two Chicanos from the Los Angeles newspaper *La Raza* who saw the police murder Rubén Salazar on August 29, 1970, at the moratorium—and took pictures to prove it. Chicano press workers are not career-minded professional journalists who have to please their bosses. They are devoted to La Causa and to breaking the control over people's minds by the regular mass media. They have taken their stand and risked their lives along with other movement Raza. Ernesto Vigil, former editor of the Denver newspaper *El Gallo*, was imprisoned for draft resistance while Antonio Cordova of the newspapers *El Grito del Norte* and *Venceremos* in New Mexico was murdered by police while writing against police brutality.

Some of the finest art in the history of America— the continent—is now coming from the Chicano. In poetry, painting, sculpture, music, dancing, and theater, our people are bursting with creativity. The spirit behind all this art has been described by Luis Valdéz, founder of El Teatro Campesino. Although he is talking about theater, his words explain the spirit of all new art:

> What is Chicano theater? It is theater as beautiful, human, cosmic, broad, deep, tragic, comic, as the life of La Raza itself . . . Chicano theater is a reaffirmation of LIFE . . . the limp, superficial, gringo seco [dry] productions in the "professional" American theater are so antiseptic . . .
>
> Chicano theater must be revolutionary in technique as well as content. It must be popular, subject to no other critics except the pueblo [people] itself; but it must also educate the pueblo toward an appreciation of social change, on and off the stage.

Thousands of poems have been written in the last few years by Raza—men and women, small children, and campesinos. These poems are gritos of liberation. They are written in Spanish or English or a mixture, it doesn't matter; all carry the strong message of our new-found pride and our dreams of building our own nation. In theater, there is not only El Teatro Campesino but many other groups, both in the barrio and the fields. Our painters seem to be everywhere and Chicano murals can be found on public buildings, in parks, beside swimming pools. Wherever there is a wall, there is an expression of La Raza. Some very beautiful oil painting and drawing is coming from Chicanos in prison. We also have many dance groups, the best-known being the Ballet Chicano de Aztlán in Denver.

Creativity is a part of us—not just for the sake of performance and showmanship, but as a way of enjoying and expressing what is truly ours. It is part of our liberation. Today a giant treasure chest of Raza talent seems to have been opened after being locked for many years. Thousands of voices and hands and bodies are being freed to express a beauty that was buried by cultural racism. We are seeing the end of that oppression described by Abelardo Delgado in his poem, *Stupid America:*

> stupid america, hear that chicano
> shouting curses on the street
> he is a poet
> without paper and pencil
> and since he cannot write
> he will explode

stupid america, remember that chicanito
flunking math and english
he is the picasso
of your western states
but he will die
with one thousand masterpieces
hanging only from his mind

No more, our people say today, as the flowers of our art bloom everywhere.

What about the other needs of our people, like health and food? Here, too, Raza have shown a new devotion to serving *la gente*—the people. We have started "people's clinics" that offer medical and dental care at no cost or very low fees. This means a great deal to Chicanos, for whom illness has often meant a terrible financial blow—or early death because the family could not afford treatment.

The people's clinics also try to offer a new *kind* of medical care. The doctors and nurses who work in these clinics must not be like the usual "professional," who cares more about his fee than about the patient. The doctors try to prevent people from getting sick, instead of just treating them after they are sick. They also remember that the treatment of illness is a strong part of Raza culture—we have our own time-tested, natural *remedios*. All in all, the people's clinics try to relate closely to the community and develop a truly revolutionary idea about medical care.

One of the biggest concerns of Raza families is the problem of drug addiction, and here, too, our people have been organizing. We have come to realize that although government officials and police talk about campaigning against drugs, they don't really want to get our people off drugs. In some cases, the police themselves are selling drugs or getting pay-offs from the big drug pushers. So they protect the powerful syndicates, while arresting and harassing the little consumer—the drug user.

In many cases, the police realize that having our youth strung out on drugs is the best possible way to slow down the Chicano movimiento. We have been informed, for example, that police in one large city where barrio organizing was going well allowed or had thousands of LSD tablets sold at a rock-bottom price of fifteen cents to prevent the barrio youth from getting organized. So drugs are not just a personal matter, they are an enemy of our revolutionary struggle.

One of the first anti-drug programs created by Chicanos was El Proyecto del Barrio (The Barrio Project) in East Los Angeles. This was a self-help program to help addicts get off drugs. Then, in 1971, the police showed their real interests when they moved to stop the drive against drugs. That year, they arrested three Raza working with the Casa de Carnalismo, an anti-drug center.

The Casa de Carnalismo believed that one of the best ways to get off drugs was to realize that your community needs you. The Chicanos there saw that drugs make you self-centered instead of concerned with the oppression of your people and all the injustice around us. As one former addict said, "Chicanismo is the ticket to mental health." With this philosophy, the

Casa de Carnalismo had much success—too much for the police.

The three Chicanos arrested there are known as Los Tres del Barrio. They were charged with attempted murder of a federal narcotics agent. It was a frame-up and the community rose to support Los Tres. They were later convicted, but the struggle to clear them goes on. Chicanos everywhere know how urgent it is for us to get drugs out of our communities, and we are determined to do it.

Our people are working to meet other kinds of daily needs by creating co-operatives. In different parts of the Southwest, we can see Chicano co-operatives. These include groups that grow food or buy and sell it at low prices; co-op restaurants, publishing houses, art workshops, gas stations. The idea behind these new projects is not to start Chicano-run businesses that will exploit the people just as the Anglo-run businesses have always done. The idea is not "brown capitalism." The idea is to meet our people's daily needs in the spirit of La Familia de La Raza, with the community in control. All these projects, from clinics to food co-ops, are *survival programs*. But they are also something more long-range. They give our people experience in working together, experience in new kinds of work, new ideas, and they help build unity.

"We resign as members of the Church . . . and not as believers of the Christian faith and the true principles of the Catholic, Apostolic, and Roman Church, to which we will return when once again it becomes the church of the poor and the forsaken."

These are the words of Pedro Arias, one of twenty-one Catholics who took part in a peaceful protest in Los Angeles on Christmas Eve, 1969. Pedro Arias was a member of Los Católicos por La Raza, an organization of priests and ordinary Catholics. His words express the feeling of many Raza today, who are deeply spiritual, but who also know the true history of the Church. We know that it played a large role in the conquest of Mexico and we know that it has been taking from the poor for too many years.

Los Católicos por La Raza was the first Raza organization to raise its voice against Church policies. It published a partial list of Church property in Los Angeles, showing that this property had a value of *at least* one billion dollars. The group then commented, "Blessed are the poor (they say) for they shall inherit the kingdom of heaven. The CHURCH, it seems, is quite satisfied in inheriting Los Angeles County."

Los Católicos por La Raza supported the student blow-outs but when they went to ask the Church for help in getting better education, they found police at the door. They tried to talk to high Church officials and were insulted, then thrown out. Thus, on Christmas Eve of 1969, they held a peaceful protest against the Church's financial policies and the twenty-one people were arrested. Several were beaten by police. Ten were later convicted of "inciting to riot."

While the Católicos have been struggling in Los Angeles, we find Chicanos everywhere taking a new approach to religious ideas and customs. More and more young people are getting together according to old Mexican customs, and being married by a member of the family or a close friend. Young couples are baptizing their own babies. Our ceremonies are serious but also full of color and gay music, because these express the spirit of our people. All this is part of rediscovering our own souls and developing our spirits. All this is part of building Aztlán.

Chota . . . chango . . . la placa . . . la jura . . . cochino . . . marrano . . . all these words of ours mean the same thing: COP. Many people in the United States do not know what COP means to minority peoples, they do not know how many Chicanos are beaten and murdered by police day after day. We are not talking here about Chicanos working in *el movimiento* or on the scene of a protest demonstration. We are talking about ordinary Raza whose only crime is that they are brown.

Just in the last few years, in just one state—California, there have been many unarmed Chicanos killed by police. The names of a few of them are: Vicente Gutiérrez, Arturo Varela, Rómulo Avalos, Mario Barreras, Paul Meza Aguilera, Jr., Jesse Manuel Villa, David Aguayo, Ray Hernandez, Mario Armando Romero, Danny García. Many were young teen-agers. In one case, a seventeen-year-old youth was shot by police and then chained to his hospital bed for three weeks. Two hours after he was dead, his body still lay shackled to the bed.

Dozens of stories of near-killing can also be told. For

example: Alfredo Brian, age sixteen, was shot by police
in el barrio de Cuatro Flats, East Los Angeles. A cop
had been shot to death earlier (members of the community say he shot himself accidentally in a scuffle)
and the police swept down on the barrio with guns
and helicopters. They arrested seventy persons,
smashed down the doors of people's homes, and beat a
fifteen-year-old boy so badly that he wasn't recognized
by his mother. Later they spotted Alfredo Brian in a
dark corner, and pumped seven bullets into his body—
firing at him even while he lay still on the ground.
Somehow Alfredo lived, but his jailers beat him at least
twice. Gangrene set in from his wounds, and his foot
was amputated after authorities refused to let private
doctors in to treat him.

One of the worst incidents was that of the police attack on the Anguiano home in Los Angeles. A chota
was shot (but not killed) one night. Police surrounded
the Anguiano house on the suspicion that his attackers
were inside. For an hour and a half, they fired bullets
and tear gas at the home. Eight children, ages one and
a half to fifteen, were inside with their mother. When
the house caught fire, police continued firing and the
mother fled from the house with the children, dodging
bullets. She was grabbed by police, choked, hit, and
thrown into a police car while she screamed in protest
—afraid that some of the children might still be in the
burning house.

Her brother, who had been sleeping in a converted
garage behind the house, was shot when he came outside to see what was happening. Mrs. Anguiano's step-
father, who lived nearby, also tried to go to her help

and was stopped by police who then forced him at gunpoint to lie down on the street—where he listened to the cries of the mother and children. Mrs. Anguiano was held in jail for four days, then released, and the charges were dropped.

Such horrors are not limited to the Southwest. In Milwaukee, Wisconsin, police attacked a crowd demonstrating for winter clothing needs in 1970. José Puente and Ernesto Chacón were arrested. The following year, police attacked Chicanos protesting on behalf of José and Ernesto, and broke up their march with billy clubs. In East Moline, Iowa, six Chicanos were arrested at a bar in December 1968 and beaten so brutally that the whole community organized in protest. It is the same everywhere. A Chicano may be moving his own furniture into his own house, and that is enough for police to suspect him of robbery. If a Chicano is found with a hundred dollars in his pocket, police assume he is a thief. If he doesn't have the "right" expression on his face, he may end up with a cracked skull.

All the abuse that our Raza receives from the chota is not just a coincidence, or just because some police enjoy being brutal. The cop is a tool of the entire legal system, and when he hurts defenseless people he does it with the blessing of the entire legal system. He knows that the courts and government officials will back him up. He can count on the support of judges like Gerald S. Chargin of California.

During a 1969 trial, Judge Chargin found a Chicano in his early teens guilty of a sexual crime. Then he told the boy: "You are just an animal. You are lower than an animal . . . Mexican people, after 13 years of age, it's perfectly all right to go out and act like an animal . . . We ought to send you out of the country—send you back to Mexico . . . You ought to commit suicide . . . You are lower than animals and haven't the right to live in organized society—just miserable, lousy, rotten people . . . Maybe Hitler was right. The animals in our society probably ought to be destroyed because they have no right to live among human beings." These words of Judge Chargin can be found in the transcript, the official record of the boy's trial.

Judge Chargin was more open in his racism than most judges, but actually he was just saying out loud what many judges think and practice. We must understand that the legal system of the United States today carries out laws that were written by the colonizer to suit himself. The laws work well today for the rich white people who control this country. They almost never work well for poor, non-white people. We see here a double standard of justice, and so our people often call it JUST-US—meaning that it's a justice by and for the ruling class only.

How does this double standard work? In Albuquerque, New Mexico, in 1968 a policeman shot sixteen-year-old Tommy Valles to death inside a shed from which he could not escape. Police said they had chased Tommy because he was riding in a car which they believed to be stolen. He jumped out and ran into the shed. According to police, Tommy threw a sharp piece of scrap metal at an officer who approached the shed, and hit him. The officer then shot Tommy dead. The car, it turned out, belonged to Tommy's mother. The

killer of Tommy not only went free, without a trial; local businessmen held a luncheon in his honor.

When Pete García of the same city killed a chota,
after the cop had shot him almost fatally in the back
for no reason, it was a different story. Pete had clearly
fired in desperate self-defense, using the cop's gun, as
many witnesses testified. He was brought to trial, and
the first time the jury could not reach a verdict. They
just were not convinced of Pete's guilt. So he was tried
again and found guilty. Then the conviction was appealed, and the state Supreme Court decided Pete was
innocent. Yet the state had to try him again—and again
he was found guilty. Three trials of one man, not for
the sake of justice but because the state just couldn't
accept Pete's innocence.

A famous case that shows just how "justice" works
against Raza is that of Los Siete—The Seven—in San
Francisco's Mission District. On May 1, 1969, an officer known for his harassment and brutality against
young Chicanos was shot to death. Gio Lopez, Gary
Lescallet, Mario Martínez, Rodolfo "Tony" Martínez,
Danilo "BeBe" Melendez, Jose Ríos, and Nelson
Rodriguez—Los Siete—were charged with the crime.
Six of them were caught, and jailed from that day to
November 1970. They were held *without bail*—even
though three of them had proof that they were not
even near the scene of the killing at the time. The
press, with its screaming headlines and distorted reports, made them sound like hoodlums instead of the
students and community workers that they were.

When the trial of Los Siete finally started, evidence
came out that the officer supposedly killed by Los Siete

had in fact been killed accidentally by another, drunken cop. The entire case against them fell apart and they were acquitted of the murder charge. But the police were enraged that this one time the system hadn't worked the way they thought it should. From the moment Los Siete were freed, the police tormented them with false arrest, harassment, beatings, and a final murderous attack that left one of them near death. All those not jailed finally went underground—driven there by men who are supposed to "protect" us and our rights. They had spent almost a year and a half in prison for no crime, gone through a seventeen-week trial—and still were not free men.

The case of Los Siete also revealed the way another part of the U.S. legal system works: the grand jury. This is the body that brings formal charges, called indictments, in important crimes. The grand jury that charged Los Siete was entirely white and middle class. It knew nothing of lying, racist police or life in the barrio. And this is the situation everywhere. Chicanos almost never get to serve on the grand juries, and even if they do, the number chosen is never close to the percentage of Chicanos living in the area. The same holds true for ordinary juries, with extremely rare exceptions.

A 1970 report by the U. S. Civil Rights Commission, based on a two-year study, confirmed this whole picture of how "justice" does not work for Raza. The report said that "there is widespread evidence that equal protection of the law in the administration of justice is being withheld from Mexican-Americans." The report described excessive police violence and harsh treatment of our people, who are often arrested on insufficient grounds. It confirmed that we do not get adequate legal representation, are charged excessive bail, are excluded from juries, and receive penalties higher than those given to whites for the same crimes. So there it all is, written down, confirmed, in an official government report—but nothing has been done to change the situation.

All this experience with the police, the courts, and the government has taught La Raza that if we want to change the situation, we must do it ourselves. We must organize for survival. As a result, fear has been replaced by anger in many places. Our people have started community patrols that regularly go through a barrio, checking on police action. They take cameras, tape recorders, and witnesses with them to record any cases of abuse.

We have also organized legal defense committees to stop our people from being railroaded and to expose how "law-and-order" really operates in a community. In the case of Los Siete, the defense committee not only worked to free the brothers, but "Los Siete de La Raza" became the name of a community organization with its own newspaper, a free breakfast for school children program, a restaurant, and a people's clinic. Thus the case of Los Siete served to create a solid social awareness never to be forgotten in the Chicano community.

Because of the double standard of justice that we mentioned before, hundreds of Raza have been doomed to long jail terms although they are often innocent. One of the most common reasons for innocent poor people being behind bars is that we cannot afford to hire our own lawyers, so we are assigned "public defenders." The public defenders get less money for such cases than for private clients, so they usually don't bother to make a good case. They will often advise a defendant to plead guilty, even if innocent, saying that he will then get a lighter sentence. But often this doesn't work and an innocent man lands in jail. In other cases, our people have been railroaded by pure racism: the mere word of a white person against theirs, and the judge chooses to believe the white person.

With Chicanos awakening all over the country, our people in prison have also begun to move and organize. The *pintos*—Chicano prisoners—have started groups to learn more about our culture and history, to develop Chicanismo behind bars. Ex-cons and others in the "free" world have formed groups like MAYO to help the pintos. Thanks to their joint efforts, prisons are being visited by Chicano teachers, speakers, teatro groups, dancers, and poets. The pintos hold special fiestas on Raza holidays, with Chicano food and music. They are publishing newsletters, organizing workshops of writers and artists, and holding art shows.

The new feeling of Chicanismo among the pintos is one of pride and hope. One of their meetings with MAYO visitors is described by a prisoner in California who calls himself "Sleepyboy del Barrio First Flats":

> . . . I like to holler out loud, "VIVA MAYO!"
> One MAYO council member hollers out, "VIVA MAYO" and "VIVA!" we say; "VIVA LA CAUSA," "VIVA!" we say; "VIVA LA REVOLUCIÓN," "VIVA!" we answer. "VIVA LA RAZA NUEVA" and we say again, "VIVA!" . . . when we're doing this we holler with all our hearts and at the same time we're loudly clapping . . . now we all

kick back and have our heads clear, our ears open and
our hearts open for all information. We always have
good discussions and speakers, we talk about our problems in the institution and the problems in the institution and the problems out there.

After the JUNTA meeting I leave with my crazy
home-boys and we talk about the Movimiento. I feel
so great that I learned something, which I did. It's a
beautiful feeling I have in my Brown Soul, I just
can't describe it, but every Chicano feels the same
damn way, Brown and Proud.

The feeling of brotherhood, the new pride of our
pintos, has helped them to organize with other inmates
to try and change such prison conditions as bad food,
filthy cells, beatings by guards, lack of medical attention. In the Washington state prison, Chicanos joined
with Indians, Blacks, and white prisoners to hold the
longest non-violent strike in U.S. prison history. At Fol-
som Prison in California, Chicanos joined with others
to support the creation of a California Prisoners' Union.
Although interracial conflict still exists, prisoners of all
colors are now saying: we will not let the prison authorities play one group against the other.

The wardens and guards have moved to suppress
Chicano protest in many ways. They always try to play
Chicanos and Blacks against each other. Sometimes
they transfer a leader to another prison but often they
beat and tear-gas the men. Then they tell lies to the
news media about what really happened.

A Chicano who has revealed much of the truth
about what goes on behind prison walls is Luis Tala-
mantez, in San Quentin prison. A revolutionary poet
from Los Angeles, Luis has written: "I am a 20th cen-

tury revolucionario of a world state with no barriers to the brotherhood of man. I do not want to belong to the Amerikan Fascist State."

Luis was already known for his courage and militant spirit when, on August 21, 1971, George Jackson was killed by guards at San Quentin. Luis had the cell next to George Jackson. All the prisoners on that block, including six Chicanos, said that George had been murdered—not while trying to escape, but murdered in cold blood. All of them were then chained and beaten by guards. Hugo Pinell, a pinto from Nicaragua, was one of those most seriously hurt.

Luis, Hugo, and four Black prisoners have been charged with many crimes from the events of August 21. Chicanos say: "George Jackson was murdered for being a revolutionary—will Luis and Hugo be next?" Yet the spirit of Luis and Hugo triumphed in a message smuggled out to the people. It said in Spanish: "All prisoners suffering at this moment feel the support of the people and by knowing this, we know we will win. All of us are strongly united and whatever happens to one, we shall all accept together."

The police and the prisons are one kind of repression in uniform, but there is another that strikes just as much fear and hatred into the hearts of many Raza. This is La Migra—the U. S. Immigration Service, the Border Patrol.

We have already told about the mass deportations of the 1930s, when thousands of our people were driven out of the United States—even though many of them were citizens. This nightmare returned in the summer of 1973, when La Migra rounded up and deported a total of ten thousand or more Raza from the Los Angeles area during a period of about one month, according to lawyers who became involved in these cases. Six hundred were grabbed on the first day alone. Immigration agents carried out a Gestapo-like dragnet operation, picking up people off the street, at bus stops, in their homes at night, and even inside churches. If the people could not produce proof of U.S. citizenship on the spot, they were arrested and kicked out of the country into Mexico. There were many violations of civil and human rights. Señora Velia Limón, for example, who is a U.S. citizen, reported in a sworn statement that she heard children screaming next door and ran to see what was happening. When she arrived and went in, an agent of La Migra tried to handcuff her, throwing her on the couch in the process. No wonder that a Chicano newspaper announced: HITLER HAS RISEN IN THE SOUTHWEST!

The excuse given for the dragnet operation was that the Mexicanos and Latinos were responsible for high prices, inflation, unemployment, and other economic problems. But Raza believed that the government was just trying to blame the Latinos for problems it couldn't solve. We also believe that the government was trying to distract the public's attention from corruption in La Migra. Just before the dragnet began, the public learned that La Migra was being investigated by a Federal Grand Jury for taking bribes from aliens and alien smugglers, and for forcing Mexicanas to give them sexual favors in exchange for letting the women enter the United States.

Thanks to strong protests, the dragnet slowed down

after a while. But La Migra is still there, terrorizing our people when they choose to do so and helping the rich growers overpower the striking campesinos.

Students, batos locos, campesinos, city workers, poets, artists, pintos—all have been deeply stirred by the new spirit of Chicanismo, the call for Aztlán and social revolution. The spirit and goals of today have special meaning for La Chicana—the woman.

It seems just recently that the Raza woman was portrayed as the quiet, stoic, brown-eyed beauty who endured all and made an obedient wife, a good housekeeper, a loving mother. Both the Church and the colonizer's culture told her to be this and nothing else, without question. And she often was. But as she has become more politically aware, doubts and whispers came to her mind. "Why do I see my children disappear and become strangers?" she wondered. "Why do the police beat my boys and jail them for nothing?" Why, why, why?

As the movement of Chicanismo has grown stronger, as we have begun to uncover our roots and rediscover ourselves, the Chicana, too, has made a great discovery. She has realized that women have long played a very important role in the history of the mestizo. La Chicana has sweated in the fields as a campesina; La Chicana has struggled to get a job in the city or a welfare payment; La Chicana has had to fill a dozen different roles in order to survive. Many times she has been both father and mother to her children.

The history of Mexico shows the woman as a fighter

on the front lines, as a revolutionary whose courage matched that of the men. To struggle for our people is nothing new, it is a destiny. So La Chicana of today is again beginning to move toward her destiny. She realizes that her strength lies in removing that European mask of so-called female roles. This includes removing the idea of being possessed and owned by men, removing any idea that limits her participation in today's struggle.

One of the first things that the aware Chicana has come to realize is that the woman is the first teacher of the child. So she must be the first to combat the colonized mind, she can prevent gringo values from passing on to the generations that follow. She can have the main responsibility for bringing La Raza home to itself and its own values. As one active Chicana stated, "If we have complaints to our men, we have ourselves to blame many times. We bear them, we raise them, we better start deciding what we are going to teach them. Not when they are ten years old, or eighteen or twenty, but when they are born—when they are babies."

It is the Chicana who can lead in the battle against materialism and competitive values, within herself and her family as well as her people. She can build a strong, true life style by not supporting that majority system with one penny more than necessary. All this and more she can do with the endurance and strength that are La Chicana *de hoy*—today's Chicana.

Across the country today, we see Chicanas moving with that strength. The campesinas are the backbone of the farmworkers' movement. It was also Chicanas who held out in the Austin, Texas, furniture company

strike and the Silver City, New Mexico, hospital workers' strike of 1971. Chicanas have organized special
protest marches and they have edited many of the Chicano movement papers. They have started organizations to help La Chicana coming out of prison—whose
problems are as bad as those facing the men and can
be even worse because she must often fight an uphill
battle to get back children taken away from her by the
courts.

The struggle for welfare rights has produced many
strong Chicana leaders. The best known is Alicia Es-
calante of Los Angeles: a small woman, hardly five feet
tall, whose life is typical of many Chicanas in the city
except that Alicia went to bat for her friends and
neighbors. Anything she learned, she shared and put to
use for others. She has devoted her full life and all her
time to helping welfare mothers.

Originally from a very poor family of El Paso, Texas,
Alicia later moved to Los Angeles. At the age of sixteen
she was forced to leave school and go work. She married and had four children within five years. Caught in
the cycle of poverty and oppression that faces so many
Chicano families, she and her husband were finally di-
vorced. During those years, Alicia was on and off the
welfare roles, working as a waitress, living in housing
projects, trying to hold her family together. She later
formed the East Los Angeles Welfare Rights Organization to provide help for women in the area, and to encourage them to fight for their rights—something our
women are usually afraid to do, for fear of losing the
little they have.

Alicia participated in the Mass held by Los Católicos por La Raza in 1969, and was arrested on a charge of "assault with a dangerous weapon" when she hit a cop with her shoe. This charge was later dropped but she continued to be harassed by the law. The city attorney of Los Angeles is reported to have sworn that he would put her behind bars and she did go to jail.

Alicia had opened an office, next to the welfare office, where she provided such services to welfare mothers as translating and informing recipients of their rights. One day she entered the welfare office of a social worker to use the telephone and was asked to leave. Alicia refused to leave and demanded to use the telephone, which was for the use of recipients. A quarrel ensued in which the social worker charged Alicia with having "threatened" her and a warrant was issued for Alicia's arrest. She turned herself in and in 1972, Alicia was sent to jail for forty days in Los Angeles.

But Alicia is too strong to let such experiences bother her. She is typical of the Chicana in the city who, by having to fight for herself and her children over the years, has acquired a strength to move mountains.

This kind of strength was recognized by the 1970 National Chicano Conference in Denver, where a women's workshop took place. Out of the workshop came a resolution that expressed the feeling of most Chicanas today. On the one hand, the women resolved "not to separate but to strengthen Aztlán, La Familia de La Raza." This simple statement meant that Chicanas would not adopt an anti-male attitude. We could not afford to; our struggle for survival as a people is too hard and dangerous for us to think of not using all human resources—men, women, and children.

The Denver workshop went on to resolve that:

"1. All women must participate according to their capacity in all levels of the struggle.

"2. We encourage all Chicanas to meet in their own groups for the purpose of education and discussion.

"3. Self-determination of the women, in terms of how they will implement their goal of becoming full human beings and of participating totally in the struggle for La Raza, must be respected.

"4. We must change the concept of the alienated family, where the woman assumes total responsibility for the care of the home and the raising of the children, to the concept of La Raza as the united family."

Many meetings of Chicanas have taken place besides that one in Denver. In May 1971, a National Chicana Conference was held in Houston, Texas.

In November 1972, Chicanas participated in a third world women's conference in San Anselmo, California, for the purpose of defining third world and third world concerns. (Third world means the colonized and formerly colonized peoples of the world.) Seven of us made up the Chicana caucus. We presented our mestizo history as the Chicano nation of Aztlán, and we learned of other views and struggles. To learn of other struggles and peoples was no threat to our Chicanismo but an affirmation of our struggle and what is yet to come. We came together aware of our differences but with the realization of what brought us together; *a deep concern for the necessity of unity around the issues affecting humanity, on a long-term, world basis.* We recognized that we must create an awareness of the links between the struggles within the United States and world struggles.

The Chicana's involvement in the movimiento has led to a growing awareness of the limitless power of sisterhood and the possible achievement of world consciousness and a new humanity. The feeling of the third world was expressed as follows:

> To see and speak with these women of the third world was
>   to see oneself.
> There were blacks who looked like me,
> There were Indians who looked like me,
> There were Asians with traces of me.
>   All were pieces of struggles;
>   pieces of reality;
>   pieces of flesh . . .
>   All were pieces of me . . .

As we Chicanas become more active, more aware, more alive, more ready to fight, we become more total human beings. It is this feeling of freedom and liberation that we seek today for every man, woman, and child of La Raza. We have learned that once a spirit has tasted of that freedom, once we have learned to love our people and ourselves freely, there is no turning back. A woman or man who has breathed the air of true equality will never submit to chains, to exploitation, to rulers.

14

Your Whip Is My Sword

A TELEVISION COMMENTATOR interviewed a Chicano youth not long ago and when the talk ended, he said: "I like everything that you Chicanos are doing, but I don't buy your Plan de Aztlán." This comment seems very expressive of the white society, and we shall answer it very clearly. You see, Uncle Stars and Stripes, La Raza has had to come up with something that *we* want, something that is *ours*, NOT something you will "buy." We don't care what you think of us any more. We do not "buy" you and your society.

For over one hundred years, we made accommodations and concessions for you. You stood over us as a master with a whip. Your society never respected the Mexican as a human being, as an equal. We did not ask that you love us; we just hoped that you would learn to see us as humans and respect us as humans. But you, your nation, treated us as if we weren't there at all—or worse.

So we have quit pulling at your coattails and saying, "Hey, meester." We are no longer asking for your approval—and if we did, we are sure that you would whip us into line, build a bureaucracy, and call out points of order for another hundred years. But we don't ask for your approval. We want to be rid of you. You came to this country as a guest and became the master. You moved into our homes and took over. Now we are going to build our own homes and homeland, using our own hearts, our own spirit.

Many say, "But you are going to overthrow our government, our democracy." We can only listen to this and shake our heads in pity at their blindness. It was never "our" government, or "our" democracy. We and most of the world are today telling the gringo: "get out." We have come to realize that the so-called democracy is a giant fraud. We see how the capitalist system of the United States has forced it to go outside its own boundaries in order to continue existing. In the name of "progress," the United States has swallowed up 67 per cent of the world's resources for the benefit of only 8 per cent of the world's population. Today we can see clearly that the "progress" of the United States is not being used or shared as science that could help humanity, but is instead being used as a power to keep control over humanity. Inside its own boundaries, the United States is "progressing" itself out of existence—swallowing up resources and people on a road that leads to total destruction. If the white society will poison its own people for the sake of profit—as it has done with the pesticides—then where does the madness end?

We reject the gringo's violence, his destruction, his competition, his whole insane society. We have studied the gringo's mind and society, and we see how they work. As we see more of the truth, we rid ourselves of the influence of that mind and society. We uncover the truth about ourselves, we stop looking to Anglo sociologists and other "experts" to find out what we are. We tell the gringo: go write about what you know best, study and write about yourself, expose your own sickness.

There is room in the Raza movement for the Anglo who sincerely wants to help. We would like best for Anglos to clean their own house instead of helping us to build ours. But if they choose to help, then we have had much experience over the years as to just when, how, and where they can fit in. We have learned that there are many who call themselves amigos, but few who prove to be true amigos. Those who truly want to help must first of all be willing to accept Raza leadership. They must realize that they will be followers, not leaders and not spokesmen. The Anglo finds it very difficult to be a follower, for he has been born and raised in a system that teaches white superiority. He may say that he wants to help us build our house, but he will often end up telling us how to build it.

The Anglo who truly wants to help must also realize that he has to contribute to us *as a people*. He will have to work with us in an unselfish manner—not for personal satisfaction. This may sound easy and simple, but it is not. Few people can actually work for others without demanding some kind of recognition. Few Anglos can be counted upon to come through in time of our need and against their personal needs, rooted in their values and society. But some can. Some do recognize that their own freedom can never be real until all peoples are free. When a person realizes this, then the people's interest becomes self-interest—and in that moment, selfishness ends.

Today, as we look back on our history—on what the Raza has suffered and is still suffering, on all the injustices done to our people and all the oppression—we can see its merits. It has served as a crucible that hardens and makes people more able to endure. This is why an oppressed people is stronger than the oppressor will ever be. We have endured Mr. Gringo and his whip. We have endured his lashes, we have endured his raging mania as he lashed at us with his screams of "turn white, damn it, turn white!"

But Mr. Gringo is no more. It is his own whip that has stirred us. His own whip awakened us. To Mr. Gringo, the Chicano now says: you have failed miserably. You tried to make me feel guilty by labeling me a failure. But it is you who are guilty. You failed yourself and your people. You tried to make me your slave, but it is you who are enslaved. You tried to pain me with your whip, but now it is you who howls with pain. You called me culturally deprived, but it is you who has no culture. You told me that I had a problem, that I was a problem, but it is you who has the problem; YOU are THE problem.

And now your whip has become my sword. I have turned the shame you taught me into pride. You made Mexican into a dirty word, now I make it into a word of strength and beauty. I am no longer tortured by your mad mind, I am no longer the slave. As I watch now, I see you and your whip sprawl, and you cry out in anguish with all your power, all your wealth, all your luxuries. You reek of fatal disease.

You call yourself progressive, but you are only a progressive machine that does not dare to be human. You call yourself a conqueror because you seek ways to conquer and harness nature—instead of seeking knowledge of how to live in harmony with nature. You respect nothing, and in your so-called progressiveness you have come to the brink of death.

Yet you refuse to see what you have done to yourself. You refuse to look at the giant whip you have built—a whip around humanity, a whip around the world, and a whip around yourself. You keep saying that you live in peacetime, while you make war and kill millions. When the young men come home in coffins, you say "look at the moon," "look at your color TV sets," "look at the abundance." And you continue to lash at the world.

But slowly that whip is winding itself around you and tightening its grip. Your own sons and daughters look on, and they want to be free of you. All over the world, those whom you have oppressed and exploited cry "Enough!" and declare that they will fight for liberation.

We Raza are not alone. We have allies all over this country, all over the world—in America, Asia and

Africa, even in Europe. They, too, want to be rid of you. We all step up now to have our day in the world court of humanity and you have no choice but to bow. For your whip is gone, it has become my sword. *Tu riata es mi espada*—your whip is my sword.

VIVA LA RAZA, RAZA, RAZA . . .

E. M.
E. V.

Index

ELIZABETH (BETITA) MARTÍNEZ is a writer, editor and activist in the Chicano movement. Under the name Elizabeth Sutherland, she published *Letters from Mississippi* and *The Youngest Revolution*. Born in Washington, D.C., of a Mexican father and U.S. mother, she worked as an editor in book publishing for five years and then became books and arts editor of *The Nation* magazine. From 1963 to 1968, she worked with SNCC in New York and the South. In 1968, she moved to New Mexico, where she founded the Chicano newspaper *El Grito del Norte* (Outcry of the North), and served as its editor for five years. She has traveled throughout the Southwest as well as in Mexico, Cuba, China, Vietnam, Europe, and other countries.

ENRIQUETA LONGEAUX Y VÁSQUEZ is a writer and active participant in the Chicano movement. She was born and raised in Colorado of Mexican-Tarascan parentage. While living in Denver, she was active in community affairs and worked closely with the Crusade for Justice. She has lived and traveled in many parts of the Southwest. Señora Vásquez has published articles in *El Grito del Norte* and other Chicano newspapers, including a well-known column *"Despierten, Hermanos"* (Wake Up, Brothers). She is presently writing and doing independent research for the Colegio Jacinto Treviño, a Chicano college in Texas.